The Collected Works of Paddy Chayefsky
THE SCREENPLAYS

VOLUME II

The Collected Works of Paddy Chayefsky
THE SCREENPLAYS

VOLUME II

The Hospital
Network
Altered States

APPLAUSE
BOOKS
NEW YORK • LONDON

An Applause Original
The Screenplays Volume II

The Hospital Copyright © 1971 Simcha Productions, Inc.

Network Copyright © 1976 Metro-Goldwyn-Mayer Inc. and United Artists Corporation. All rights reserved.

Altered States Copyright © 1978 Simcha Productions, Inc.

All inquiries regarding publication rights, including anthology and transla-tions should be addressed to: Rights Department, Applause Books, 211 West 71st Street New York, NY 10023.

Library of Congress Cataloging-in-Publication Data

Chayefsky, Paddy, 1923-1981.
    The screenplays / Paddy Chayefsky.
        p.   cm. -- (The collected works of Paddy Chayefsky ; 3-4)
        Contents: v. 1. Marty, The Goddess, The Americanization of Emily -- v. 2. The Hospital, Network, and Altered states.
        ISBN 1-55783-193-9 (v. 1) : $16.95. -- ISBN 1-55783-194-7 (v. 2) : $16.95
        1. Motion picture plays. I. Title. II. Series: Chayefsky, Paddy, 1923-1981. Works.   1994 ; 3-4.
        PS3505.H632A19   1994 vol. 3-4
        812'.54--dc20   94-24706
                                                                                                      CIP

British Library Cataloging-in-Publication Data

A catalogue record for this book is available from the British Library.

Applause Books
211 West 71st Street   406 Vale Road
New York, NY 10023   Tonbridge Kent TN9 1XR
Phone (212) 496-7511   Phone 073 235-7755
Fax: (212) 721-2856   Fax 073 207-7219

First Applause Printing 1995

Printed in Canada

This collection is dedicated to the memory of its author, Paddy Chayefsky, and to the enormous gift of his talent and insight which fills these pages.

—Susan Chayefsky

An enormous debt of gratitude is owed to Karen Jaehne, who provided invaluable help on this publication. With care and uncommon dedication, she edited the screenplays and contributed greatly to compiling this work. She has our great thanks.

The following people were of special assistance in the preparation of these volumes, and their help is gratefully acknowledged: Susan Brown, Dan Chayefsky, David Cleaver, Barbara Cramer, Herb Gardner, Howard Gottfried, Arthur Hiller, Andrew Pontious, Arthur Schlesinger, Jr., J. Stephen Sheppard, Paul Sugarman, Ken Swezey, and all the staff at Applause.

Contents

The Collected Works of Paddy Chayefsky

The Stage Plays

•

The Television Plays

•

The Screenplays Volume I
Marty, The Goddess, The Americanization of Emily

•

The Screenplays Volume II
The Hospital, Network, Altered States

THE HOSPITAL

1971

*Original Story and Screenplay
by* PADDY CHAYEFSKY

Produced by HOWARD GOTTFRIED

Directed by ARTHUR HILLER

CAST CREDITS

DR. HERBERT BOCK	George C. Scott
BARBARA DRUMMOND	Diana Rigg
DRUMMOND	Barnard Hughes
MRS. CHRISTIE	Nancy Marchand
SUNDSTROM	Stephen Elliott
MILTON MEAD	Donald Harron
GUERNSEY	Roberts Blossom
DR. IVES	Robert Anthony
DR. SCHAEFER	Lenny Baker
MRS. CUSHING	Frances Sternhagen
NURSE DEVINE	Lorrie Davis
MRS. REARDON	Cynthia Belgrave
NURSE PEREZ	Julie Garfield
NURSE CAMPANELLA	Angie Ortega
MISS LEBOW	Carolyn Krigbaum
HITCHCOCK	Jordan Charney
INTERN AMBLER	Paul Mace
DR. EINHORN	David Hooks
DR. BRUBAKER	Robert Walden
WILLIAM MEAD	Andrew Duncan
DR. LAGERMAN	Lou Polan
DR. IMMELMAN	Jacqueline Brooks
RESIDENT	Christopher Guest
DR. WELBECK	Richard Dysart
MARILYN MEAD	Katherine Helmond
POLICE CAPTAIN	Bill Lazarus
MR. BLACKTREE	Arthur Junuluska
WOMEN'S LIBBER	Marilyn Sokol
YOUNG ACTIVIST DOCTOR	Bruce Kornbluth
BLACK PANTHER	Nat Grant
MILITANT LEADER	Milton Earl Forrest
DR. CHU	Sab Shimono
DR. SPEZIO	Rehn Scofield
NURSE ARONOVICI	Stockard Channing
PARANOID LADY	Anita Dangler
DR. MALLORY	Barnard Hughes

THE HOSPITAL. DAY. MAY, 1971.

PANORAMIC VIEW of The Hospital—a vast medical complex, a sprawl-
ing pastiche of architecture extending ten blocks north and south on First
Avenue and east to the river.

The Hospital was founded in the late 19th century, and there are still a few
begrimed Victorian Bedlams and Bastilles among the buildings. Mostly
though, it is Medical Modern 1971, white and chrome and lots of glass and
concrete shafts and rotundas. A spanking new Community Mental Health
Clinic towers among the tenements at the northern end of the complex. On
the far side of First Avenue, a twenty-story apartment house with recessed
balconies and picture windows to house the resident staff has just recently been
completed, and next to it, eight ghetto buildings are being demolished to make
way—according to the construction company's sign—for a new Drug
Rehabilitation Center, to be completed in 1973, we should all live so long.
This is where the shattering SOUNDS OF CONSTRUCTION are coming
from. A block length of generators and cement and demolition machines are
POUNDING, CRASHING, SCREAMING. Traffic HONKS and
BRAYS up First Avenue.

It is a cold spring morning—10:00 A.M.

A 1966 station wagon pulls up to the Holly Pavilion.

A tiny, fragile, white-bearded OLD MAN, almost lost in his overcoat, is
helped from the rear of a station wagon and slowly led to the entrance doors
by a middle-aged nurse.

NARRATOR On Monday morning, a patient named Guernsey, male,
middle-seventies was admitted to the hospital complaining of chest
pains.

HOLLY PAVILION. EIGHTH FLOOR CORRIDOR.

The old man is now in a wheelchair pushed by a hospital orderly down the
corridor.

NARRATOR   He had been referred by a nursing home where the doctor had diagnosed his condition as angina pectoris. Now it is axiomatic that nursing home doctors are always wrong.

ROOM 806.

The old man, shirtless, is propped on the edge of the bed, wheezing. DR. SCHAEFER, a young intern in white-uniform, perches beside him with the old man's chart in his lap, taking down his history. The other patient in the two-bedded room, a MIDDLE-AGED MAN, is comatose and all rigged up with I.V.'s and catheters.

NARRATOR   The intern who admitted Mr. Guernsey, however, accepted the diagnosis and prescribed morphine, a drug suitable for angina but not at all suitable for emphysema, which is, unfortunately, what the old man actually had. Within an hour...

EIGHTH FLOOR CORRIDOR.

Two orderlies rush the old man's bed with, of course, the old man in it, past the Nurses' Station and into a waiting elevator.

NARRATOR   ...the patient became unresponsive and diaphoretic and was raced up to Intensive Care with an irregular pulse of 150, blood pressure 90 over 60, respiration rapid and shallow.

INTENSIVE CARE.

An oxygen mask is applied to the old man's face by the resident.

NARRATOR   The resident on duty now compounded the blunder by treating the old man for pulmonary edema. He gave him digitalis, diuretics and oxygen. This restored the old man's color...

EIGHTH FLOOR CORRIDOR.

The elevator door opens. Two orderlies wheel the sleeping man on his bed back around the Nurses' Station and down the corridor to his room.

NARRATOR   ...and he was sent back to his room in the Holly Pavilion, ruddy complected and peacefully asleep.

ROOM 806. EVENING.

The old man is back in his room sleeping serenely, his tiny body making barely a ripple in the white sheet that covers him. The room is in hushed shadows. A yellowish light diffuses into the room from the half-opened bathroom door. The other patient in the room remains as before, comatose and silent.

NARRATOR   In point of fact, the patient was in CO_2 narcosis...

ROOM 806.

All the lights are on now. NURSE PENNY CANDUSO and an orderly are wrapping the old man in a post-mortem shroud. BRUBAKER, the senior resident, is giving hell to Schaefer, the intern.

NARRATOR   ...and died at seven-thirty that evening.

The shrouded body of the old man is wheeled out of the room. CAMERA STAYS on the vacated bed.

NARRATOR   I mention all this, only to explain how the bed in Room 806 became available.

PAN from bed to Schaefer, now alone in the room and regarding the empty bed with frowning interest. Schaefer is a scraggly young fellow, bespectacled, with a contemporary mess of hair and a swinging unkempt moustachio. HOLD on Schaefer.

NARRATOR The intern involved was a prickly young buck named Schaefer who had a good thing going for him with a technician in the hematology lab. In the haphazard fashion of hospital romances, Dr. Schaefer had been zapping this girl on wheelchairs, stretchers, pantry shelves...

Dr. Schaefer moves for the phone on the table between the two beds.

NARRATOR   ...in the kitchen, in the morgue, in the dark corners of corridors...

Schaefer speaks softly into the phone.

NARRATOR   ...standing up, sitting down—so you can imagine what an available bed meant to him.

SCHAEFER   *(on phone)* Hey, Sheila, this is Howard, Sheila. Hey listen. I got us a bed for tonight. A real, honest-to-god bed.

FREEZE on CLOSE-UP of the beaming, lubricious Schaefer on phone as

CREDITS AND MUSIC ERUPT ONTO THE SCREEN—

THE HOSPITAL

INTERSPERSED WITH CREDITS, the following scenes:

ROOM 806. NIGHT.

Dark. Just a bit of moonlight streaking through the not quite closed bathroom. The hallway door opens, and a young woman, carrying a top coat, slips quickly in giggling like hell, followed by Schaefer, who is likewise giggling and admonishing her to be quiet. Her name is SHEILA. Sheila notices the other patient in the room sleeping away and looks questioningly at Schaefer, who reassures her as he removes her coat. After which he strips off his own white jacket and trousers and hangs them in the armoire. The girl asks in a hoarse whisper if they're going to get totally nude and wonders if that's such a good idea. For an answer, Schaefer fondles her crotch. They both giggle, they both shush each other, they giggle again; they're both stoned. The girl unzippers her dress. The dark room is filled for the moment with the flurry of undressing, flung garments, elbows, legs and arms, bumpings into each other, and Sheila saying between giggles, "Boy, I sure hope nobody walks in."

They eventually wind up on the unoccupied bed, and the scene ends looking ACROSS the sleeping profile of THE PATIENT in the other bed as Schaefer and his girl thump away at each other with much creaking of springs, moans, groans, giggles and the white-limbed patterns of fornication.

ROOM 806.

Dark, silent, hushed. The fun and games are over. Sheila is in front of the armoire. She slips back into her dress, after which she tiptoes back to the bed where Schaefer is deeply asleep, smiling in postcoital peace. Sheila bends, shakes his shoulder.

SHEILA *(whispers)* I'll see you.

Schaefer smiles, grunts, sleeps on.

END OF CREDITS.

FADE OUT.

FADE IN:

THE HOSPITAL. 6:30 A.M. NEXT MORNING, TUESDAY.

A cold newly-dawned sun shines down on the vast sprawling complex of the hospital. Desultory early morning traffic on First Avenue.

HOLLY PAVILION, EIGHTH FLOOR.

The night shift of nurses is closing out another night's work, which has been on the whole uneventful. The head nurse, MRS. REARDON, hunches over her paperwork. NURSE ELIZABETH RIVERS sits at the desk beside her, resting her head on the palm of one hand. NURSE'S AID J.C. MILLER crosses with an armful of linens. She disappears into the pharmacy and supply areas behind the Nurses' Station. In the west corridor, NURSE LUCINDA PEREZ glances at her watch, then pads down to Room 806. She enters.

ROOM 806. DAY.

A cold gray light cheerlessly illuminates the room. Nurse Perez checks the I.V. on the comatose patient who is in the bed nearest the door. Then she turns to regard the other bed—which gives her pause.

NURSE'S P.O.V.: Intern Dr. Schaefer is lying on this bed, rigid, eyes dilated, pupils staring unseeing. An I.V. tube sticks out of his naked right arm. Nurse Perez doesn't quite know what to make of the fact that Dr. Schaefer is lying on that bed with an I.V. tube sticking out of him looking dead. Frowning, she reaches out a tentative hand to shake his naked shoulder.

NURSE PEREZ Doctor Schaefer....

There is, of course, no response. A terrible suspicion enters Nurse Perez's mind, and she closes her eyes and sighs a long shuddering sigh. Then she opens her eyes and, with a second and briefer sigh, reaches for Schaefer's neck to take his pulse. Clearly, the result is not encouraging. She sighs another short sigh and regards Schaefer's unblinking, dilated pupils. It's all a bit too much for her; she shuffles to the window and stares out into the gray morning where things are a little more comprehensible. Once again, she returns to the bed, regards Schaefer's death mask. She raises the bedsheet and, for one short but appreciative moment, considers Schaefer's naked body. She lets the bedsheet carefully down. She sighs again.

NURSE PEREZ *(trying again, with little hope)* Doctor Schaefer?

She sighs, turns and leaves the room.

EIGHTH FLOOR CORRIDOR.

Nurse Perez, frowning and pursing her lips, moves slowly back to...

EIGHTH FLOOR, NURSES' STATION.

Head Nurse Reardon is still bent over her paperwork.

NURSE PEREZ Listen, did you know Doctor Schaefer was in Eight-O-Six, because he's dead?

MRS. REARDON *(late forties, continues her painstaking paperwork, grunts)* What?

NURSE PEREZ I'm just telling you, Dr. Schaefer is dead.

MRS. REARDON *(works on; after a moment, looks up)* What do you want, Perez?

NURSE PEREZ Look, I don't know what the hell this is all about, but Dr. Schaefer is in Room 806 with an I.V. running and he's dead. I didn't even know he was sick.

MRS. REARDON *(regards Perez a moment)* Perez, what the hell are you talking about? *(appeals to Nurse Rivers coming out of the floor pharmacy)* Do you know what the hell she's talking about?

NURSE PEREZ Well, maybe I'm going crazy. I don't know. Isn't Room 806 the patient Guernsey? I mean, did something happen I don't know about?

MRS. REARDON Perez, I don't know what you're talking about.

NURSE PEREZ This is the nuttiest thing I ever saw. Dr. Schaefer's in Room 806 dead.

MRS. REARDON What Dr. Schaefer? Our Dr. Schaefer?

NURSE PEREZ Our Dr. Schaefer. The one who's always grabbing everybody's ass.

MRS. REARDON *(to Nurse Rivers)* Do you know what she's talking about? I don't know what she's talking about. *(to Perez)* What do you mean Doctor Schaefer's in Room 806 dead?

NURSE PEREZ I mean, he's lying on the far bed, stone dead, and with an I.V. tube sticking out of him. And if you don't believe me, maybe you just ought to get up and look for yourself.

With a short, irritable sigh, Mrs. Reardon abandons her paperwork and heads down the west corridor, followed by Nurses Perez and Rivers. CAMERA TRACKS as Mrs. Reardon turns to Nurse Rivers.

MRS. REARDON All right, maybe you'd better call Mrs. Christie.

Phone RINGS.

BOCK'S HOTEL ROOM.

Dark. Venetian blinds drawn. TV set on, a gray coarse-grained square. PHONE RINGS.

DR. HERBERT BOCK, 53 years old, a large man, bulky, disheveled, apparently fell asleep in a chair while watching television the night before. The bed still has its spread on but is rumpled. Bock is in trousers and shirt, collar opened, barefooted. PHONE RINGS. The reading lamp is the only light in the room except for the sheen of gray hissing from the television. Newspapers litter the floor. Books, two-day-old plates of food, yesterday's mugs of coffee, cigar-stuffed ashtrays, a shirt, a pair of pants, a winter overcoat, a battered gray fedora have been slung about. PHONE on the bedtable RINGS again, begins to penetrate the sotted sleep of the man. Two bottles of booze, one empty, and a clump of glasses are on the coffee table in front of Bock. He grunts, opens an eye. PHONE RINGS. Bock suddenly exsufflates in a snorting grunt. He stands, shuffles to the bed, a big, sodden fellow, picks up the receiver, interrupting its next RING. He sinks, sitting on the bed.

BOCK   This is Dr. Bock...Yes, Mrs. Christie, what is it? It's all right, I'd be getting up in a few minutes anyway...I'm sorry I missed that. Would you say it again? Yes, I know him, Schaefer, the stud with the glasses, who fancies the nurses... I'm afraid I don't understand that, what do you mean? Was he sick? I mean, was he...uh, what was the cause of death? Was he being treated? I don't understand. What was he doing in the bed? You did say he... Look, Mrs. Christie, did you call the office? Good, well, I'll... No, no, it's all right. I'll be getting my wake-up call any minute anyway.

He returns the receiver to its cradle, sits disoriented, unbuttoning his shirt.

HOSPITAL. MORNING. 8:00 A.M.

LONG SHOT of the hospital, now alive and jumping. Taxis pull up and out of the large U-shaped drive. A noisy picket line of about twenty chanting protesters parade with signs in an uneven ellipse.

GRUMBLING PROTESTERS *(chanting)* Two-four! Help the poor!

*Most of the placards are slogan-y: "PEOPLE YES! DOCTORS NO!"—
"CURE POVERTY! HEAL THE POOR!" Two protesters move toward
the street, waving and yelling at an approaching car. One, a young white
fellow wears a sandwich board that goes into the matter at some length:
"WE PROTEST THE EVICTION OF 386 BLACK FAMILIES AND
THE DESTRUCTION OF THEIR HOMES TO SERVE THE
EXPANSIONIST POLICIES OF THIS IMPERIALIST HOSPITAL."*

*In the back seat of the car sits JOHN SUNDSTROM, handsomely graying,
tanned, early fifties, the Director of the Hospital. He looks up. That young
demonstrator, DR. IVES, a sandy-haired bespectacled man of 30 in a white
doctor's coat, sidles to the car's open rear window angrily shouting.*

DR. IVES What do you say, Sundstrom? How much longer do you think
our monopolistic, exclusionary, racist policies will work?

PROTESTER We're the hope!

*Sundstrom lowers his window and gives his driver directions. He exits in the
BACKGROUND parking area, where he notices Bock emerging from his
car. Sundstrom waits for him.*

SUNDSTROM So how's it going, Herb?

*Bock's sour glance says it all. He locks his car, joins Sundstrom, and the two
men start down the concrete ramp.*

BOCK *(after a moment)* One of my interns dropped dead this morning.

SUNDSTROM Really? I'm sorry to hear that. I understand you've
moved out to a hotel.

BOCK Yes.

SUNDSTROM It got that bad with Phyllis?

BOCK It's been that bad for twenty-four years. Are you going to be solicitous?

SUNDSTROM Yes.

BOCK Oh, God.

They trudge across the U-shaped entrance drive, pausing to let a car pass.

SUNDSTROM Listen, Herb, I'm the guy who brought you into this hospital, so I think I can skip the diplomatic overtures. Marty stopped me in the hall yesterday, very upset. He had just had lunch with you and said you sounded suicidal. Marty tends to be extravagant, but he's not the only one. Jack Singer mentioned the other day you've been boozing it up a lot. And let's face it, you've been sloughing off. I understand you haven't even been doing rounds.

BOCK I'm going to do rounds today.

They pick their way around the shuffling line of protesters—many with Afro haircuts and tinted glasses, including a black minister and four young white activists.

HOSPITAL, HOLLY PAVILION, EXECUTIVE CORRIDOR.

Early-arriving secretaries chat in the doorways. The corridor itself connects to the Bryce Pavilion (pediatrics, gynecology and obstetrics), so a steady stream of traffic moves back and forth. Bock and Sundstrom enter the corridor and slow to a halt to continue their chat by a wall.

SUNDSTROM Herb, want a couple of days off?

BOCK No.

SUNDSTROM Go down to Montego Bay, get drunk, get laid, get a little sun.

BOCK For God's sake, John, I'm fifty-three years old with all the attendant fears. I just left my wife after twenty-four years. Standard case of menopausal melancholy.

SUNDSTROM Maybe you ought to have a talk with Joe Einhorn.

BOCK I don't want to see a psychiatrist. Stop worrying about me. All I have to do is get my ass back to work, and I'll be fine. I'm sorry I've caused you concern.

He sets off down the long corridor to the elevators. MILTON MEAD, the Administrator of the Hospital, comes out of one of the offices, waves a good morning to Bock, who acknowledges him and plods on. Mead comes up to Sundstrom, now moving toward his own office.

MILTON MEAD Sid just called from St. Luke's, and he's heard that the demonstrators up there are planning a march to join the bunch down here.

SUNDSTROM Oh, God. *(He wraps his arm around Mead's shoulders, ushering him into his office area.)* Did you call the cops?

MILTON MEAD Yes.

HOLLY PAVILION, EIGHTH FLOOR. 8:15 A.M.

The elevator door opens. Out comes Bock, overcoat unbuttoned now. He clumps to the Nurses' Station. An unusual number of nurses seems to be there. Through the doorway of the floor pharmacy, we can see Nurse Rivers of the night shift being comforted by Nurse Perez of the night shift and Nurse Edwards of the morning shift. The head morning nurse, MRS. DONO-VAN, is at the desk hunched over her paperwork. (Nurses are always hunched over their paperwork.) NURSE FELICIA CHILE is also seated at the desk doing some paperwork. Head Nurse Donovan looks up briefly as Dr. Bock approaches.

MRS. DONOVAN *(back to her paperwork)* They're all in Eight-O-Six, Doctor.

BOCK What happened?

MRS. DONOVAN I think I'll just let Mrs. Christie tell you about it.

Bock lumbers off for the west corridor through a press of activity. Kitchen workers trundle creaking portable carts, nurse's aids and attendants pop in and out of doorways bearing trays and used dishes. A robed patient or two ambulates along the hall. Morning rounds have just started, which means a clump of white-jacketed, white-trousered young doctors are gathered in a gaggle at the far end. The group includes senior resident MONROE BRUBAKER, junior resident HARVEY BIEGELMAN, interns SAM CHANDLER and IRVING AMBLER and another medical student, all lounging outside a door discussing the condition of the patient within.

Chandler is presenting the case from a handful of notecards in his hand. The others lean against the walls, listening. They wear shirts and ties with the exception of Ambler, who is new to the floor and still in the canonical white tunic under his jacket. They are all in their twenties and have swinger side-burns and occasional mustaches. When he spots Dr. Bock, senior resident Brubaker turns the rounds over to Biegelman and joins Bock just outside 806.

BRUBAKER *(as he approaches, rolls his eyes)* Oh boy.

BOCK What happened?

BRUBAKER I've seen some pretty good snafus, but this one...I mean, there's a certain splendor to this one. One of the night nurses, a float, thought Schaefer was a patient and plugged an I.V. into him. He was a diabetic, you know.

BOCK What do you mean, a nurse plugged an I.V. into him?

BRUBAKER Oh, it's really a screwed-up story, Doctor. You see, what happened was we had an old man in that bed who died last night, so the bed was available. And you know Schaefer. He's Sammy Stud.

BOCK And he talked a nurse into zapping him on that bed.

BRUBAKER   I think it was a girl from hematology he's been running with.

BOCK   My God, it's a Roman farce.

The door to Room 806 opens, and an Assistant Administrator named HITCHCOCK pokes his head out.

HITCHCOCK   I thought I heard you out here, Doctor.   *(He too rolls his eyes heavenward in an expression of incredulity.)*

Bock makes a noise and goes into...

ROOM 806.

Aside from Hitchcock, the room includes MRS. CHRISTIE, the Director of Nurses, a fusty forty-six, in streetclothes; Head Night Nurse, Mrs. Reardon, in uniform; Head Evening Nurse, MRS. DUNNE, mid-fifties, who had apparently been called in from home because she's in mufti and wearing a winter coat; and, of course, the comatose patient and the dead Dr. Schaefer. Mrs. Christie is instructing the two nurses.

MRS. CHRISTIE   I'll need one from both of you, three copies, and I suggest you do that right now. The forms are in my office...

Mrs. Dunne, on the verge of tears, head bobbing, looks up to Bock.

MRS. DUNNE   I'm really so terribly sorry about this, Dr. Bock. I...

BOCK   *(regarding Schaefer's rigid death mask)* As I understand it, one of the nurses inadvertently administered an I.V. to Schaefer here. How the hell could that happen?

HITCHCOCK   Listen, I think we ought to straighten this out somewhere else.

MRS. CHRISTIE   Yes, very good idea. Oh God, what a mess.

They all file out now, Bock in the rear into....

HALLWAY, NURSES' STATION AND LOBBY AREA.

They all go along to the Nurses' Station where Mrs. Reardon and Mrs. Dunne disappear into the rooms behind. Mrs. Christie leads Hitchcock and the trailing Bock to the TV-solarium; but Dr. Brubaker is now holding his rounds there. He stands, quietly expounding on the uses of heparin, a deco- agulant. One of the patients last night had hemorrhaged consequent to inju- dicious use of that drug. Listening, the other young doctors make notes. Mrs. Christie leans against the wall. Apparently, the conference is to take place in the corridor. Background activity continues normally.

MRS. CHRISTIE *(with a sigh)* Well, these things happen, of course.

HITCHCOCK I suppose I'd better call the Medical Examiner.

BOCK I still don't know what happened.

MRS. CHRISTIE Well, it took an hour to get it sorted out. It seems a patient named Guernsey died last night in Eight-O-Six, but that information wasn't given to the night nurses. These things happen.

Bock has begun to get the drift. A curious state of apathy settles over him.

MRS. CHRISTIE *(rattling on)* At any rate, according to the cardex, the patient Guernsey was down for twenty-five milligrams of Sparine Q-6-H, so Mrs. Reardon sent Nurse Perez to give him his twelve o'clock shot. Meanwhile, it seems Dr. Schaefer had usurped that particular bed for his own purposes. Dr. Brubaker suggests it was for a love tryst, and some weight is given that hypothesis by the fact that Dr. Schaefer was naked.

BOCK *(trying to give his attention to this)* I get the drift, Mrs. Christie. In other words, Nurse Perez went in and sedated Dr. Schaefer thinking it was the patient Guernsey. My God! What I don't understand...

MRS. CHRISTIE If I may finish, Doctor. Well, after Perez gave him his shot, she noticed the I.V. on the bed had been pinched off, and she reported that back to Mrs. Reardon, who then assigned Nurse Rivers to restart the I.V. *(Bock sighs.)* Now Rivers was a float. She didn't even know the staff people on the floor, and nobody knew what the patient Guernsey looked like anyway, since he'd only been admitted that morning.

BOCK So she plugged an I.V. into him.

MRS. CHRISTIE Yes.

BOCK How much?

MRS. CHRISTIE A liter.

BOCK *(The doctor in him intrudes into his lassitude.)* A five percent glucose solution won't kill anybody. Did he have any other ancillary conditions? He wasn't dehydrated, was he? Didn't anybody bother to go in to check him during the night, even under the impression he was merely a patient? Was he hyperasthmolic? Did he have a bad heart? He must have had some kind of thrombosis. I want the post done here, Mr. Hitchcock. And you and I better have a little chat, Mrs. Christie, about your excessive use of float nurses.

MRS. CHRISTIE I've got nearly a thousand nurses in this hospital.

BOCK *(gathering rage)* And every time one of them has her period, she disappears for three days. My doctors complain regularly they can't find the same nurse on the same floor two days in a row. What the hell am I supposed to tell that boy Schaefer's parents? That a substitute nurse assassinated him, because she couldn't tell the doctors from the patients on the floor? My God, the incompetence here is absolutely radiant! I mean, two separate nurses walk into a room, stick needles into a man—and one of those was a number eighteen jelco!—tourniquet the poor sonofabitch, anchor the poor sonofabitch's arm with adhesive tape, and it's the wrong poor sonofabitch! I mean, my God! Where do you train your nurses, Mrs. Christie? Dachau!? *(He is aware his voice has risen and is attracting attention. He lowers his voice.)*

All right, wrap him up and get him down to Pathology. I'm especially interested in his blood sugar. A liter of glucose never killed anybody. Your ladies must've done something else to him.

MRS. CHRISTIE Will there be anything else, Doctor?

BOCK No.

HITCHCOCK Before you call the family, Doctor, I wish you'd talk to Mr. Mead about this. We'd like, naturally, to avoid litigation.

Bock heads abruptly down the corridor to the elevators.

HOLLY PAVILION, SEVENTH FLOOR, CORRIDOR.

A corridor of offices. This is the Department of Medicine, where Bock and all the senior staff members of the department have their offices. It's quiet, since most of the staff are away at their various specialties about the hospital.

Bock comes up the corridor still wearing the overcoat he arrived in some hours ago. He has only managed to unbutton it in all the time it has taken him to reach the corner office. Gilt lettering on the door reads: DEPARTMENT OF MEDICINE and below that DR. HERBERT E. BOCK.

BOCK'S OFFICE, OUTER OFFICE.

Small office with two desks. As Department Chief, Bock gets two secretaries. Both are at their desks, one on the phone, MISS GLORIA LEBOW, and the other rattling away on the IBM, MISS STEPHANIE McGUIRE.

MISS LEBOW *(mouthing)* Coffee?

It would seem not. Bock waves a listless hand, exits into...

BOCK'S PRIVATE OFFICE.

The modestly imposing office is lined with medical tomes. Bock slips out of his coat and jacket and hangs them in the closet. In shirtsleeves with his tie a bit askew—fastidiousness in dress is not Bock's strong point—he crosses to his desk and sits, breathing more heavily than his small exertions would seem to warrant. He seems exhausted. There is a KNOCK on the door. Miss Lebow enters, holding a filing envelope stuffed with papers.

MISS LEBOW A few things have been piling up. Would you like to go into them?

A guttural noise indicates yes. Miss Lebow pulls up a chair, opens her folder.

MISS LEBOW A quickie. Dr. Esterhazy wants to start hiring temporary people to cover the summer vacations. He says last year some of the replacement people didn't receive their checks until they waited six months. He wonders if you could do something about getting these people paid more promptly.

She places a sheet of paper on the desk in front of Bock. He tries to give his attention to it.

MISS LEBOW *(drones on)* Miss Aronovici complains the lab reports are coming in slow into the E.R. I called Dr. Immelman about that, and she said three microscopes have been stolen out of her lab in the last two months. Charley Waters also complains about pilferage. I've clumped all those together for you...*(She lays a sheaf of memos in front of Bock, who stares at them blankly.)* Now, as you know, Doctor, we've agreed to take over the local ambulance cases as part of the hospital's commitment to the community, and it's created a serious overload in the E.R. I don't know why this was dumped in our lap, but...

Bock obviously isn't up to all this. He waves a limp hand to stop Miss Lebow's morning report.

BOCK *(staring at his desktop)* Find out if Dr. Einhorn is in his office yet.

MISS LEBOW Which Dr. Einhorn? Ophthalmology or Psychiatry?

BOCK Psychiatry. *(suddenly stands)* Never mind. I'll look in myself.

He lumbers across the room and out into...

BOCK'S OUTER OFFICE.

...and down past Miss McGuire, rattling away on her IBM, and out into...

HOLLY PAVILION, SEVENTH FLOOR, CORRIDOR.

...down past several closed doors, stopping at a door marked DEPARTMENT OF PSYCHIATRY, DR. JOSEPH EINHORN. He enters.

DR. EINHORN'S OFFICE, SECRETARY'S OFFICE.

A secretary at her desk, sips coffee and reads a paperback novel.

BOCK Is he in?

The doctor is obviously in. He can be seen through the open door sitting at his desk writing in a notebook. Bock leans in.

BOCK Can you give me a few minutes, Joe?

EINHORN *(short, chunky, bespectacled, late fifties)* Of course.

Bock goes in, closes the door behind himself.

DR. EINHORN'S OFFICE.

Bock looks only at the floor.

BOCK *(ill at ease)* I've been having periods of acute depression recently. Apparently, it's becoming noticeable. A number of people have remarked on it. Anyway, John Sundstrom thought it might be a good idea if I spoke to you about it.

EINHORN Do you want to sit down, Herb?

BOCK No. I'm not good at confessional. *(He ambles around.)* Well, what can I tell you? The last year, two, three...it goes way back, I suppose. I can remember entertaining suicidal thoughts as a college student. At any rate, I've always found life demanding. I'm an only child of lower-middle-class people. I was the glory of my parents. My son the doctor. Well, you know. I was always top of my class. Scholarship to Harvard. The boy genius, the brilliant eccentric. Terrified of women, clumsy at sports. God, Joe, how the hell do I go about this?

EINHORN I understand you just separated from your wife.

BOCK I left her a dozen times. She left me a dozen times. We stayed together through a process of attrition. Obviously sado-masochistic dependency. My home is hell. We've got a twenty-three-year-old boy I threw out of the house last year. A shaggy-haired Maoist. I don't know where he is, presumably building bombs in basements as an expression of his universal brotherhood. I've got a seventeen-year-old daughter who's had two abortions in two years and got arrested last week at a rock festival for pushing drugs. They let her off. The typical affluent American family. I don't mean to be facile about this.

Indeed, he does not. He is horrified by the fact his eyes are wet and he is verging on tears. He turns away quickly.

BOCK I blame myself for those two useless young people. I never exercised parental authority. I'm no good at that. Oh, God, I'm no good at this either. Joe, let's just forget the whole thing. I'm sorry I bothered you.

He starts for the door.

EINHORN How serious are your suicidal speculations, Herb?

BOCK *(at the door)* I amuse myself with different ways of killing myself that don't look like suicide. I wouldn't want to do my family out of the insurance.

EINHORN Digitalis will give you an arrhythmia.

BOCK   A good toxologist would find traces. Potassium's much better. Sixty milli equivalent. Instantaneous. Of course, then you're stuck with how to get rid of the hypodermic. Forty milli equivalent. Gives you plenty of time to dispose of the evidence.

EINHORN You seem to have given considerable thought to the matter.

BOCK   You ought to know a man who talks about it all the time never does it.

EINHORN   I don't know. I see a man who's exhausted, emotionally drained, riddled with guilt, and has been systematically stripping himself of his wife, children, friends, isolating himself from the world. Are you impotent?

BOCK   Intermittently.

EINHORN   What does that mean?

BOCK   It means I haven't tried in so long, I don't know. Let's just drop the whole thing, Joe. I feel humiliated and stupid. All I have to do is pull myself together and get back into my work. I'm sorry I troubled you. Take care of yourself. I'll see you.

Before Einhorn can say a word, he slips away and disappears into his own office.

HOLLY PAVILION. 8:30 A.M.

The score of protesters outside the pavilion still move in an uneven ellipse and shout: "Two—Four! Help the Poor!" Ives, the bespectacled demonstrator who shouted at Sundstrom earlier, is removing his sandwich boards and giving them to his replacement. He hurries across the walk and into...

HOLLY PAVILION, LOBBY.

Ives cuts through the congestion of people and moves swiftly up the long cor-

ridor leading to the Farkis Building, unbuttoning his overcoat as he goes into...

THE FARKIS BUILDING, FIFTH FLOOR.

...and comes out, as the elevator opens. This is a laboratory floor, and the corridors are empty except for a white-uniformed orderly leaning against a wall and for one young woman in a white smock in the background, who waves to the young man before disappearing into one of the rooms. Ives fishes out a ring of keys and unlocks the door to his own lab. He enters into...

FARKIS BUILDING, NEPHROLOGY LAB.

Dingy and cheerless place, as labs go. Ives hangs his coat in the cupboard, loosens his tie, unbuttons his suit jacket, squats on a stool, reaches over for a loose file on the work table, opens the file and begins to read the papers inside.

A door CLICKS open behind him, and without looking up, he waves briefly to whoever has entered. CAMERA DOLLIES to FULL SHOT of Ives frowning over his notes. We are suddenly conscious of a white-uniformed presence behind him. We know it's medical personnel, but we can't see the face. Ives starts to turn to the presence behind him, when suddenly a small hospital sandbag is whipped down on his head, and he slumps forward, his forehead thumping against the black surface of the lab table.

DISSOLVE TO:

HOSPITAL. NOON.

HIGH ANGLE SHOT establishing the passing of hours. Sun high overhead, traffic on First Avenue an impenetrable river of HONKS and HOOTS. At a crosswalk, a loose procession of fifty or so shouting demonstrators, bearing placards, flows toward the main gates. Their posters read: "FIGHT DOPE—NOT DOPES!" "DRUGS YES! TRANSPLANTS NO!" and "SAVE OUR KIDS FROM THE SKIDS!" which is what they now chant: "Save our kids! From the Skids!" The demonstration moves through a handful of city cops where our original group of twenty still ramble around, chanting: "Two—Four! Help the Poor!"

HOLLY PAVILION, EIGHTH FLOOR.

The staff elevator doors open and Bock comes out, wearing his long white doctor's coat unbuttoned. Hanging about the Nurses' Station are Dr. Brubaker and a few young men in white. They come quickly to respectful attention at Bock's entrance. CLATTERING TRAYS dominate the lunchtime atmosphere.

BOCK All set?

BRUBAKER Yes, sir.

The doctors move off toward the solarium on the east corridor overlooking the river. They pass a curious quartet of people consisting of a very handsome YOUNG WOMAN in her late twenties in an out-of-fashion miniskirt (She has great legs, long and tanned.); an ELDERLY MAN, uncomfortable in city clothes and unmistakably an INDIAN; a tall overcoated man in his forties wearing a MINISTER's white collar; and a DISTINGUISHED MAN dressed in fashionable gray who is trying to persuade the young woman of something. The young woman and the Indian stand absolutely still, silent, impassive. The minister is more fidgety.

BOCK *(to Brubaker en passant)* Who's that exotic group?

BRUBAKER *(murmurs)* You got me. They've been here about an hour.

ONE YOUNG DOCTOR I think they're with the old man in Eight-O-Six.

Bock and Brubaker, trailed by young doctors, move into the TV room.

BOCK Dr. Perry said he picked the tuberculosis and the liver nodes for today, right?

BRUBAKER Yes, sir.

BOCK Good. Because that's the one I studied up. A hell of a case.

EIGHTH FLOOR, TV ROOM.

Some twenty-five or thirty young doctors, two or three of them black, three or four of them women, fill the room. At Bock's entrance, they find places around the walls, sofas, soft chairs and benches. The TV set has been pushed into a corner, and a large portable blackboard has been set up. This is the Chief of Service Round, attended by every available intern and resident. Somebody closes the door, just as two young doctors come hurrying in.

BOCK All right, who's presenting?

EMERGENCY AREA, WAITING ROOM.

People of all ages sit around on aluminum chairs arranged around the walls of the room. All are in streetclothes. Some speak to each other. A line of people, extending into the hallway and holding their charts, waits for a lady from the accounting department taking Blue Cross numbers. This lady from accounting is MRS. CUSHING, late forties, bespectacled and testy. She calls out at large.

MRS. CUSHING Is there anybody seated who hasn't been to see me first? Is there anyone here who hasn't given me their health insurance number?

Her phone RINGS. She picks it up.

MRS. CUSHING Emergency Room... Well, I don't know, Sybil. What's his name?

To a man on line at her desk, thrusting his chart out to her.

MRS. CUSHING Would you wait a moment, please. I'm on the phone, can't you see I'm on the phone? *(rummaging through a stack of charts, large paper forms in quadruplicate)...* Of course not, do they ever? *(hangs up, takes two charts from the desk, pushes through the waiting line)* Would you mind, please. I have to get through, do you mind?

She makes her way to the door and goes out into...

EMERGENCY AREA, ENTRANCE LOBBY.

...which is congested. Mrs. Cushing enters...

EMERGENCY, ADMITTING AND TREATMENT ROOMS.

NURSE *(on phone)* Give me that one again...thirty-two?

Facing the desk are six curtained treatment rooms, mostly open to view. Behind the desk are a supply room and another treatment room. Both are occupied, the former by a PARANOID LADY wringing her hands in a paranoid rush and listened to by a very patient young intern.

PARANOID LADY They follow me everywhere. Three big black men. Naked, completely exposed. Right in the street. Hanging down to their knees. Disgusting. They're waiting out there for me now...

...and in the other room, a man in his thirties is being treated for some sort of head lacerations. In one treatment room, the Chief of Emergency Service, DR. SPEZIO, a man in his late thirties, along with an intern, an anesthesiologist and a nurse, is bent over a naked and comatose young black woman of eighteen, covered somewhat with a sheet. She's a junkie, being intubated, i.e. a small endotracheal tube has been inserted into her mouth. This is the most melodramatic of the varied activity here.

A middle-aged man complaining of chest pains is lying clothed in another treatment room; a nurse attends him.

An asthmatic middle-aged woman sits in still another room being administered her 500 mg. of amenophylene subcutaneously.

The curtains on another room are drawn for privacy. On chairs in the corner sit a teenage boy with a badly sprained ankle and an elderly man bathing his hand in an enamel basin held in his lap.

A young mother with a five-year-old daughter with a badly cut arm is being attended to by the back wall. The Emergency Room Nursing Supervisor, MISS ARONOVICI, a pretty woman in her mid-twenties, is sterilizing the little girl's wound.

Mrs. Cushing makes her way to Miss Aronovici. They detest each other.

MRS. CUSHING Did you call upstairs and tell them to admit a patient named Mitgang?

MRS. ARONOVICI *(continuing to treat the little girl)* The concussion?

MRS. CUSHING I don't know. They just called me. They said you didn't fill out the chart. And where do you come off sending anyone up to Admitting without my okay?

Miss Aronovici turns to Mrs. Cushing, regarding her sweetly.

MRS. ARONOVICI Sally, would you get the fuck out of here. The patient's in the Holding Room. You want his Blue Cross number, you go in and you get his Blue Cross number.

Mrs. Cushing elbows back through the line of patients waiting at the Admitting desk..

MRS. CUSHING Do you mind, please...

There are now three nurses behind the desk, all of them on phones. One nurse calls to Dr. Spezio.

NURSE O.P.D. wants to know how that asthmatic they sent down is.

DR. SPEZIO *(just leaving the group around the junkie)* She's fine. We'd like to keep her here a little while.

Spezio heads for the door where he is intercepted by Mrs. Cushing.

MRS. CUSHING May I see you a moment, Doctor, if you don't mind.

DR. SPEZIO *(sighs, calls back to the triage nurse)* I'll be right back.

He goes out, followed by Mrs. Cushing, into...

EMERGENCY AREA, LOBBY.

Spezio and Mrs. Cushing move between laundry and supply carts.

MRS. CUSHING *(thrusting some papers at the doctor)* If you don't mind, Doctor, is this your handwriting?

Spezio stops, sighs, examines the paper.

MRS. CUSHING Am I supposed to read that? Was it a sprain? Was it a broken wrist? I can't read that scribbling. I mean, I have to bill these people. I know you doctors are the ministering angels, and I'm just the bitch from the Accounting Department, but I have my job to do too. I mean, if you don't mind, Doctor...?

DR. SPEZIO *(studies the paper)* The kid had a collar fracture. We had him in the O.R. We reduced it and we gave him a small cast.

He strides off.

MRS. CUSHING *(calls after him)* But did you give him a sling? You must have taken X-rays. How am I supposed to make up the charges?

She turns into...

EMERGENCY AREA, HOLDING ROOM.

Designed to hold patients who've been examined and wait to be admitted to a room upstairs, it's in fact used for examination, treatment, storage. The room is quiet. Two male patients lie on comfortable stretchers, apparently sedated and resting. Mrs. Cushing turns to the patient immediately to her right as she enters. To the still figure she poses her questions.

MRS CUSHING Are you Mitgang?

She gets no answer from that bed. From another direction, a voice.

MITGANG I'm Mitgang.

She turns to Mitgang. Something bothers her about the first patient. She finds Mitgang's chart tucked in under his pillow, takes out her pencil.

MRS. CUSHING Do you carry Blue Cross, Blue Shield, Mr. Mitgang, if you don't mind?

Mitgang, eyes closed, emits a sound.

MRS. CUSHING Do you have your card with you? *(no answer)* Do you know your number?

Negative grunt from Mitgang.

MRS. CUSHING Mr. Mitgang, you're not leaving this room until I have this information.

NURSE *(enters for some chore)* Will you leave that man alone?

In a fit of temper, Mrs. Cushing throws the chart and her pencil down on the floor.

MRS. CUSHING *(indicating the other patient)* Do you mind if I at least ask this gentleman to fill out his chart?

She pulls his chart from under his pillow, bends and retrieves her pencil from the floor, straightens. She speaks to the silent patient.

MRS. CUSHING May I have your A.H.S. policy number, sir?

No answer. CAMERA MOVES SLOWLY IN on the patient. We now recognize him as the bespectacled young activist Dr. Ives, so recently coshed over the head with a sandbag.

MRS. CUSHING *(looming)* Do you carry Blue Cross? Blue Shield?

Mrs. Cushing stares at the patient. He is not breathing. Behind her, the nurse exits carrying whatever she came for. Mrs. Cushing turns to her, but she is gone. Frowning, Mrs. Cushing backs out ...

...as Dr. Spezio and others come down the corridor.

MRS. CUSHING   *(as Spezio approaches, with spiteful relish)*   I think one of your patients in here is dead, Dr. Spezio.

DR. SPEZIO   *(enters the Holding Room)*   Why do you say that, Mrs. Cushing?

MRS. CUSHING   Because he wouldn't give me his Blue Cross number, Dr. Spezio.

HOLDING ROOM.

Spezio regards the death mask of a face.

DR. SPEZIO   Oh, Christ.

He moves quickly forward to raise the dead man's eyelid. Behind him, a nurse enters. He wheels on her angrily.

DR. SPEZIO   How the hell long has this man been lying here? Isn't this that doctor who came in around nine o'clock?

MILTON MEAD'S OFFICE. 2:00 P.M.

MILTON MEAD, late thirties, lean, efficient but under constant strain, is having his daily staff luncheon conference, which consists of a CHIEF ENGINEER, the ASSISTANT ADMINISTRATOR OF PERSONNEL, three residents in administration, including Hitchcock, sandwiches and coffee.

CHIEF ENGINEER   I mean, they gave me a hard time, Con Ed. "For Pete's Sake," I said, "this is a hospital. One of our feedlines just blew..."

Mead's phone RINGS and he picks it up.

MILTON MEAD Yeah? *(It's another annoyance; he sighs with irritation.)*

CHIEF ENGINEER I mean, it's lucky we traced it in time.

MILTON MEAD *(on phone)* No, I'll be right up. *(hangs up, stands)* Have we covered about everything?

ADMINISTRATIVE RESIDENT   Dr. Kish has been driving me nuts with the O.R. schedule.

MILTON MEAD He's supposed to see me about that.

He moves across his office into...

MEAD'S SECRETARY'S OFFICE.

Actually a communal office with desks for three secretaries.

MEAD'S SECRETARY *(looks up to Mead from talking on the phone)* This is the Emergency Room. One of the doctors just died of a heart attack.

MILTON MEAD *(pauses)* One of our staff?

MEAD'S SECRETARY I think so.

Mead frowns, leans back into his own office.

MILTON MEAD   *(to Hitchcock)*   Tom, you want to go down to the Emergency Room? One of our doctors just died.

HITCHCOCK What? Another one?

MILTON MEAD Yeah, see what that's about. *(en passant to secretary)* I'll be on Holly Eight. I'll be right back.

HOLLY PAVILION, EIGHTH FLOOR.

The staff elevator door opens, and Milton Mead comes out. He has appar-

ently been buttonholed in the elevator by a woman in a doctor's coat, DR. IMMELMAN, Pathology, who follows him out...

DR. IMMELMEN It's no longer pilferage, Milton. It's reached the point of piracy. That's the third microscope this month.

MILTON MEAD Why don't we get together on this sometime this afternoon, Fran?

DR. IMMELMAN One o'clock?

MILTON MEAD One o'clock will be fine.

He turns left and heads for...

HOLLY PAVILION, EIGHTH FLOOR, NURSES' STATION.

...where Head Nurse Donovan is bent over her paperwork. In the background, we see normal morning hospital activity. Nurse's Aid, SHAR-LENE STONE, takes towels into a room. R.N. Felicia Chile comes out of another, bearing her enamel tray of instruments.

Also in the background, the curious quartet from before—the beautiful woman, the elderly Indian, the minister, Dr. Sutcliffe. Mead hardly notices them as he makes for the desk.

MRS. DONOVAN *(without pausing or looking up)* Your brother's in the room, Mr. Mead.

MILTON MEAD What room is it?

MRS. DONOVAN Eight-O-Six.

Mead bobs his head thank you and heads for the west corridor.

EIGHTH FLOOR, ROOM 806.

As Milton Mead enters, his elder brother, WILLIAM MEAD, mid-forties, a smaller and manifestly nervous man, is seated sullenly puffing a cigar, fidgeting, still wearing his coat and hat. He looks up briefly when Milton enters and avoids his brother's eye. His wife, MARILYN, late thirties, is standing in suppressed exasperation, staring out the window. Out of respect for the COMATOSE PATIENT, the ensuing agitated scene is held in whispers.

MILTON MEAD   For heaven's sake, Willie, you're going to be in the hospital for two lousy days. What're you making such a fuss about?

WILLIAM MEAD   You're supposed to be such a big wheel here.

MILTON MEAD   There are no private rooms available. If they brought in Jesus Christ fresh off the cross, I couldn't get Him a private room.

WILLIAM MEAD   I'm not going to stay in a room with a dying man...

MARILYN MEAD   He's not dying. They'll screen him off. You won't even know he's here.

MILTON MEAD   If you want a private room, go on home, and I'll call you the first one that comes up. But you're the one who phoned me in a panic, you're going on a vacation. For heaven's sake, Willie, they'll cut this polyp out tomorrow morning. You'll be home Thursday, you'll be in Miami Friday. Marilyn, will you talk some sense into this lunatic?

MARILYN MEAD   Well, you said it, he's a lunatic.

WILLIAM MEAD   Big wheel, can't even get me a private room.

MILTON MEAD   I'll get you a tranquilizer...

He exits.

EIGHTH FLOOR, TV ROOM.

Bock—excited, vivid, alive—is in full flush with his lecture. He moves around in front of the blackboard, chalk in hand. The blackboard itself is scrawled with formulae and diagrams.   He is writing the words "full abdomen," as the fifth in a list reading "(1) parexia, (2) hepatomegaly, (3) splenomegaly, (4) episodes of arthralgia."   The audience is forty young doctors rapt with attention.   There is a good deal of note-taking.

BOCK   ...five, a full abdomen contrasted to wasting elsewhere; six, ascites with a protein content above four grams; unexplained anemia, leukopenia, unexplained elevation of the serum gamma globulin level, especially abnormal flocculation tests, and of course, a positive P.P.D. All these findings assume special significance among Negroes. This has been a very commendable workup, as commendable a workup of an F.U.O. as I can remember. The staff of this floor is to be applaud-ed.   *(spots Brubaker among the others)* It's a reportable case, Brubaker. Write it up.   *(a brief, rare smile)* Well, let's go have a look at the girl.

He rumbles toward the door. The class of doctors dissolves into hospital mur-murs and mutters and a general dispersal. They follow Bock out to...

EIGHTH FLOOR, EAST CORRIDOR.

...where Dr. Sutcliffe, the beautiful young woman, the elderly Indian and the minister are engaged in agitated discussion. The girl and the Indian retain their stoic impassivity. Dr. Sutcliffe leaves them and moves down the corridor to the counter of ...

EIGHTH FLOOR NURSES' STATION.

SUTCLIFFE   Nurse! Nurse, who's the Senior Resident on this floor?

NURSE   That would be Dr. Brubaker. But I'm afraid he's at Chief of Service rounds right now.

Sutcliffe points off right.

SUTCLIFFE   That's...this way?

The nurse nods indifferently.

ACROSS to Bock coming out of the TV room, followed by some dozen young doctors. Bock is in very good spirits indeed. He quizzes his young doctors en route:

BOCK   I wonder if there might not be some correlation between hepatic tuberculosis and drug addiction. Presumably, there was an early consideration of S.B.E.

BRUBAKER *(off-screen)* Yes, sir. We discounted it after repeated blood cultures were negative.

BOCK You, Ambler. Is that right, Ambler?

AMBLER Yes, sir.

BOCK What else do you look for in bacterial endocarditis?

AMBLER *(nervous)* Some sort of embolic phenomena, sir.

BOCK Good.

SUTCLIFFE *(flagging Brubaker)* Dr. Brubaker, I wonder if I could see you for a moment?

Brubaker detaches himself from his group to join Sutcliffe. CAMERA STAYS with Bock and his entourage, following them down the east corridor, Bock still happily conducting class. Bock strides into...

ROOM 819.

Past two beds, they group around the foot of a third bed on the right side of the room. Bock checks the patient lying in the bed.

BOCK Still a little icteric. Who's got an opthalmoscope?

One of the young men hands his to Bock, who leans over the patient to look through it.

BOCK Did anyone note Roth spots?

The doctors exchange a look as Bock rises, moves toward them, laughing.

BOCK Well, don't worry about it. There aren't any. Ambler, you're our big man on S.B.E. What was the latex-fixation?

BIEGELMAN It wasn't done, sir.

BOCK Don't you think that's an important test to differentiate S.B.E. from miliary T.B.?

BIEGELMAN *(off-screen)* No, s...

BOCK Not you, Biegelman. Ambler.

AMBLER Well, there's about a seventy percent incidence of false-positive latex in S.B.E.

Bock hands the opthalmoscope to Ambler.

BOCK You have been reading up. If the diagnosis were S.B.E., would a positive latex indicate anything in the therapy?

AMBLER We'd expect the latex to become negative.

BOCK If...?

AMBLER If the antibiotic therapy were successful.

BOCK Are you applying for your internship here?

AMBLER I'm not sure.

BOCK Come and see me. *(to the patient, helping her up)* Would you sit up for a minute?

Bock turns to the off-screen patient, helping her sit up and forward, percussing her back as the students look on.

EIGHTH FLOOR, EAST CORRIDOR.

Brubaker and Sutcliffe are now both involved in discussion with the woman, the Indian and the minister, as Bock drifts through the background, followed by the band of young doctors now dispersing. Bock crosses past the foreground group to the staff elevator. He pushes the button. Brubaker approaches Bock. They confer quietly in the hallway.

BRUBAKER We've got a little thing over here, Doctor. The girl over there is the daughter of the patient in Eight-O-Six. He is at the moment comatose and requires intravenous feeding and meds.

The elevator comes and goes, disgorging some, taking on others. Bock, who greeted Brubaker with a rare, benign smile, has begun to look a bit sodden. Poor Brubaker, aware of the gathering storm in Bock's demeanor, sighs and continues regardless.

BRUBAKER The thing is, the daughter wants to take the father out of the hospital and back to Mexico where they live. The patient's name is Drummond. He's apparently a Methodist missionary, and he and his daughter run some kind of religious mission among the Apache Indians. The daughter claims to be a licensed nurse, so she can give the necessary I.V. treatment. I certainly don't think he should be let out of this hospital. The Attending—he's the guy in gray over there—concurs.

Bock squints at Brubaker.

BOCK All right, wait a minute. Let me have all that again.

BRUBAKER As a matter of fact, Doctor, this is Dr. Biegelman's case.

BOCK Never mind the professional ethics, what happened?

BRUBAKER *(sighs)* I don't know why I'm covering for that sonofabitch in Farkis Pavilion anyway. *(sighs and begins)* The patient, a man of fifty-six, was admitted to the hospital ten days ago for a check-up, in good health, no visible distress. We did the mandatory work-up on him. Blood cultures, stool, L.E. preps, chest, E.K.G., all negative. But there was apparently some evidence of protein in his urine. I don't know how that sonofabitch in Farkis Pavilion ever found out about it. Maybe he had some kind of deal with one of the girls in the lab. Anyway, he turned up the next day, conned the patient into signing an authorization for a biopsy...

BOCK What sonofabitch in Farkis Pavilion?

BRUBAKER Some post-grad fellow named Ives. Elroy Ives. I never met him. He's on one of the immunology research programs.

BOCK Are you trying to tell me some post-grad fellow came up here and did a biopsy on the patient?

BRUBAKER Yes, sir. He conned Biegelman with that old story about...

BOCK ...protein in the urine?

BRUBAKER Yes, sir.

BOCK And he biopsied the man?

BRUBAKER And he nicked a vessel, and at two o'clock in the morning, they woke up Biegelman because the nurse found the patient in shock. Biegelman called the kidney people for a consult right away. What was there to see? The man was sour and bleeding. We spoke to this fellow Sutcliffe, and he referred us to a surgeon named Welbeck...

BOCK Welbeck?! That barber!

BRUBAKER You ain't heard nothing yet. So we finally got Welbeck around four in the morning. He said, go ahead. So they laid on the surgery for eight. Welbeck turns up, half-stoned, orders an I.V.P., clears him for allergies...

BOCK ...without actually testing.

BRUBAKER Right.

BOCK And the patient went into shock...

BRUBAKER ...and tubular necrosis. They lopped out the bleeding kidney, ran him back to the room, and we sat around waiting for three days to see how obstructed he was. Fever began spiking like hell, euremia, vomiting, so we arranged hemodialysis. He's putting out good water now. But some nurse goofed on his last treatment. A leak in the tube, something. His blood pressure plunged. They ran him right up to I.C.U., checked out vital signs, all normal except he's comatose. That was two days ago.

BOCK In short, a man came into this hospital in perfectly good health, and, in the space of one week, we chopped out one kidney, damaged the other, reduced him to coma and damn near killed him.

BRUBAKER Yes, sir.

A great sad serenity has settled over Bock.

BOCK You know, Brubaker, last night I sat in my hotel room, reviewing the shambles of my life and contemplating suicide. Then I said "No, Bock, don't do it. You're a doctor, a healer. You're the Chief of Medicine at one of the great hospitals of the world. You're a necessary person. Your life is meaningful." Then I came in this morning and find out one of my doctors was killed by a couple of nurses who mistook him for a patient because he screwed a technician from the nephrology lab...

BRUBAKER Hematology, sir.

BOCK And now you come to me with this gothic horror story in which the entire machinery of modern medicine has apparently conspired to destroy one lousy patient. How am I to sustain my feeling of meaningfulness in the face of this? You know, Brubaker, if there was an oven around, I'd stick my head in it. What was the name of that sono-fabitch from Farkis Pavilion again?

BRUBAKER Ives, sir. Elroy Ives. Somebody ought to ream his ass.

The gathering storm erupts. Rage suffuses Bock's face. Out of respect for the hospital corridor and the people working around him and Brubaker, he keeps it glacial. But there is no mistaking the volcanic fury he feels.

BOCK *(barely containing himself)* I'm going to ream his ass. And I'm going to break that barber Welbeck's back. I'm going to defrock those two cannibals. They won't practice in my hospital, I'll tell you that!

BRUBAKER What'll I tell the girl, sir? She says we have no legal right to stop her from taking her father out. She's willing to sign an A.O.R. form.

BOCK Let him go. Before we kill him.

The elevator door opens. A couple of nurses come out. Bock strides in.

SEVENTH FLOOR, DEPT. OF MEDICINE CORRIDOR.

Bock advances in a cold fury down to his office. He wrenches the door open.

BOCK'S OFFICE, OUTER OFFICE.

Miss Lebow and Miss McGuire clatter away at typewriters. Sitting on a chair in the crowded office is a senior staff doctor, a man in his late forties, wearing a coat similar to Bock's. He is DR. LAGERMAN. He looks up from the magazine he's been leafing through as Bock storms in.

DR. LAGERMAN Hi, Herb...

Bock acknowledges him with a brusque nod, storms over to Miss Lebow.

BOCK Get me Dr. Gilley. Put him on page if you have to. I want to talk to him right now. I don't care if he's operating. *(wheels around to Miss McGuire)* And you get me some monkey named Ives. Ives. I-V-E-S, first name Elroy. He's in the Farkis Pavilion.

DR. LAGERMAN   Herb...

BOCK   I want to talk to you, Joe. Would you mind coming into my office?

He strides, followed by Dr. Lagerman, into...

BOCK'S PRIVATE OFFICE.

...and *slams the door shut behind him.*

BOCK   Have you got some punk named Ives rotating in your department?

DR. LAGERMAN   Listen, Herb...

BOCK   *(sits at his desk)* I also want to know what the hell kind of a dialysis room you're running. I just came from...

The phone RINGS. Bock seizes it.

BOCK   Yeah...Gilley? Put him on. Bock. Didn't you tell me a couple of months ago you were going to cut off all privileges for that assassin, Welbeck? Yeah. Wellbeck. He just butchered another one of my patients ... Oh, come on, Harry! The man's a buccaneer! I want him brought before the Medical Executive Committee.... He's in your department, Harry, not mine. He's putatively a surgeon!... I'll be here! *(slams receiver down, stares at Lagerman)* Listen, Joe, I think you should know that you've got a research guy in your department named Ives who's been doing some very dubious biopsies. We're having enough trouble squeezing grants out of the Nixon administration...

DR. LAGERMAN   Ives is dead, Herb. That's why I'm here.

This gives Bock pause. He blinks at Lagerman.

BOCK What do you mean, Ives is dead?

DR. LAGERMAN   I mean he's dead.   He had a heart attack in the Emergency Room.

BOCK He had a heart attack in the Emergency Room?

DR. LAGERMAN Yeah.

BOCK *(blinking)* What the hell is this? Some kind of plague? *(stands)* Where is he now?

DR. LAGERMAN They were just taking him down to Pathology.

HOLLY PAVILION, FIRST FLOOR, PATHOLOGY DEPT.

Bock, Lagerman and Hitchcock have gathered across the shrouded figure of Dr. Ives on a stretcher. We are in the lab section of Pathology; in the background, through the glass part of the door separating the lab from the surgery room, we can see the autopsy on Dr. Schaefer being performed.

Schaefer's naked white cadaver is stretched out on an operating table. He has been opened up and all his vital organs are being excised. It's bloody. The autopsy is being performed by DR. BREWSTER, the Resident in Pathology, dressed in surgical scrub.

HITCHCOCK   ...and the next thing anybody knew, about three hours later, Mrs. Cushing from Accounting came in and said there was a dead man in the Holding Room.

BOCK You don't find anything grotesque about all this?

HITCHCOCK What do you mean?

BOCK I mean, at half past eight this morning, we meet over a doctor who's been killed intravenously, and here we are again, four hours later, with another doctor who had a heart attack in the Emergency Room.

HITCHCOCK   Well, what're you suggesting Doctor? Do you think we have a mad killer stalking the halls of the hospital? Presumably, Dr. Ives died of a heart attack and Schaefer in a diabetic coma. People do die of these things. It's all perhaps coincidental, but I don't think I'd call it grotesque.

BOCK   How long are they going to be on Schaefer's post?

He knocks on the glass window of the door separating the laboratory from the operating room. Dr. Brewster turns from his gory chore. Bock makes a gesture saying, "How much longer?" Brewster raises ten blood-drenched rubber-gloved fingers. Bock turns and shuffles across the lab for the door out.

BOCK   *(pauses at door, to Lagerman)* I don't suppose you'd like to call next of kin?

DR. LAGERMAN   No thanks.

BOCK   *(deeply depressed)* Oh God, I need a drink.

He goes down...

THE PATHOLOGY CORRIDOR

...and is soon lost in the normal traffic of the area.

THE HOSPITAL. NIGHT.

CRASH of THUNDER. CRACKLE of LIGHTNING. A horror-film rainstorm lashes the vast dark complex of buildings.

SEVENTH FLOOR, DEPT. OF MEDICINE CORRIDOR.

Dark, empty, silent. One lonely light at the lobby end of the long, closed corridor of offices. The door to Bock's office stands ajar and issues a trace of light.

BOCK'S OFFICE.

ACROSS the silent, dark, typewriter-covered desks of the two secretaries through the doorway to Bock's private office, we can see Bock at his desk, lit by the desk lamp. He has a bottle of booze on his desk. He gets up from his desk. He has made a decision.

HOLLY PAVILION, EIGHTH FLOOR.

The corridors are silent; the night lights are on, subdued. Head Evening Nurse Mrs. Dunne is back at her desk, hunched over paperwork. Resident Brubaker passes by.

EIGHTH FLOOR, PHARMACY.

Nurse SHERLEE DEVINE, a black woman in her mid-twenties, has a porcelain tray on the shelf onto which she puts a small jar of alcohol, cotton swabs, a wrapped hypodermic needle and syringe. She moves out into...

NURSES' STATION.

...where Mrs. Dunne looks up as she passes.

NURSE DEVINE   Mead.

Mrs. Dunne nods. Nurse Devine makes her way silently down the sleeping doors to...

ROOM 806.

Dark, sleeping. The bathroom light is on, but only a thin stream of yellow light trickles through the door. THUNDER CRASHES. William Mead sleeps fitfully. The other patient is entirely curtained off. Nurse Devine sets her tray on Mead's bedtable, turns on the goose-neck lamp, keeping it from his eyes. She unwraps the hypodermic syringe, sets in the needle, draws the required dosage, reaches over and gently shakes Mead by the shoulder.

NURSE DEVINE (*softly*) Mr. Mead...Mr. Mead, I have an injection for you.

Mead sleeps on. Expressionlessly, Nurse Devine extracts Mead's right arm from under the sheets, wets a swab with alcohol and rubs down the vein. The needle slides into Mead's vein. OVER THIS, we begin to hear a distant sibilant HISSING, indistinct like the leakage of a bad heart. There is also an occasional distinctly human but not quite civilized sound.

CAMERA PULLS BACK SLOWLY to Nurse Devine withdrawing the needle, looking up, for she too has heard the soft, strange sounds. They emanate from behind the curtains of the other bed. Nurse Devine returns the syringe to the tray, gathers her things and pads silently around Mead's bed to Drummond's bed. With her free hand, she opens the curtains a little and stares in.

NURSE DEVINE What the hell is going on in there?

NURSE DEVINE'S P.O.V.: The Indian and BARBARA DRUMMOND bend over Drummond performing some pagan ritual. The HISSING is Barbara's contribution to the ceremony. (It sounds like pis-pis, and is in fact an imitation of the nighthawk, meant to appease the spirit of the thunder.)

The old Indian has stripped to the waist and marked his body with smears of dye and tule pollen. He wears a ceremonial hat, a sort of beaded beanie. He holds a small buckskin bag of pollen in his cupped palms and is facing north, east, south and west, offering the bag and prayers under his breath as he does. A beaded amulet lies stretched across the white sheet covering the comatose Drummond.

When Nurse Devine draws the curtains, Barbara frowns at Nurse Devine, holds a cautioning finger to her lips and draws the curtains closed again. Nurse Devine, carrying her porcelain tray, exits.

EIGHTH FLOOR, NURSES' STATION.

Bock comes out of the elevator, jacketed now, fairly drunk but holding it well.

He heads for the Nurses' Station as Nurse Devine comes down the west cor-
ridor. Bock grunts at Mrs. Dunne and goes into...

PHARMACY.

...where he quickly runs his finger along the second shelf until he comes to the
bottle of potassium which he filches off the shelf and slips into his pocket. He
rummages through the drawers for a hypodermic syringe. Through the open
doorway, we see Nurse Devine making her way swiftly up to Mrs. Dunne at
the desk.

NURSE DEVINE   Well, honey, we got a witch-doctor in Eight-O-Six,
and you better go in there. You know that Indian that was sitting in
Eight-O-Six all night? He's still there, and the girl's there, and they're
doing some voodoo in there, and I ain't kidding.

Behind Mrs. Dunne, Bock appears in the doorway to the pharmacy where he
stands listening.

MRS. DUNNE   *(looking up)* What are you talking about?

NURSE DEVINE   I mean that Indian's in there, half-naked and going
pis-pis-pis with a little bag. You just better get in there, Mrs. Dunne.

Mrs. Dunne, annoyed, gets up and heads for the west corridor, followed by
Nurse Devine and by an intrigued Dr. Bock at a few paces behind.

NURSE DEVINE   *(to NURSE WEITZENBAUM, coming out of another room)*
You want to see somethin', baby? You jus' come here.

As the small procession bears down, Barbara Drummond slips out of that
room to intercept them.

BARBARA   *(keeping her voice low)*   Look, it's a perfectly harmless
ceremony, nothing to get excited about. It'll be over in a few minutes
anyway. Mr. Blacktree is a shaman who gets his power from the thunder, and it's imperative he conclude his rituals while the storm is still
going on.

NURSE DUNNE Visiting hours were over at nine o'clock, Miss.

Bock reaches for the door to the room.

BARBARA All that's going on in there, Doctor, is a simple Apache prayer for my father's recovery.

Bock makes a vague noise, neither contradicting her nor assenting, and continues around her into...

ROOM 806.

As Bock slides in, a bit of the corridor light comes in with him. The curtains have been left sufficiently open to reveal Mr. Blacktree. He is still stripped to the waist and marked with crosses of pollen. He extends two twigs to the four directions after which he places the twigs carefully on the white sheet covering Drummond in a pattern around the amulet already there. Behind Bock, Mrs. Dunne can be seen peeking in. The Indian is oblivious to both of them. Bock watches it all with interest for a moment and then backs out into...

EIGHTH FLOOR CORRIDOR.

...closing the door after him.

BARBARA The markings he's made on my father's arms are from the pollen of the tule plant. The twigs have no significance other than they've been struck by lightning and are consequently appeals to the spirit of lightning. It's all entirely harmless, a religious ceremony, not a medical one.

BOCK You don't seriously believe all that mumbo-jumbo will cure him?

BARBARA On the other hand, it won't kill him, Doctor.

They regard each other levelly.

BOCK *(grunts)* Okay. Go ahead.

He wheels and clumps off for the stairway exit.

BARBARA Thank you.

Nurse Weitzenbaum opens the door of the room and peeks in. At the stairway exit, Bock pauses to look back at all the women in front of Room 806.

BOCK Miss Drummond, are you still taking your father out?

BARBARA Yes. I still have to arrange an ambulance service. Is there a phone around I could use?

BOCK Use my office.

BARBARA Thank you.

Bock exits. Barbara edges past Weitzenbaum, who is still peeking into the room.

ROOM 806.

Barbara comes in, gathers her coat and purse from a chair and moves to the Indian, now occupied with what seems to be the rolling of a cigarette. The two exchange a brief dialogue in Apache. The old Indian nods. Barbara turns and exits, taking Nurse Weitzenbaum out with her and closing the door. The room is dark and hushed again. Blacktree lights his cigarette and "sends the smoke up," a ritual which consists of puffing smoke to each of the four directions, muttering in Apache "May all be well" after each puff.

CAMERA SLOWLY PANS to the other bed where William Mead sleeps fitfully. The Apache words and pis-pis-pis penetrate Mead's drugged sleep. He opens one eyelid and stares glazedly at the dark air. The SOUNDS persist. Blacktree chooses this moment to sidle out from behind the curtains and continue his ritual in the less-confined space at the head of Drummond's bed. It's quite a sight for a nervous, sedated man to wake to. Thunder RUMBLES and the rain SLASHES and a sudden, savage STREAK of lightning illuminates it all.

Mead figures it's all a bad dream and, after a moment of dully regarding the odd spectacle, closes his one eye and goes back to sleep.

BOCK'S OFFICE, OUTER OFFICE.

Barbara Drummond comes in. Bock has apparently turned the lights on for her, but Bock himself is not immediately visible. She looks through the half-open door to Bock's private office, and there he is, staring blankly at the bottle. Barbara starts to say something, thinks better of it, lays down her coat, and looking around, spots a Manhattan classified directory which she hauls up from its shelf and sets on Miss Lebow's desk. She sits, quickly flips through the pages.

Barbara flips through the directory. Bock is partially visible in the background at his desk. He sits soddenly. Barbara finds what she wants, opens her purse and takes out two airplane tickets. She dials. The CLICKING of the dial catches Bock's ear. He looks up for a moment.

BARBARA   *(on phone)*   Hello. I'd like to arrange an ambulance for one-thirty tomorrow afternoon...Thank you...

REVERSE ACROSS Bock at his desk with Barbara partially visible at Miss Lebow's desk. All he can see are her great long tanned legs.

BARBARA   *(in background on phone)*   ...Drummond, first name, Barbara. I'll pay cash...

Bock stands a little unsteadily and moves around his desk to get a better look at those legs.

BARBARA   *(on phone)*   No, you're to pick up my father, Drummond, Edward, at the Manhattan Medical Center, Holly Pavilion, Room Eight-O-Six. It's a stretcher case. I presume you provide the stretcher.

She senses Bock watching her, turns, smiles. She's a very beautiful girl. She returns to the phone.

BARBARA   He's to be taken to American Airlines, Yes...No...Kennedy

Airport, Flight Seven-Two-Nine to Yuma, Arizona. I'll accompany the patient....Yes, thank you.

She returns the receiver to its cradle. When she looks up again, Bock is no longer there. She returns the flight tickets to her purse, snaps it shut, stands and moves to the doorway, enters a step into...

BOCK'S OFFICE.

Bock, back at his desk, looks up.

BOCK You believe in witchcraft, Miss Drummond?

BARBARA I believe in everything, Doctor.

BOCK Like a drink?

BARBARA Yes.

Bock drains his glass and pours her a hefty shot of bourbon.

BARBARA *(from the door suddenly)* My father, you should know, was a very successful doctor in Boston, a member of the Harvard Medical Faculty. He was a widower, and I was his only child. He was not an especially religious man, a sober Methodist. One evening, seven years ago, he attended a Pentecostal meeting in the commons rooms at Harvard and suddenly found himself speaking in tongues. *(She takes her drink and crosses to the sofa.)* That is to say, he suddenly sank to his knees at the back of the room and began to talk fluently in a language which no one had ever heard before. This sort of thing happens frequently at Pentecostal meetings, and they began to happen regularly to my father. *(She sits.)* It was not unusual to walk into our home and find my father sitting in his office, utterly serene and happily speaking to the air in this strange foreign tongue. I was, at that time twenty years old and having my obligatory affair with a minority group, in my case a Hopi Indian, a post-graduate fellow at Harvard doing his doctorate in the aboriginal languages of the Southwest. One day, I brought the Indian boy home just as my father was sinking to his knees in the entrance foyer in one of his trances. The Indian wheeled in his tracks and said, "Well, I'll be a sonofabitch." You see, my father was speaking an Apache dialect, an obscure dialect at that, spoken only by a ragged band of unreconstructed Indians who had rejected the reservation and were living in total isolation in the Sierra Madre Mountains of northern Mexico. Well! What do you say to that, Dr. Bock?

BOCK *(who has been staring at her as if she were insane)* What the hell am I supposed to say to that, Miss Drummond?

Barbara throws back her head and roars with laughter.

BOCK I'm sitting here boozing and, all of a sudden, you start telling me some demented story about your father's religious conversion.

BARBARA No, no, you miss the point, Doctor. Not my father's conversion—mine. You see, I had been hitting the acid pretty regularly at that time. I had achieved a few minor sensory deformities, some suicidal despairs, but nothing as wild as fluency in an obscure Apache dialect. I mean, like wow, man! I mean, here was living afflatus right before my eyes! Within a week, my father had closed his Beacon Hill practice and set out to start a mission in the Mexican mountains. And I turned in my S.D.S. card and my crash helmet and followed him. It was a disaster, at least for me. My father had received the revelation, not I. He stood gaunt on a mountain slope and preached the apocalypse to solemnly amused Indians. I masturbated a great deal. We lived in a grass wickiup and ate raw rabbit and crushed piñon nuts. It was hideous. Within two months, I was back in Boston, a hollow shell and dizzy with dengue, disenchanted with everything. I turned to austerity, combed my hair tight and entered nursing school. I became haggard, driven and had shamelessly incestuous dreams about my father. I took up with some of the senior staff at the hospital. One of them, a portly psychiatrist, explained I was generated by an unresolved lust for my father. I apparently cracked up. One day, they found me walking to work naked and screaming obscenities. There was talk of institutionalizing me, so I packed a bag and went back to my father in the Sierra Madre Mountains. I've been there ever since. That's three years. My father is, of course, mad as a hatter. I watch over him and have been curiously content. You see, Doctor, I believe in everything.

She pauses, her story over. Throughout, Bock has been trying to keep his glowering eye on the desktop. During her long narrative, he once seized the bottle and took a swig. Mostly he is finding the experience murkily sensual. His glance keeps darting out from under his brows to surreptitiously look at the beautiful long tanned legs; or, when she bends for the drink she set on the floor, to peer down the flapping open scalloped neck of her dress; she is bra-less.

She, on the other hand, has been crossing and uncrossing her legs, bending, stretching, so that her short dress has ridden up almost to her waist and is saved from utter exhibitionism only by the darkness of the shadows. She seems unaffected by Bock's voyeuristic interest in her, but she is surely not unaware of it. It is hard to believe she is not courting his attention.

BOCK Now what was that all about, Miss Drummond?

BARBARA I thought I was obvious as hell. I'm trying to tell you I have a thing for middle-aged men.

BOCK I admire your candor.

BARBARA You've been admiring a lot more than that.

Bock looks up, and they suddenly find their eyes locked. The dark, dense air in the room fairly steams with incipient sexuality.

BOCK *(looks down again)* You're wasting your time. I've been impotent for years.

BARBARA Rubbish.

With a crash of his fist on the desktop, Bock stands; he is in a drunken rage.

BOCK *(lurches about)* What the hell's wrong with being impotent? My God, you kids are more hung up on sex than the Victorians! I've got a son, twenty-three. I threw him out of the house last year. Pietistic little humbug. He preached universal love and despised everyone. He had a blanket contempt for the middle class, even its decencies. He detested my mother because she had petit bourgeois pride in her son the doctor. I cannot tell you how brutishly he ignored that rather good old lady. When she died, he didn't even come to the funeral. He thought the chapel service an hypocrisy. His generation didn't live with lies, he told me. "Everybody lives with lies," I said. I grabbed him by his poncho, dragged him the full length of our seven-room despicably affluent middle-class apartment and flung him out. I haven't seen him since. But do you know what he said to me as he stood there on that landing on the verge of tears. He shrieked at me: "You old fink! You can't even get it up anymore!" That was it, you see. That was his real revolution. It wasn't racism and the oppressed poor and the war in Vietnam. The ultimate American societal sickness was a limp dingus. Hah! *(He lurches about, laughing rustily.)* My God, if there is a despised and misunderstood minority in this country, it's us poor impotent bastards. Well, I'm impotent and proud of it! Impotence is beautiful, baby! *(He raises a militant fist.)* Power to the Impotent! Right on, baby!

BARBARA *(smiling)* Right on.

BOCK *(stares drunkenly at her)* When I say impotent, I don't mean merely limp. Disagreeable as it may be for a woman, a man may sometimes lust for other things, something less transient than an erection, some sense of permanent worth. That's what medicine was for me, my reason for being. When I was thirty-four, Miss Drummond, I presented a paper before the annual convention of the Society of Clinical Investigation that pioneered the whole goddam field of immunology. A breakthrough! I'm in all the textbooks. I happen to be an eminent man, Miss Drummond. And you want to know something, Miss Drummond? I don't give a goddam. When I say I'm impotent, I mean I've lost even my desire for work, which is a hell of a lot more primal a passion than sex. I've lost my raison d'etre, my purpose, the only thing I ever truly loved. It's all rubbish anyway. Transplants, antibodies, we manufacture genes, we can produce birth ectogenetically, we can practically clone people like carrots, and half

the kids in this ghetto haven't even been inoculated for polio! We
have assembled the most enormous medical establishment ever con-
ceived, and people are sicker than ever! We cure nothing! We heal
nothing! The whole goddam wretched world is strangulating in front
of our eyes! That's what I mean when I say impotent! You don't know
what the hell I'm talking about, do you?

BARBARA Of course, I do.

BOCK I'm tired, I'm terribly tired, Miss Drummond. And I hurt, and
I've got nothing going for me anymore. Can you understand that?

BARBARA Yes, of course.

BOCK Then can you understand that the only admissable matter left
is death?

*He suspects he is going to cry and turns quickly away. He sits heavily and
fights his tears.*

BARBARA Sounds to me like a familiar case of morbid menopause.

BOCK Oh Christ.

BARBARA Well, it's hard for me to take your despair very seriously,
Doctor. You obviously enjoy it so much.

BOCK Oh, bugger off. That's all I need now, clinical insights. Some
cockamamie twenty-five-year-old...

BARBARA Twenty-seven.

BOCK ...acidhead's going to reassure me about menopause now. Look,
I'd like to be alone, so why don't you beat it? Close the door and turn
off the lights on your way out.

They are both suddenly conscious of a third presence in the room. They look to the door where Mr. Blacktree, fully clothed again and carrying his coat, is standing in the doorway. Barbara uncrosses her long legs and stands.

BARBARA   *(crossing to the door)*   Mr. Blacktree disapproves of my miniskirt, but it was the only thing I had to come to the city with. Back at the tribe, I wear ankle-length buckskin.

BOCK   Swell. Just close the door and turn off the lights.

Barbara regards his hunched form and, murmuring in Apache, she exits, closing the door. In the subsequent hush, thunder RUMBLES and CRASHES. Wind sweeps the rain against the window panes.

The sounds go unheeded by Bock, still as marble. Slowly, he raises his head and sighs and then fishes about in his jacket pockets to bring out the bottle of potassium and syringe. He takes off his jacket, rolling up his shirtsleeve, poking about for the vein. He removes his trouser belt, which he ties tightly about his upper arm for a tourniquet. Now, he tears the wrapping of the syringe and fits the needle to it. Fiddling about in the pockets of his jacket, he finally finds a crumpled pack of cigarettes. He lights one and returns to the business of killing himself, puffing expressionlessly as he does. Thunder RUMBLES and rain SLASHES. He carefully draws just the right amount of potassium from the bottle to the syringe, peering at the procedure against the light of his desk lamp. He sets the cigarette on the ashtray, switches the hypodermic to his right hand, holds his left arm rigidly out under the light of the lamp...

BARBARA'S VOICE   *(off-screen)*   What're you shooting, Doc?

He turns slowly to the doorway, his bare left arm still rigidly extended, the belt dangling, the hypodermic clenched in his other hand. Barbara is perfectly framed in the doorway. He stares at her, slowly suffusing with the numb, blind, total rage of the aborted suicide. The thunder CRASHES.

BOCK   *(barely gets the words out)*   Leave me alone...

She approaches the desk affably, turns the potassium around to read the label.

BARBARA   Potassium. You take enough of this stuff, it'll kill you, Doc. *(moves toward the couch)*   It occurred to me that I might have read you wrong, that you really were suicidal. So I came back.

Bock's rage erupts. He crashes the hypodermic syringe down, shattering it. The potassium puddles on the wood.

BOCK   *(hysterical rage)*   Who the hell asked you!

He moves around the desk, a shambling bear of a man, a leather belt dangling dementedly from his arm, tears coursing down his cheeks. He advances on her in a stuperous shuffle.

BOCK   Who the hell asked you!

She regards his lumbering approach with a faint, grotesquely sensual smile. He reaches with his naked left arm to the neck of her dress and, with one savage wrench, rips her stark naked, sobbing through hysterical tears.

BOCK   Leave me alone! Why the hell don't you leave me alone!

He is on her, crushing her down into the shadows of the couch, ravenous at her neck and shoulders in a brutish assault, sobbing.

BOCK   Why didn't you let me do it? Who the hell asked you!

Throughout the scene, CAMERA MOVES SLOWLY IN through the flesh and fury to an INTENSE TWO-SHOT of this terrified act of love. Then slowly over Bock's plunging shoulder to the woman's face. She gasps at the moment of penetration, then her lovely face slowly shapes into smiling serenity. Bock sobs; even in the shadows we can see the path of the tears on his cheek.

ABRUPT SILENCE.

OUTSIDE THE HOSPITAL, NIGHT. 4:00 A.M.

The quiet, black streets glisten wetly in the puddles of lamplight.

THE STEINMETZ PAVILION, TENTH FLOOR.

The night shift is finishing up. THERESA CAMPANELLA, R.N., a high-strung girl in her early twenties, stands at a water tap holding a glass and popping some pills in her mouth. To the room:

CAMPANELLA   Well, I'll see you.

TENTH FLOOR CORRIDOR. NIGHT.

Campanella comes out of the Dialysis room, puts on her coat and walks to...

HOLLY PAVILION LOBBY. NIGHT.

Campanella moves down the empty corridor. All the doors are closed now; only the overhead light in the background of the corridor glows weakly. Campanella puts a cigarette in her mouth, pauses to look for matches; she hasn't any. Scowling with annoyance, she continues to the lobby and stops by a partially visible white-jacketed figure reading a newspaper.

CAMPANELLA   Do you have a match, Doctor?

She takes the matches, lights her cigarette, inhaling deeply, when he suddenly sandbags her from behind. She goes down.

BOCK'S OFFICE. DAYBREAK, WEDNESDAY.

Covered by Bock's overcoat, Barbara tosses and turns on the couch in a small nightmare. Through the windows comes the first gray wash of dawn. FULL SHOT of Barbara, awake and up on one elbow on the verge of a scream. She looks around the room. It is dark, empty, silent.

ACROSS Barbara looking through the door to the secretarial office. It is likewise dark, but suddenly the lights go on and, a moment later, Bock enters. He holds a container of coffee in each hand and has something white draped over his forearm. From under Bock's bulky coat, Barbara watches him lumber to his desk, where he sets the containers of coffee down. He drops the whitish garment over the back of a chair and then sits. He hoists a bulging

*folder of correspondence from his filing tray and hunches to work, reading.
After a moment, he regards the silent figure on the couch across the room.*

BOCK You wouldn't be awake.

BARBARA What time is it?

*He rises, picks up the second container and white dress from the chair. She
reaches out an arm for the coffee. Bock holds up—a nurse's uniform.*

BOCK I swiped this for you out of the nurses' locker room. I'll make
good on your dress. I'm afraid it's torn beyond repair. Buy yourself a
new one or, if you like, give me your size and I'll send it on to you.
But I want to talk to you about that.

BARBARA Talk to me about what?

BOCK About your father. You really shouldn't move him in his
condition. I just had a look at his chart. There's no reason to presume
brain damage. You know as well as I you can't predict anything in
these instances. He could pull out of that coma at any time. I think
you should let him stay here. I'll personally look after him.

*He has perched on the edge of the couch, and she rests her cheek against the
long, bent curve of his back, smiling.*

BARBARA Is this your way of saying you'd like me to stay in town a few
more days?

He turns to look at her, smiles back.

BOCK Well, that would be nice, too.

She sips her coffee.

BOCK What do you say, Miss Drummond?

BARBARA   I expect you can call me Barbara, considering you ravished me three times last night.

BOCK   Three times?

BARBARA   Oh, look at him, pretending he didn't count. You were as puffed up as a toad about it. Punched a couple of holes in your crusade for universal impotence, didn't it? I think we're on a first name basis by now. I'll call you Herb.

BOCK   Let's give your father a week, Barbara, what do you say?

BARBARA   *(A frown darkens her face.)*   No, I don't want my father in this hospital. I had a dream about this hospital. *(Some of the terror shows on her face.)* I dreamt this enormous starched white tile building suddenly erupted like a volcano, and all the patients, doctors, nurses, attendants, orderlies, the whole line staff, the food service people, the aged, the lame—and you right in the middle—were stampeding in one hideous screaming suicidal mass into the sea. *(She stares at him wide-eyed, reliving the dream.)* I'm taking my father out of here—and as quickly as I can.

They stare at each other, she in terror, he with affection.

BOCK   You're a real fruitcake, you know?

She sets her coffee down on the couch and decides to wear Bock's overcoat rather than use it as a cover. She searches for the sleeves. Bock assists her.

BARBARA   Well, let me put it this way. I love you. I fancied you from the first moment you came lumbering down that hallway upstairs. I said to Mr. Blacktree, "Who's that hulking bear of a man?" The Apaches are reverential about bears. They won't eat bear meat; they never skin bears. Bear is thought of as both benign and evil, but very strong power. Men with bear power are highly respected and are frequently said to be great healers.

By now she's standing, the overcoat reaching her toes. She looks down at Bock perched on the couch.

BARBARA   I said to Mr. Blacktree, "That man gets his power from the bear."

BOCK   Swell.   Now, look, do you have a hotel, some sort of accommodations where you can stay for a week or so?

Barbara reaches for her coffee, sips, moves around in her tent of a coat.

BARBARA   All right, let me put it this way, Herb. My father and I accept the implacability of death. If he dies, he dies, but I'm taking him out of here and back to Mexico about one o'clock this afternoon. I want you to come with us, because I love you and want children.

BOCK   I'm afraid Mexico sounds a little too remote for me.

BARBARA   We could use you down there, you know.   There's a curiously high incidence of T.B. And you'd be a doctor again, Herb. You'd be necessary again. If you love me, I don't see what other choice you have.

BOCK   What do you mean, if I love you?   I raped you in a suicidal rage. How did we get to love and children all of a sudden?

BARBARA   Oh, for heaven's sake, Herb, I ought to know if a man loves me or not. You must have told me half a hundred times last night you loved me. You murmured it, shouted it; one time, you opened the window and bellowed it out into the street.

BOCK   I think those were more expressions of gratitude than love.

BARBARA   Gratitude for what?

BOCK   Well, my God, for resurrecting feelings of life in me I thought dead.

BARBARA Well, my God, what do you think love is?

BOCK Okay, I love you, and you love me. I'm not about to argue with
so relentless a romantic. Well, then, since we have this great passion
going for us, I don't see why you won't stay on here in New York for
a week or ten days...

BARBARA It's up to ten days now.

BOCK As long as it takes for your father's condition to improve.

BARBARA No. I've had these prophetic dreams for seven nights. Seven
is a sinister number. The meaning of these dreams is very clear, seven
times as clear. I am to get my father and you out of this hospital
before we are all destroyed.

BOCK *(throws up his hands)* You're certifiable! My God, half the time
you're a perfectly intelligent young woman, and then suddenly you
turn into a goddam cabalist who believes in dreams, witchcraft and
bear power! And I don't like the way you dismiss my whole life as
unnecessary. I do a lot of healing right here in Manhattan. I don't
have to go to Mexico for it. I also teach. I send out eighty doctors a
year into the world, sometimes inspirited, at least competent. I've
built up one of the best damned departments of medicine in the world.
We've got a hell of a heart unit here and a hell of a kidney group. A
lot of people come into this hospital in big trouble, Miss Drummond,
and go out better for the experience. So don't tell me how unnecessary I am.

BARBARA *(who's been slipping into the nurse's uniform)* Yeah?

BOCK Yeah.

BARBARA So how come, eight hours ago, you were trying to kill
yourself with an overdose of potassium?

BOCK Where are you going now?

This last in reference to Barbara crossing to the secretaries' office, zippering her uniform.

BOCK'S SECRETARIES' OFFICE.

BARBARA *(gathering her coat and purse)* My hotel. I have to check out. Mr. Blacktree doesn't speak any English.

BOCK *(from the connecting doorway)* Well, you're coming back, of course.

BARBARA Of course. I have to settle the bill here and pack my father. And I think you need a few hours alone to make your decisions.

BOCK What decisions?

BARBARA You're a very tired and very damaged man. You've had a hideous marriage and I assume a few tacky affairs along the way. You're understandably reluctant to get involved again. And, on top of that, here I am with the preposterous idea you throw everything up and go off with me to some barren mountains of Mexico. It sounds utterly mad, I know. On the other hand, you obviously find this world as desolate as I do. You did try to kill yourself last night. So that's it, Herb. Either me and the mountains or the bottle of potassium. I'll be back in an hour or so. I'll be in my father's room.

She slips into her coat and exits, as Bock looks after her thoughtfully, then turns back to his own office.

BOCK'S OFFICE.

He shuffles around distractedly, not knowing how to articulate the exuberance he feels. Suddenly, he opens the window, leans out and bellows to the empty air.

BOCK All right. I love you! *(softly)* My God!

FIRST AVENUE, CONSTRUCTION AREA. DAWN.

A construction sign fills the screen. It reads ON THIS LOCATION, THE NEW YORK MEDICAL UNIVERSITY CENTER WILL BUILD A DRUG REHABILITATION COMMUNITY CENTER, TO BE COM-PLETED IN 1973. E.F. SCHLAGER & CO., CONTRACTORS. Suddenly, the sign comes crashing down into CAMERA. It has been wrenched off the wooden fence protecting the row of tenements and brown-stones being demolished. About a dozen young and loud militants have torn it down.

CAMERA PANS to show the row of houses behind the fence, two of which have already been reduced to rubble; the others have been boarded up. The demolition generators and cranes are parked silently along the curb. In the dark of 5:00 A.M., three black families, carrying children, and children car-rying household effects, mattresses, pots, pans, bags of groceries, etc., are repossessing the condemned buildings.

FIRST AVENUE, CONSTRUCTION AREA. DAY, 10:00 A.M.

Strong sun overhead. The street has been roped off, and police are all over the place. A sparse crowd of a hundred or so throng the sidestreets off First Avenue. Signs read, "People Sí, Doctors No." A Channel 11 mobile news crew, newspaper photographers, and a radio newscaster are recording the sit-uation with desultory interest.

A POLICE CAPTAIN stands in the middle of the cordoned street, bull-horning the occupiers of the condemned brownstones, who can be seen through the broken windows.

POLICE CAPTAIN I repeat. I'm asking you to come out peacefully. These buildings are condemned and unfit for habitation.

A piece of brick arches down from the roof of a building and cracks the street a few feet from the Captain.

POLICE CAPTAIN *(sighs, tries again)* You people are possessing this building illegally and in violation of the law. I'm asking you to come out peacefully...

HOLLY PAVILION, ENTRANCE LOBBY. DAY.

A small press conference is going on in a corner of the lobby. Reporters cluster, and TV cameras surround the Press Representative of the Hospital, a young woman in her thirties named EVELYN BASSEY, who is trying to read a statement, squinting under her mod glasses at the blaze of lights set up by the camera crews.

MRS. BASSEY *(reading)* ...complete sympathy with the tenants. So the hospital has assumed the responsibility of finding 400 housing units in good buildings. The hospital wishes to point out that this particular row of buildings on First Avenue was condemned by the City before the hospital acquired ownership, and even then, only after responsible leaders in the community had approved the building of our new drug rehabilitation center.

SUNDSTROM'S OFFICE.

SUNDSTROM *(explodes on the phone)* Goddammit, Barry, I've got a dozen community leaders waiting for me in the library! We've been trying to work out some kind of negotiable formula for two years! And with no help from you people in the Urban Affairs Division, I might add!

DR. WELBECK appears in the doorway. He's in his fifties, gray, distinguished and very tanned with terribly, terribly kindly old country doctor eyes. He wears a camel hair topcoat. He smiles benignly and twinkles at Sundstrom from one of the leather chairs across the desk from the Director.

SUNDSTROM *(hardly notices Welbeck)* And I'm not going to throw all that down the drain because some cockamamie activist group is showboating for the television cameras! You get those people out of those buildings before a wall collapses or a fire breaks out and we've got a riot on our hands!... Okay!

He hangs up, sighs, turns to the man across the desk.

WELBECK *(smiles, twinkles)* Having your troubles, eh? Well, I won't take much of your time. My name's Welbeck. I've been associated with this hospital for six years, and, yesterday afternoon, Dr. Gilley called me to say he was cutting off my privileges at the hospital. Do you know anything about it?

SUNDSTROM *(glances at his watch)* It's news to me.

WELBECK He said he sent the report on.

SUNDSTROM I'll probably get it tomorrow. Report on what?

WELBECK Well, I'm not sure myself. I did a nephrectomy on a man about seven days ago. Emergency, called in at four in the morning. The man was hemorrhaging, he'd gone sour...

SUNDSTROM Welbeck, I'm terribly sorry, but I do have this meeting. *(crosses to the door)* In any event, there's nothing I can do about it. If Gilley wants to cut your privileges, he's Chief of Surgery, it's within his province. You'll have to have the hearing...

He exits, followed by Welbeck into the...

DIRECTOR'S SUITE, SECRETARIES' OFFICES.

Buzzing now. Typewriters clicking. Phones ringing.

WELBECK I have a laparotomy laid on for this morning. I assume I'll be allowed to go through with that.

SUNDSTROM Of course.

WELBECK *(huffing a little)* I've been associated with this hospital for six years...

SUNDSTROM Now, now, Welbeck. It seems to me I've had your

name down here before for something...*(to his secretary en passant)* I'll be in the staff room.

He and Welbeck pass out into the...

EXECUTIVE CORRIDOR.

Flowing with a normal stream of traffic, Sundstrom and Welbeck turn right and head down to the last room of the corridor. Something comes to him, and Sundstrom pauses.

SUNDSTROM   Wait a minute.   You're the fellow with the Medicaid collecting business who incorporated and went public, right? I mean, something like that? Milton Mead was telling me about you just the other day. You're a whole medical conglomerate. You've got a Factoring service, a computerized billing company, and a few proprietary hospitals, a few nursing homes.   Good heavens, Welbeck, you shouldn't be brought up before a committee of mere doctors. You should be investigated by the Securities and Exchange Commission. You'll have to go through with the hearing, Welbeck. I don't interfere in these things.

He opens the door of the staff room and strides in. Even before he enters, we get a blast of angry voices, both male and female. For the moment the door is ajar, we see a harried Milton Mead being assailed by angry blacks and Puerto Ricans and young white activist doctors.

HOSPITAL LIBRARY.

VOICES   *(all overlapping)*   ...no goddam halfway house, no way, baby! We ain't gonna wait 'til 1973 to deal with this problem! We want to kill the drug thing right now!... imperializing the Blackaporican community, and we reject the bourgie-ass middle-class black traitors and flunkies who are selling out the Blackaporican proletariat masses to the expansionist, racist policies of this shit hospital! ...

WOMAN   Let's get back to the abortion issue!

VOICE Sit down, Woman!

WOMAN   What the hell does the male establishment know about abortions?

There's an agitated reaction in the crowd.

BLACK WOMAN   Who the hell raised the issue of birth control? The issue at hand is the control of drug addiction in this community and in the ghetto generally.

A black man jumps up and points off right.

BLACK MAN   We don't want no goddam abortion...

A white doctor jumps in from the left.

WHITE DOCTOR   Let's ...let's get down to the core of this matter.

More murmuring. A Che Guevara–styled revolutionary moves toward Mead and Sundstrom at the table.

MAN The point is that this hospital is the landlord for those buildings and they should've turned them down.

Angrily, he leans over the table facing Sundstrom.

MAN   Those buildings are imperialistic extensions of the medical establishment. This hospital ought to be rebuilding those tenements, give those people decent housing.

Sundstrom raises his hands for quiet and starts to rise. The hostile din has gotten to him.

SUNDSTROM Please, please, please!

HOLLY PAVILION, ROOM 806.

William Mead is transferred from his bed to a rolling stretcher by an order-ly in shirt and trousers and by Nurse Felicia Chile. Nurse Chile tucks Mead in. He opens his eyes to look at her drowsily.

WILLIAM MEAD *(under sedation)* You know, I hallucinated last night. I hallucinated there was an Indian doing a war dance in here.

NURSE CHILE *(affably)* You weren't hallucinating, Mr. Mead. There was an Indian in here last night.

WILLIAM MEAD *(staring through his sedation at her)* There was?

They wheel him out into...

HOLLY PAVILION, SURGICAL AREA CORRIDOR.

Mead is wheeled down the corridor by the orderly. At the far end, an anes-thetized patient, blue in the harsh light, fresh from surgery, is being wheeled into a recovery room.

Surgery is busy and efficient but not as clinically tidy as we'd like. Linens and equipment and surgical gear are piled into corners or on empty stretch-ers. Green-uniformed nurses, doctors and orderlies go in and out of the many doors flanking the corridor. This is the non-sterilized area, where doctors and nurses confer in the corridors; three black orderlies await an assignment, sit on stretchers, chuckle, mutter. Phones can be heard RINGING. The order-ly wheeling Mead turns left into the...

SURGICAL AREA, CENTRAL PLAZA.

...a small, cluttered central area with the office of the Operating Room Nursing Supervisor on the right and the Holding (for Anesthesia) Room on the left. The O.R. is like the Emergency Ward, desperately busy but staffed by people grown so accustomed to it that they display a calm, almost casual but febrile efficiency. A large blackboard faces the Supervisor's Office with the

*day's schedule of operations neatly chalked in. It is full. A middle-aged sur-
geon, still in his overcoat, is studying the schedule.*

*A green-uniformed NURSE swings through the glass doors from the
Operating Room area to lean into the Supervisor's Office.*

NURSE Dr. Norris says about half an hour.

SECOND NURSE Tell Shirley it was just an ovarian cyst.

*The THIRD NURSE leans back into the Supervisor's Office to relay this
information.*

THIRD NURSE Shirley, it was just an ovarian cyst!

This is apparently good news, for we hear someone saying

VOICE *(off-screen)* Oh, thank God.

*An orderly rumbles by with an E.K.G. machine. O.R. Nursing Supervisor
DOROTHY KIMBALL, a pleasant lady in her late thirties, leans out of her
office to speak to one of the lounging orderlies.*

MRS. KIMBALL *(handing the orderly a slip)* All right, Jerry, go up to
Holly Six.

*The orderly detaches himself from his cronies and exits. It is into this atmos-
phere of subdued febrility that William Mead is wheeled.*

ORDERLY *(to Mrs. Kimball)* William Mead from Holly Eight.

MRS. KIMBALL Hold him there, Tom. We've got somebody coming
out right now.

*Indeed, a stretcher is being wheeled out of the Holding Room. The patient is
sedated and covered. As the orderly wheels her past CAMERA, we may recognize the pale, sleeping profile of Miss Campanella, the nurse who had been*

coshed with a sandbag not many scenes ago. A CIRCULATING NURSE comes through the glass doors, examines the chart dangling from the stretcher.

MRS. KIMBALL *(to this nurse)* Who's that? Mangafranni?

CIRCULATING NURSE *(checking wristband)* Yeah. *(to orderly)* Number three, Marty.

The orderly wheels the silent Miss Campanella off to Operating Room Three, as Dr. Welbeck, in his natty blue suit, carrying his camel coat, turns in from the outer corridor and examines the blackboard. He goes back to...

OUTER CORRIDOR.

...Welbeck crosses, opens a door and enters...

SURGEONS' LOCKER ROOM.

All four walls are lined with lockers. Shelves and cartons of green surgical clothes, caps, masks, trousers, shoe-coverings. Obviously, surgeons dress for their operations here. Two surgeons, one middle-aged and the other a young RESIDENT, are changing. The resident turns to Welbeck on his entrance and says:

RESIDENT It's legal for a doctor to incorporate in New York, isn't it, Doctor?

WELBECK *(en route to phone)* Since last September. If they had that when I was your age, I'd have put away a couple of million by now. *(dials)* It gives you a variety of deferral devices, profit-sharing for example. Let's say you pick yourself an October 31-fiscal. You declare a bonus payable in '71. An accrued item payable to a principle share-holder must be paid within two and half months after the close of the year to get the deduction in the prior year. But your corporation doesn't pay that tax, because we've eliminated the taxable income with the bonus. With two taxable entities, you can bury a hell of a lot of expenses...*(on phone)* Hello, this is Welbeck, any messages?... Well,

I'm at the hospital. I have to cut open some guy in a couple of minutes. I'll try to make it as fast as I can. How urgent did he say it was?... Well, Dr. Hogan made those arrangements with the underwriters. The Registration Statement was filed with the S.E.C. well over a year ago.... If he calls again, have me paged here. *(hangs up, turns back to the attentive young doctors to conduct his class in medical finance while changing into surgical scrub)* The really big money is in health leasing, of course. Dr. Hogan, the eminent orthopedic surgeon, and I incorporated a leasing company and went public last year. I hold a controlling interest in a number of proprietary hospitals, nursing homes and rest farms, and I've been leasing hospital equipment to my own hospitals at excessive rates. Why, you ask, am I draining my own hospitals? Well, my hospitals are taxed at 48 percent, and I'm giving my leasing company a hell of a price-earnings ratio, which'll balloon the market value of the stock. I hold three hundred thousand shares of that stock, lettered of course, but in a year, I'll dump those shares at a capital gain and walk off with a bundle...

OPERATING ROOM THREE.

Just like on TV—well, almost. The surgeon, DR. MALLORY, a bad-tempered man in his fifties, sits on a stool with his gloved hands wrapped in a towel, waiting for the two surgical RESIDENTS to finish painting the operable area, which happens to be the abdomen. It's a hysterectomy. The patient is sheeted except for the small square of abdominal area.

DR. MALLORY Mangafranni, right?

SCRUB NURSE Right.

DR. MALLORY *(grumbles to one of the residents)* What do you say, huh? We're not going to hang it in the Louvre, you know.

The anesthesiologist, DR. CHU, injects pentathol in the I.V. tube.

DR. CHU Bring a mask over.

The RESIDENT ANESTHESIOLOGIST trundles over the oxygen tank, takes the hypodermic syringe from Dr. Chu, who now applies the oxygen mask to the enmarbled profile of the patient. He studies the gauges and equipment around him at the head of the operating table.

RESIDENT ANESTHESIOLOGIST There's no pulse, Doctor.

DR. CHU What's the pressure?

RESIDENT ANESTHESIOLOGIST There's no blood pressure, Doctor.

DR. CHU No pulse. Get the tube and E.K.G.

DR. MALLORY What's the matter?

RESIDENT I can't feel a thing, sir.

The room galvanizes into the swift, silent activity of a chest massage. Dr. Mallory, standing and stretching in the back of the room, turns and moves toward the off-screen patient. He begins a vigorous rhythmic massage of the patient's rib cage over the heart.

DR. MALLORY What the hell happened?

Dr. Mallory thumps the patient's chest hard with his fist, and the others, likewise, go to work.

DR. CHU I don't know. She must have thrown an embolus. She was doing fine up to now. *(to Resident Anesthesiologist)* Did you check the gasses?

RESIDENT ANESTHESIOLOGIST I did, sir.

DR. CHU The only time I ever saw anybody conk out like this, some jerk switched the nitrous oxide and the gas lines.

The scrub nurse is applying electrode paste to the defibrillators. Dr. Mallory yanks the sheets and hospital shirt off the patient and begins very rigorous massage of the exposed ribs; we can hear one rib crack.

DR. MALLORY   Get the damn leads on. For Chrissakes, what the hell is this?!

RESIDENT   She's just a young woman, sir.   Do you think we should open the chest?

DR. MALLORY   *(defibrillating)* She's fifty-three, you buttonhead!

RESIDENT   *(off-screen)* Bicarb?

Dr. Chu, who has been inserting some suprel and bicarbonate into the tube of the patient's I.V., is frowning at her rigid, white-capped face. He leans over to check the E.K.G. readings.

DR. CHU   She's fibrillating, Doctor.

Mallory straddles the patient. He's doing heavy heart massage.

DR. MALLORY   Jesus H. Christ!

DR. CHU   Okay, stop for a minute...Doctor...

Dr. Chu pushes back, the operating cap on the patient's head, revealing jet-black hair.   Mallory starts to massage again.

DR. MALLORY   *(barking at the scrub nurse)* You got those paddles ready?

Dr. Chu stares blankly at the patient's face, then looks up at the sweating surgeon, perched on the operating table, rhythmically crushing away at the patient's rib cage.

DR. CHU   I may be crazy, Doctor, but I don't think this is your patient.

Dr. Mallory, now pausing for a moment, looks up. He is beaded with sweat.

DR. MALLORY   What the hell are you talking about?

He massages away.   Another rib cracks.

HOLLY PAVILION, BOCK'S OFFICE.

The Supervisor of Nurses, Mrs. Christie, is sitting on a chair reading a report. Bock, now in his doctor's coat, is hunched over his desk, hands clasped.

BOCK Now, I don't want to get into an institutional hassle with you, Mrs. Christie. The malpractice here is monumental. As you see, Dr. Schaefer's blood sugar was twenty-three. No glucose solution is going to do that. The only thing that will do that is at least fifty units of insulin, probably more. The only presumption is that one of those nurses on the Eighth Floor shot fifty units of insulin into Schaefer's blood stream, either by injection or through the I.V., although how in God's name...

Mrs. Christie's electric pocket-pager BEEPS.

MRS. CHRISTIE I'm very sorry, Doctor. *(reaches for a phone)* May I?

Miss McGuire leans in from the secretaries' office.

MISS McGUIRE *(to Bock)* Doctor, did you ask the head nurse on the eighth floor to let you know when a Miss Drummond got there?

BOCK Yes.

MISS McGUIRE Well, she just got there.

BOCK Thank you.

MRS. CHRISTIE *(on phone)* Oh, dear me, Dorothy. I better get right down there directly. Have you called the O.O.D.? And you better call Dr. Gilley. And you better call Mr. Sloan.... Yes, I'll be down directly. *(hangs up; to Bock)* I'm very sorry, Doctor, but there's a real nasty one in the O.R. They've just operated on the wrong patient...

O.R. NURSING SUPERVISOR'S OFFICE.

Crowded now. The administrative resident, Hitchcock, is here and a uni-

formed man in his fifties, MR. SLOAN, the Chief of Safety and Traffic. Sloan represents the Hospital's security force. Mrs. Kimball is at her desk, on the phone.

MRS. KIMBALL   *(on phone)*   ...well, I don't understand, is she back in her room? When did she get back to her room? Who brought her back?... *(she stares at Hitchcock)* She's back in her room.

HITCHCOCK   Who?

MRS. KIMBALL   Mrs. Mangafranni, the woman who was supposed to have been operated on...*(calls to a nurse passing)* Are they still working on that woman in Three?

NURSE   Yeah.

MRS. KIMBALL   *(back on phone)* I'm sorry, Mrs. Fried, would you say that again?... Well, nobody in this office sent her back up... Well, all right, Mrs. Fried, I'll have to call you back.

She hangs up, stands, goes out into...

THE OPERATING AREA, PLAZA.

...where three orderlies lounge about.

MRS. KIMBALL   Did any of you take a woman named Mangafranni out of the Holding Room back up to Holly Five around ten o'clock?

Apparently, none of these three. Mrs. Christie turns in from the outer corridor. Normal Operating Room activity flows by: patients wheeled to and from their various surgeries, surgeons checking the blackboard, staff doctors, orderlies keeping the noise level low but steady.

MRS. CHRISTIE   *(to Hitchcock in the doorway)* What happened?

Hitchcock shrugs helplessly.

MRS. KIMBALL *(to Mrs. Christie)* I don't know what happened. A patient named Mangafranni was scheduled for a hysterectomy at ten o'clock—Dr. Mallory. I talked to Sylvia in the Holding Room who admitted her, so she was here. And now I just spoke to Mrs. Fried on Holly Five, and she says an orderly brought Mrs. Mangafranni back to her room about twenty minutes ago. Now Mrs. Mangafranni is in her room sleeping.

MRS. CHRISTIE Well, who's the woman in the operating room?

MRS. KIMBALL I don't know.

Mrs. Kimball, Mrs. Christie, Hitchcock and Sloan push through the glass doors to the crossroads of the operating rooms. Through each window, we see operating crews hacking away.

MRS. CHRISTIE Is she dead?

MRS. KIMBALL Well, they had to open her up, and that's not good.

They gather in anticipation outside O.R. Three and peer over each other's shoulders into the room where the operating crew is hunched over the open-heart massage. The masked circulating nurse looks up, notices the audience at the door, and gives a hopeless shrug.

HITCHCOCK I better get Mr. Mead.

HOLLY PAVILION, THE STAFF ROOM.

Milton Mead is sitting in a back seat of the Staff Room—a lounge with couches, easy chairs and magazine racks—gives half an ear to the several opinions being simultaneously expressed by:

LADY FROM WOMEN'S LIB ...abortion? The clinic should be under the supervision and entirely staffed by women and administered by a member of the Women's Committee for Medical Liberation!

and by

YOUNG WHITE ACTIVIST ...let's get to the core of the matter which is the criminal and gangster collusion between the American medical establishment and the drug, insurance and tobacco companies who, through their combined racketeering efforts, have produced a dual system of health care. Everything for the rich and nothing for the poor!

and by

BLACK PANTHER ...abortion clinic! That's genocide, baby! You're just killing off blacks! We consider proliferation elemental to the class struggle!

and by

SUNDSTROM *(who has lost his cool altogether and is screaming right along with everyone else)* ...for God's sake! We've got eleven people in these buildings, and we've got to get them out of there! We can rectify the injustices of the world tomorrow, but right now, for God's sake, can we get those people out of those buildings? Will you people please listen to me? Will you people please shut up and listen to me? Will you people please call a halt to this participatory democracy and address ourselves to the immediate problem?!

During this maelstrom, the phone at Mead's elbow RINGS. Mead answers it, listens, nods, returns the receiver, stand and slips out of the room into the delicious silence of the...

HOLLY PAVILION, EXECUTIVE CORRIDOR.

...where Hitchcock emerges from the Administration offices. The two men move down the hall toward each other.

MILTON MEAD How long ago did this happen?

HITCHCOCK About half an hour.

MILTON MEAD Have you called the Medical Examiner?

HITCHCOCK Not yet.

MILTON MEAD Well, you'd better do that now. And you better call
the precinct station house as well.

OPERATING ROOM THREE.

*Dr. Mallory is wrenching off his blood-drenched rubber gloves and flinging
them to the floor in a rage. The door to the room opens, and Mrs. Kimball,
Mrs. Christie and Mr. Sloan enter. Dr. Mallory is stupefied with anger. Dr.
Chu, blessed with Eastern containment, blandly gathers his equipment
together, nods to Mrs. Christie.*

DR. CHU Good morning.

MRS. CHRISTIE Good morning, Doctor.

DR. CHU This is really something, isn't it? I thought she looked a
little different when they brought her in. I even said to one of the
nurses, "She looks a little younger without her dentures." I'd only
talked to her half an hour before.

MRS. CHRISTIE Does anybody know who she is?

*Dr. Mallory can only stare at her numbly. He turns and stares numbly at
Mr. Sloan.*

MRS. CHRISTIE *(to Mrs. Kimball, examining the chart dangling from the
operating table)* What's her chart say?

CIRCULATING RESIDENT Her chart says Mangafranni. Her bracelet
says Mangafranni. The only thing that isn't Mangafranni is the
woman.

Dr. Mallory finally explodes.

DR. MALLORY Jesus H. Christ! I've been chopping out three

uteruses a day for twenty years, and is it too much to expect for you people to bring in the right goddam Jesus Christ uterus?!

DR. CHU I had just been talking to her in the Holding Room. She was perfectly fine. A little drowsy. I thought it was funny that when they brought her in, she was out cold.

DR. MALLORY *(shuffling around in aimless circles)* Jesus H. Kee-rist!

Mrs. Christie stares down at the face of the dead patient on the table, who has had her chest spread wide open so that the organs are exposed.

MRS. CHRISTIE Well, we'll just all have to stay here until Mr. Mead or someone from the O.O.D. comes back.

DR. MALLORY Well, I'm not taking the rap for this! I've already got one malpractice suit pending, and I'm not taking the rap for this one!

HOLLY PAVILION, ROOM 806.

William Mead's bed is empty. The Reverend Drummond's suit, still on its hanger, is lying on it. Drummond himself lies comatose and rigged out with I.V.s and catheters. Barbara Drummond is packing her father's things into an open one-suiter valise. The door opens. She looks up. It's Bock. They look at each other—two people in love.

BOCK Look, you're not going. I love you, and I'm not going to let you go.

He picks up the suit lying on the bed.

BOCK Come on, let's start putting your father's things back. He's staying here. *(hangs the suit in the closet)* I'll find an apartment somewhere. I'm staying in a filthy little hotel room. We can't use that.

His eyes are caught by a white doctor's uniform hanging in the armoire along with the suits and overcoats of the two patients in the room. He bends over to peer at the nameplate over the breast pocket.

BARBARA I can't make it here, Herb. I'll crack up. I cracked up once already. One week here, and I'd be running naked through the streets screaming again. I can retain my sanity only in a simple society.

BOCK For God's sake, Barbara, you can't seriously see me living in a grass shack hunting jackrabbits for dinner? Be sensible for God's sake.

BARBARA I am being sensible. What is it you're so afraid of leaving here? Your plastic home? Your conditioned air? Your synthetic clothes? Your instant food? I'm offering you green silence and solitude, the natural order of things. Mostly, I'm offering me. I think we're beautiful, Herb.

BOCK *(utterly in love)* You make it sound almost plausible.

BARBARA I don't know why you even hesitate. What's holding you here? Is it your wife?

BOCK No, that's all over. I suppose if I'm married to anything, it's this hospital. It's been my whole life. I just can't walk out on it as if it never mattered. I'm middle-class. Among us middle-class, love doesn't triumph over all. Responsibility does.

BARBARA Herb, don't ask me to stay here with you, because I love you, and I will. And we'll both be destroyed.

He turns to her again. They both look away.

BARBARA I've got the bill here to pay yet.

BOCK I'll come with you.

She gathers her raincoat and goes. Bock follows her out into the...

HOLLY PAVILION, EIGHTH FLOOR, CORRIDOR.

...where Dr. Joseph Lagerman, Head of Nephrology, perhaps remembered

from an earlier scene, has been waiting for Bock. He joins them en route to the elevators.

LAGERMAN Herb, you asked me to find that dialysis nurse.

BOCK What dialysis nurse?

Barbara has continued walking. Bock starts to follow her.

BARBARA I'll go pay the bill.

LAGERMAN The one who goofed on your patient, Drummond.

Bock turns back to Lagerman.

LAGERMAN Well, her name is Theresa Campanella, but you are not going to believe this, Herb. She died on the operating table in O. R. Three about an hour ago.

Barbara is disappearing into an elevator. Bock starts after her, then turns back to Lagerman.

BOCK What do you mean, she died on the operating table in O.R. Three?

They hurry down the corridor to the elevators.

BOCK You mean she was the one?

LAGERMAN That's the one. I just identified her.

BOCK What the hell's going on around here? Every time I try to find somebody in this hospital, they either died of a heart attack in Emergency or of anesthesia shock in an operating room.

Elevator doors open. A nurse and visitor get out. Bock and Lagerman go into...

THE ELEVATOR.

Two or three people besides the elevator operator are there, as well as a patient on a stretcher and an orderly.

LAGERMAN   Listen, I just came from the O.R. They're trying to find a Dr. Schaefer. Don't you have a kid named Schaefer in your service?

BOCK *(scowls, mutters)*   I had a Schaefer. He died yesterday of an overdose of insulin. What do they want Schaefer for?

LAGERMAN   The Holding Room nurse says there was a Dr. Schaefer hanging around the Holding Room. It wouldn't have been your Schaefer anyway. The nurse says it was senior staff, a middle-aged man.

BOCK   There's no senior staff named Schaefer in this hospital.

LAGERMAN   I told them that. I said, I don't know any senior staff around here named Schaefer. They've got detectives down there, everything. It's a whole big investigation.

The elevator stops at the seventh floor. The doors open and Bock and Lagerman stroll into...

HOLLY PAVILION, SEVENTH FLOOR, CORRIDOR.

Bock lumbers down the west corridor, turns into...

ROOM 806.

William Mead, sedated and apparently zonked out cold, is being transferred from a stretcher back into bed by an O.R. orderly and nurse's aid. Bock rolls back the curtains around Drummond's bed revealing the comatose patient, his face sculptured against the white pillow, an I.V. tube in his right arm, a catheter projecting from under the sheet. Bock lowers the protective railing, leans in, takes the man's pulse on his neck, raises one closed eyelid, then the other. The pupils stare vacuously back at him; the eyelids drop closed as soon as they are released.

In the background, the orderly and aid finish tucking in William Mead and exit, wheeling their creaking stretcher out. The room is shockingly silent. Bock goes to the window and frowns in thought.

HOLD ACROSS the patient Drummond, on Bock in the background at the window with his back to us. Suddenly, Drummond's eyes open. He lies rigid, his eyes staring dementedly into the air above him.

Slowly, his left hand reaches out and carefully withdraws the catheter from his bladder, lays it on the white sheet beside him, and silently reaches over to withdraw the I.V. needle from his right arm. He lets the needle dangle, drip-ping onto the bed. Carefully, he twists out from under his sheet, swings his legs over the side of the bed and sits up.

REVERSE ACROSS Bock at the window, pondering. With a swift lash of movement, the double tubes of a stethoscope are whipped over his head and tightened around his throat.

DRUMMOND *(mad as a hatter)*   I am the Fool for Christ and the Paraclete of Caborca.

CLOSE TWO SHOT of Bock being strangled, Drummond's face frozen in bland dementia behind him.

BARBARA'S VOICE *(off-screen)*   For heaven's sake, Dad! What the hell's going on?

Drummond pauses in his strangling and, releasing the poor man altogether, turns to his daughter in the doorway.

CAMERA DOLLIES to include all three—Bock recuperating; Drummond staring madly; and Barbara infuriated with her father.

BARBARA *(annoyed)* We all thought you were at Death's Door! What're you doing out of bed?

Drummond, abashed, stands there, a scolded schoolboy, a rawboned figure in a hospital shift, a stethoscope dangling from his right hand.

BARBARA *(to Bock)* What happened? Did he say anything to you?

BOCK *(sufficiently recovered)* As a matter of fact, he said, "I am the Fool for Christ and the Paraclete of Caborca." And you'd better close the door, because if he's going to tell everyone who walks in here he's the Fool for Christ and the Paraclete of Caborca, they'll put us all away. He's already killed two doctors and one nurse.

DRUMMOND I am the wrath of the lamb and the angel of the bottomless pit.

BARBARA What do you mean he killed two doctors and a nurse?

BOCK I mean, he's killed two doctors and a nurse! And he just tried to kill me! He has something against doctors. Somehow he got hold of a thousand units of insulin and put it in Dr. Schaefer's intravenous solution. And somehow he got Dr. Ives to die of a heart attack in the middle of the Emergency Room. And somehow he got a dialysis nurse named Campanella to die of anesthesia shock on an operating table! *(opens the closet, points to the white doctor's uniform hanging there)* He's been running around the hospital wearing Dr. Schaefer's uniform. Right now, they're looking all over the place for this mysterious Dr. Schaefer. I know this all sounds as grotesque to you as it does to me, but you can see for yourself your father is not the helpless comatose patient we thought he was. Don't look at me like I'm the one who's crazy. Ask your crazy father!

DRUMMOND I was merely an instrument of God. I killed no one. They all three died by their own hands, ritual victims of their own institutions, murdered by irony, an eye for an eye, biblical retribution. Schaefer was first, you see, because he killed God. God was admitted to this hospital last Monday under the name of Guernsey...

ROOM 806. MORNING. (FLASHBACK)

A cheerless, gray sunlight fills the room as the fragile, white-haired and bearded old Guernsey (whose admittance to the hospital was the opening scene of the film) is being helped into the room by Nurse Felicia Chile. She solicitously helps the wispy old man off with his coat and jacket and hat which she puts in the armoire. With palsied fingers, the little old man unknots his stringy tie and unbuttons the collar, which is three sizes too large. In the other bed, Drummond's eyes slowly open.

DRUMMOND *(off-screen)* I was instantly aware of a divine presence.

The old man is slipping out of his clothes to expose a thin little body in a torn nightshirt.

DRUMMOND *(off-screen)* I was convinced this porcelain old man was, in fact, an Angel of the Lord...

The old man sits back, wheezing a little. Nurse Chile smiles nicely at him and takes her leave. For a moment, Drummond lies rigidly on his bed, staring dully into the air and the old man sits with his hunched back to us. The room is silent except for his rheumy wheeze.

DRUMMOND *(off-screen)* ...perhaps even Christ Himself.

After a moment, the old man rises and goes to the washbasin and, with some wheezing, spits into it. He shuffles back to bed. Dr. Schaefer comes into the room with a professional smile and the patient Guernsey's chart.

DRUMMOND *(off-screen)* Our Savior was, it seems, suffering from emphysema.

Schaefer perches on the bed beside Guernsey and begins to take his history.

DRUMMOND *(off-screen)* He was relentlessly subjected to the benefits of modern medicine. He was misdiagnosed, mismedicated, and put into shock by Dr. Schaefer; raced off to Intensive Care, where the resident compounded the blunder and induced a coma. I can tell you with authority that God is indeed dead. He died last Monday under the name of Guernsey.

CLOSE-UP of Drummond in deep shadow shows him sleeping.

DRUMMOND   *(off-screen)*   A few hours later, he appeared to me in a revelation.

ROOM 806. NIGHT, 7:00 P.M.

The room is lit only by the yellow light from the half-opened bathroom door. Guernsey walks out of the shadows, hands raised.   He shuffles to Drummond's bedside and looks down on him from his frail height.

GUERNSEY   *(softly)*   Rise up, Drummond. You are dead, now you are restored.

Drummond's eyes open and roll to the direction of the voice.

DRUMMOND'S P.O.V.:   Guernsey, dressed only in his hospital shift, is shuffling up and down the aisle of the room, hands clasped behind his back like a Mittel-European intellectual, head hunched forward—a little old man with a white beard talking to himself.

GUERNSEY   Those who killed you and those who killed me will die in our place. You are the Paraclete of Caborca, the wrath of the lamb. The angel of the bottomless pit.

Guernsey closes his eyes in religious ecstacy.

GUERNSEY   In this fashion has it been revealed to you.

Drummond starts to sob and slowly sits up in his bed, imbued with belief. He looks mutely up at the frail old man, who now raises his right hand and his face is transfigured into vast majesty.

GUERNSEY   *(thunders out)*   The age is closed! The end is at hand! The seal is broken!

So saying, he reverts to the little old man he was, wheezing a bit, and with some effort, climbs back on his bed and lies there, eyes closed. His thin, high nose projects from the whiteness of his face. He sighs the rattling last sigh of life and dies. CAMERA DOLLIES slowly to CLOSE-UP of Drummond lying motionless on his bed. His eyes are wide, glinting in the shadows, a man imbued. His cheeks are wet with tears of exaltation.

DRUMMOND *(off-screen)* Well! Not quite the burning bush perhaps but prodigal enough for me. I was to avenge the death of God and my own brutalization. I was to kill Doctors Schaefer, Ives and Welbeck and the dialysis nurse Miss Campanella, whose negligence caused my coma.

FULL SHOT of Drummond. He raises his left hand, flexing his fingers. Then he moves his other arm, his head, his shoulders. Obviously, he is regaining his faculties.

DRUMMOND *(off-screen)* I awaited a further sign from God, which was given to me later that evening. Dr. Schaefer, it seems, had arranged an assignation with a girl from the hematology lab named Sheila.

ACROSS Drummond to the now empty other bed. All the lights are on. PAN on Nurse Penny Canduso and an orderly wheeling away the wrapped body of Guernsey. Intern Schaefer, at the door, considers the empty bed with interest. Moving to the bedtable, he picks up the receiver of the phone.

SCHAEFER *(on phone)* Hey Sheila, this is Howard, Sheila. Hey listen, I got us a bed for tonight. A real, honest-to-god bed.

ROOM 806. NIGHT.

REPRISE the scene originally played UNDER CREDITS where Dr. Schaefer and his girlfriend Sheila sneak into the room and undress. Giggles and shushings, gooses and fondles.

SHEILA Boy, I sure hope nobody walks in.

During the replay, however, an additional segment is added. At one point, the girl, hanging her dress in the armoire, turns and holds something up.

SHEILA What's this in your pocket?

SCHAEFER That's my insulin. Put it back.

SHEILA What do you take insulin for? Diabetes? I didn't know you were a diabetic.

SCHAEFER It ain't contagious, don't worry about it.

They head for the unoccupied bed. CLOSE-UP on Drummond's profile.

ROOM 806.

Dark, hushed. Schaefer's girl is leaving; she tiptoes to the door, peeks out. Apparently, the coast is clear. She quickly slips out.

ROOM 806. DAY.

Drummond on his chair. Barbara perched on one side of her father's bed, Bock on the other. William Mead sleeps on.

BOCK And you put Schaefer's insulin into the I.V. jar.

DRUMMOND Yes. And then a second nurse came and plugged the I.V. jar into Schaefer. God clearly intended a measure of irony here. The hospital was to do all the killing for me. All I need do was arrange for the doctors to become patients in their own hospital. Accordingly, the next morning, I set out for Dr. Ives. I put on Dr. Schaefer's uniform, pinched some digoxine from the pharmacy and a sandbag from a utility cart, and found my way to Dr. Ives' laboratory. I coshed him with the sandbag, gave him a massive shot of the digoxine. This, you see, brought on an instant condition of cardiac arrhythmia. When he came to, I brought him down to the Emergency Room.

EMERGENCY ROOM AREA, LOBBY. DAY.

The usual E.R. crush and motion goes on in the background. Drummond escorts an obviously ill Dr. Ives to the Admitting Room. Drummond's voice under the narration explains matters to Miss Aronovici at the desk.

DRUMMOND This is Dr. Ives. He's in the Nephrology Lab. I was in there a little while ago, and he was suddenly taken ill, and I thought I'd better get him over here right away.

DRUMMOND *(off-screen)* He had at that time perhaps an hour to live. Prompt treatment would have saved his life.

They go into the...

EMERGENCY ADMITTING AND TREATMENT ROOMS.

Ives, seated on a table in evident distress, breathes heavily.

DRUMMOND *(voice-off)* As a staff doctor, he was seen without preliminaries...

An attendant takes his pulse, pressure and respiration. Ives collapses.

DRUMMOND *(voice-off)* His vital signs were taken, an electro-cardiogram...

PAN SLOWLY across the Emergency Room to catch its state of contained febrility. Every curtained treatment room is occupied, including the storage room in the back. The triage nurse and a second nurse behind the desk are busy on the phones. The triage nurse takes the history of the first in a line of five people seeking admission even as she answers her phone.

We watch Miss Aronovici and the other nurse and Dr. Spezio and his two interns, the two attendants—all busy with one patient or another.

DRUMMOND *(voice-off)* ...which revealed occasional ventricular premature contractions. An intern took his history...

ACROSS Drummond, white-uniformed, standing in the back against the filing cabinets and linens, watching the the new patients trickle and crowd in.

DRUMMOND *(voice-off)* ...and then he was promptly...

At the Admitting Desk, a MAN in his forties is being signed in by a uniformed cop.

DRUMMOND *(voice-off)*....simply...forgotten to death. Simply mislaid...

CAMERA JUST STARES at the pageant of pain.

DRUMMOND *(voice-off)* ...mislaid among the broken wrists, the chest pains, scalp lacerations, the man whose fingers were crushed in a taxi door, the infant with the skin rash, the child swiped by a car, the old lady mugged in the subway, the derelict beaten by sailors, the teenage suicide, the paranoids, drunks, asthmatics, the rapes, the septic abortions, the overdosed addicts...

EMERGENCY ROOM AREA, LOBBY.

Looking to the street doors as two ambulance attendants, bearing a seventeen-year-old black girl on a stretcher, burst in.

AMBULANCE ATTENDANTS *(shouting)* Not breathing! Not breathing!

They hurry into the Admitting Room past a nurse and into the...

EMERGENCY ADMITTING AND TREATMENT ROOMS.

...which is already galvanized into action. Miss Aronovici is at the girl's pulse even as she is being transferred to the bed that has just been cleared of Mr. Mitgang and his concussion case.

INTERN *(instructing attendant with Mitgang)* Better put him in the Holding Room.

MISS ARONOVICI   *(with the seventeen-year-old girl)*   She's taking a little pulse.

DR. SPEZIO   *(to triage nurse)*   Get an anesthesiologist, one-five-one-five...

On screen we continue watching the scene of the overdose case treatment, as the live-action sound in the room fades behind Drummond's tale.

DRUMMOND   *(off-screen)*   ...the fractures, infarcts, hemorrhages, concussions, boils, abrasions, the colonic cancers, the cardiac arrests— the whole wounded madhouse of our times...

REACTION SHOT of Drummond staring at this ceaseless panorama of pain, tears streaking down his cheeks.

MAN'S VOICE   *(off-screen)*   I wonder if I could have a minute of your time, Doctor...

Drummond turns to the voice. CAMERA PULLS BACK to include the man who had been brought into the E.R. by a uniformed cop.

DRUMMOND   I am the fool for Christ and the Paraclete of Caborca.

NAMELESS MAN   Well, it's an honor and a privilege, Doctor. I've been here ten minutes, I can't seem to get anybody to help me. I'm suffering from some sort of amnesia. I can't remember my name. As a matter of fact, it's pretty screwy. I got mugged. Two hours ago, walking out of a coffee shop on Fifty-Seventh Street and Second Avenue, eight o'clock in the morning, broad daylight, I got mugged. A sixteen-year-old girl walks up to me, shows me a knife about a yard long and says, "Give me your wallet." I thought she was kidding. I mean there's hundreds of people walking right by. Well, she wasn't kidding. "Listen," I said, "all I got's about twenty bucks." So she takes the wallet anyway. So I said, "How about leaving me my identification?" I mean, I had my driver's license, my Diner's Club, my credit cards. But she took them all, the whole damn wallet, credit cards, everything. So I stopped some guy, I said, "Hey, you see that girl there, walking away?" He says, "Yeah." I said, "She just stole my wallet, credit cards and everything." He says, "Well, that's what they want, the credit cards." So I started looking for a cop. I mean, go find a cop, right? Well, I finally find a cop. The girl's halfway to South America by now, probably bought the ticket with my credit cards. So the cop says, "What's your name?" And you want to know something? I couldn't think of my name. The girl took all my identification, you know what I mean? She took all my credit cards. So I said, "You know this is screwy. I can't think of my name." So he took me to the station house. The sergeant says, "What's your name?" I said, "I don't know! She took all my credit cards!" So they took me down here. So what do you think, Doctor? I'm nuts, right? I finally flipped.

PAN SLOWLY to Drummond who stares at the Nameless Man.

In BACKGROUND the door opens and Mrs. Cushing, the lady from accounting, enters. She calls out in her annoying voice from a chart.

MRS. CUSHING   Who's number 7-6-8-0-2-S?   Is there anybody here who is that number?

DRUMMOND *(off-screen)*   In this way was it revealed to me the manner of Nurse Campanella's death. She was to die of the great American plague—vestigial identity.

RETURN FROM FLASHBACK:

ROOM 806. DAY.

Drummond in his hospital shift, gaunt and mad as a prophet, sits rigidly on his chair. Barbara perches on her father's bed. Bock wanders disorientedly about the room, staring incredulously first at Barbara and then at her father.

DRUMMOND   So last night, I coshed Miss Campanella with a sandbag, sedated her with thorazine, shaved her, prepped her, and parked her in a corridor of the X-Ray Department for five hours.

BOCK   Why X-Ray?

DRUMMOND   Well, at X-Ray, a sedated body lying around unattended for five hours wouldn't seem unusual.

BOCK Of course.

DRUMMOND   Her operation—that is to say, Mrs. Mangafranni's operation—was not scheduled until nine-thirty. So at nine-fifteen this morning, I rang for my nurse...

BOCK You rang for your nurse?

DRUMMOND To insure one full hour of uninterrupted privacy.

BOCK Oh yes.

DRUMMOND I got up, wheeled Miss Campanella off to the operating rooms, replaced her bed with Mrs. Mangafranni's, exchanged charts and identity bracelets. She died officially of anesthesia shock. But, in point of fact, she died because she was wearing another woman's identity.

BARBARA *(to Bock)*   God, what do we do now? Let me take him back to Mexico. It's a simple world there. If you turn him in, they'll just cage him in the Rockland State Hospital for the Criminally Insane. Let me take him back, Herb.

BOCK Are you kidding? We'll both take him. I'm going with you! Get him dressed. We're getting out of here before the police put us all in Rockland State.

DRUMMOND I haven't finished my work here. I have this Welbeck to dispose of. I am the angel of the bottomless pit and the wrath of the lamb.

BARBARA Oh dear, he's having another revelation.

Bock holds Drummond's coat and hat and crosses to take his arm. He finds the entranced Drummond as rigid as a statue.

BOCK Look, that ambulance must be here by now. You go down and
get them. I'll give him a shot of something to knock him out. We'll
take him to the airport in the ambulance.

*They both hurry out of the room. Drummond remains enmarbled in his
trance. CAMERA SUDDENLY MOVES DOWN to William Mead,
whose eyes now open; he has heard it all. In background, Drummond, suddenly released from his catatonic trance, heads for the armoire and extracts
the white trousers of Dr. Schaefer's uniform. He puts them on, tucking in
the tails of his hospital shift. He notices William Mead staring at him.*

DRUMMOND You're hallucinating again.

William Mead just stares at Drummond.

EIGHTH FLOOR, NURSES' STATION AND LOBBY AREA.

*Bock and Barbara come hurrying around the corner from the west corridor.
Barbara heads for the elevators. Bock heads for the Nurses' Station. The
Eighth Floor is going about its normal 1:15 P.M. activity. Mrs. Donovan is
at her desk on the phone.*

MRS. DONOVAN   ...Edwards never showed up. I'm short-staffed
as hell. It's just me and Felicia. It's like Sunday. Nobody's here.

DR. BIEGELMAN I'll be at lunch...

*A nurse's aid, a bathrobed patient and two of his visitors stroll by. It's the
end of the lunch hour, when the kitchen workers bring used trays back.*

MRS. DONOVAN Yeah, you gotta send me somebody...Oh yeah?

*Bock moves past Mrs. Donovan and into the pharmacy where we see him
scouring the shelves for thorazine and a syringe. An elevator arrives, disgorging Milton Mead and his resident assistant, Thomas Hitchcock and, of
all people, Dr. Richard Welbeck himself. Barbara and Dr. Biegelman go into
the elevator. The doors close. Milton Mead and Hitchcock head for the west*

corridor. Welbeck, in his natty double-breasted suit and carrying his cash-mere coat, heads straight for the Nurses' Station.

MEAD We'll be in Eight-O-Six.

MRS. DONOVAN *(chuckles into phone)* ...then what did she say?

WELBECK *(to Mrs. Donovan)* I'm Dr. Welbeck. I have a patient on this floor named Drummond, and I'd like to see his chart.

MRS. DONOVAN I'll call you back.

Bock immediately emerges from the pharmacy holding a bottle of thorazine and a wrapped hypodermic syringe. He scowls at Welbeck, who scowls back.

WELBECK Oh, Dr. Bock. Can I have a few minutes of your time, sir?

BOCK No.

He starts to pass Mrs. Donovan and would continue, but Welbeck lays a restraining hand on his arm.

WELBECK Dr. Gilley tells me you're the one who initiated these proceedings against me.

BOCK I'm busy, Welbeck.

WELBECK I'd like to know what you have against me.

BOCK You turned up half-stoned for a simple nephrectomy eight days ago, botched it, put the patient into failure and damn near killed him. Then, pausing only to send in your bill, you flew off on the wings of man to an island of sun in Montego Bay. This is the third time in two years we've had to patch up your patients; the other two died. You're greedy, unfeeling, inept, indifferent, self-inflating and unconscionably profitable. Aside from that, I have nothing against you. I'm sure you play a hell of a game of golf. What else do you want to know?

Welbeck's pocket-beeper BEEPS.

WELBECK   Excuse me for a moment, Doctor.   *(He reaches over the nurses' desk for a phone.)*   This is Dr. Welbeck.   Were you paging me? *(regarding Bock with cold scorn)*   How much do you make a year, Bock? For a guy who makes a lousy forty, fifty grand...*(on phone)*   Hello, Arthur, I understand you've been trying to reach me all morning...

Bock turns and heads back for...

EIGHTH FLOOR, WEST CORRIDOR.

...and down that through the kitchen workers and strolling patients to...

ROOM 806.

...which he enters.   He is startled to find Milton Mead and Hitchcock leaning over William Mead, who is up on one elbow and in a state.

WILLIAM MEAD   I'm telling you, Milton, he pulls out all the wires and the tubes, and he gets up and puts on a doctor's uniform, and he goes out, and he murders doctors!   He just went out ten seconds before you came in!

Indeed, there is no Drummond to be seen.   His bed is empty.   Bock nods to Milton Mead and Hitchcock, who nod back, and crosses quickly to look into the bathroom which is likewise empty.

WILLIAM MEAD   And I'll tell you something else about this crazy place you got here!   There was a naked Indian in here last night doing a war dance!   That's the kind of crazy place you're running here, Milton! You got to get me out of here, Milton.   This is a crazy place, Milton!

Milton Mead's pocket-beeper BEEPS.   Milton Mead reaches for the phone.

WILLIAM MEAD   *(appealing to Bock)*   I wake up last night, there's a goddam Indian in here, a naked Indian!   What kind of hospital is this?

MILTON MEAD *(on phone)* This is Mr. Mead, are you paging me?

WILLIAM MEAD   A couple of hours later I wake up again, and the guy in that bed there is getting out of the bed...

MILTON MEAD *(to Hitchcock)* Are the police still in the building?

HITCHCOCK Yes.

MILTON MEAD You'd better get them up here. Yes.

WILLIAM MEAD All day long, he lays there like a dead man. All of a sudden, in the middle of the night, he gets out of bed! I thought I was going crazy!

MILTON MEAD *(on phone)* Yes, this is Mead. ... Oh, dear. When?...

WILLIAM MEAD   You know what he says to me? He says, you're hallucinating. Listen, I just saw a naked Indian. Now, I'm seeing a ghost. I got to figure he's right, I'm hallucinating, right?

MILTON MEAD I'll be down directly. *(hangs up)* Never rains but it pours. A fire just broke out in one of those condemned buildings. The squatters in the building came out. The police tried to arrest them and, apparently, the situation has erupted into a riot. *(to Bock as he heads for the door)* I'm sure you're wondering what this is all about, Herb.

WILLIAM MEAD   You're not going to leave me alone in this crazy place, Milton!

MILTON MEAD *(at the door with Bock)* Mr. Hitchcock is staying with you. *(to Hitchcock)* You better call the cops, Tom.

WILLIAM MEAD Milton! Milton! Milton!!!

The door slams.

WEST CORRIDOR AND NURSES' STATION.

Bock and Milton Mead stride up the corridor through the linen wagons and kitchen carts.

MILTON MEAD   I haven't the time now, and I'm not even going to try to tell you this curious story my brother just told me. I'll fill you in on it at lunch some time.

He waves his hand helplessly to indicate the utter incredulity of it all.

MILTON MEAD   *(rushes not to miss the elevator)*   Hold it!

They reach an open elevator. Mead goes in, the doors close. The doors of a second elevator then open, and Barbara comes out. She and Bock stare at each other. In background, Welbeck is on the phone at the Nurses' Station.

BARBARA   The ambulance is here.

BOCK   Yeah, but your father isn't. He's disappeared. He put on Schaefer's uniform and has gone out to do God's work, presumably the murder of Dr. Welbeck. Except, that fellow on the phone over there is Dr. Welbeck.

WELBECK   *(in background on phone)*   Oh my God, Arthur! What are you talking about? Have you talked to Dr. Hogan about this?

BOCK   And, on top of everything else, the other patient in your father's room overheard his whole confession and just told the Chief Administrator of the hospital. They're sending for the cops.

REVERSE ACROSS Welbeck on phone at Nurses' Station. In the background, Bock and Barbara stare at him.

WELBECK   *(almost apoplectic on phone)*   Oh, my God, Arthur. Well, who held title? Do the underwriters know about this yet?... Oh my God! Arthur, what're you waiting for? Arrest the son of a bitch! Turn him in!... Oh my God! When?... Of course, Arthur, call me right back. I'm at the Holly Pavilion, Eighth Floor. Please! Right away!

He hangs up.

BOCK Are you all right, Welbeck?

WELBECK All right?! That son of a bitch is trying to wipe me out! My partner, the eminent orthopedic surgeon, Dr. Noel Hogan, is a miserable thief. And he's trying to wipe me out!

MRS. DONOVAN *(extending a chart)* Mr. Drummond's chart, Doctor.

WELBECK *(angrily seizes the chart)* What room is it?

MRS. DONOVAN Eight-O-Six.

WELBECK I'm expecting a phone call. Put it straight through to me in that room.

He strides off angrily, followed by an anxious Bock and Barbara, for the...

EIGHTH FLOOR, WEST CORRIDOR.

Bock and Barbara hurry along in Welbeck's wake.

WELBECK The son of a bitch has been draining the company with phony purchase orders on another company, of which, it now turns out, his wife is the principal stockholder! Transparent fraud! I'll send him up for twenty years!

He wrenches open the door of 806, marches in, followed by Bock and Barbara.

EIGHTH FLOOR, ROOM 806.

Welbeck advances on William Mead's bed, since he is the only patient in the room. (Hitchcock is on the phone.)

WELBECK Well, Drummond, you don't seem that much the worse for the wear.

William Mead stares dully at Welbeck. Then he looks dully at Bock.

WELBECK *(to Hitchcock)* Would you mind using some other phone? I'm expecting an important call.

WILLIAM MEAD What is this? Who...who is this guy?

HITCHCOCK *(on phone)* Yes, well, I'll be at the Nurses' Desk, Sergeant. It would be futile for me to try to explain this to you over the phone.

WELBECK *(leafing through Drummond's chart)* You've got a bit of fever, Drummond, but you're coming along very well.

WILLIAM MEAD I'm not Drummond, you monkey! Drummond's the other bed!

The phone now BUZZES. Welbeck and Hitchcock both head for it.

WELBECK That's mine. *(on phone)* It's Welbeck here.... Yes, Arthur, go ahead....

William Mead is painfully trying to get off his bed.

WILLIAM MEAD I'm getting out of this nuthouse!

BOCK *(pushing him gently back)* All right, take it easy, Mr. Mead.

Hitchcock, satisfied the call is not for him, exits.

WILLIAM MEAD I came in here just to get a lousy polyp cut out.

WELBECK *(on phone)* Oh, my God, what do you mean? How many transactions were there? Bu...but Arthur, I...I borrowed against that stock! I'm in the hole for over three hundred thousand!...

WILLIAM MEAD *(appealing to the gods)* I'm a sick man! I'm supposed to have peace and quiet!

WELBECK *(on phone and apoplectic)* What do you mean, Brazil?! I just spoke to Hogan's office yesterday, and they just told me...

The phone slips from his fingers. He turns to stare at Bock and Barbara.

WELBECK I'm wiped out. The S.E.C. has suspended trading in my stock!

He keels over like a felled tree, falling face-up on Drummond's bed, his legs dangling to the floor. William Mead promptly hides his head under his sheet.

Bock moves quickly to the prostrate Welbeck, feels his throat for the carotid pulse, pulls out his stethoscope, rips Welbeck's shirt open, and listens for heart-sounds. He picks up the dangling telephone receiver, gets a dial tone.

BOCK *(on phone)* Cardiac arrest, Holly Eight.

Barbara strips off her coat. She is still in nurse's uniform. She leans into the hall and calls a passing nurse.

BARBARA We have an emergency here.

BOCK *(rips off Welbeck's natty jacket)* Breathe him.

Barbara helps Bock get Welbeck's dead weight onto the floor. On his knees, Bock straddles Welbeck's prone form, balls his fist and belts Welbeck on his chest. He begins intensive heart massage. Barbara gets down on her knees, opens Welbeck's mouth and commences mouth-to-mouth resuscitation. In the background, the P.A. system blandly echoes:

P.A. SYSTEM *(off-screen)* C.A.C. Holly Eight. Please clear all corridors.

Mrs. Donovan and aides move C.A.C. into the room, immediately followed by Intern Chandler rushing past them.

MRS. DONOVAN Where's Biegelman?

CHANDLER He went to lunch.

MRS. DONOVAN Natch. Get that other bed out of here.

William Mead, of course, is still huddled under his sheet. He peers out from under his covers in wide-eyed disbelief and ducks under again. Bock massages Welbeck's heart. Barbara continues mouth-to-mouth. Nurse Felicia Chile hurries in, pushing the emergency cart before her.

BARBARA *(to Nurse Chile as others begin moving William Mead's bed out of the room)* Give him an ambu bag and an airway.

VOICE *(off-screen)* What's been happening?

Nurse Chile has shunted the emergency cart aside to let the bed out and is extracting an ambu bag and tube from the cart's lower shelf.

CHANDLER *(to Seventh Floor Nursing Supervisor just outside door)* Watch it...

P.A. SYSTEM *(off-screen)* C.A.C. Holly Eight. Please clear all corridors.

Nurse Chile hands the Berman airway and ambu bag to Barbara, who inserts the airway and the ambu tube into Welbeck's mouth and pumps in air by hand. Bock massages away.

EIGHTH FLOOR, WEST CORRIDOR.

Mrs. Donovan and Intern Chandler finally get Mead and his bed out into the corridor where they park it. In background, emergency activity on all sides. The resident cardiologist, DR. GEOFFREY MORSE, and anesthesiologist, DR. LAWRENCE LOOMIS, both thirty-three, come hurtling around the corner.

DR. MORSE In here?

MRS. DONOVAN Yeah.

She follows Morse in as, from the lobby corner, two technicians come racing a max cart and an I.V. stand before them. Behind them, a bewildered Hitchcock moves into view, trying to determine what's going on.

HITCHCOCK *(to Intern Chandler)* Who is it?

P.A. SYSTEM *(off-screen)* Dr. Robert Jackson.

CHANDLER One of the patients had a cardiac arrest.

Hitchcock looks down at the sheeted figure hunched on the bed parked in the hallway and slowly pulls the sheet off his head. William Mead stares up at him like a hunted animal. Hitchcock covers Mead's head again.

ROOM 806.

Bock still massages, sweating bullets by now. Barbara works the ambu bag. Dr. Morse is feeling Welbeck's groin for his femoral pulse.

DR. MORSE What do you have, Dr. Bock?

BOCK Total cardiac arrest.

P.A. SYSTEM *(off-screen)* Dr. Rigby. Dr. Rigby. Dr. Lilac.

DR. MORSE How long has he been like this?

BOCK About a minute. No pulse, no heartbeat, no respiration...

If we can see anything of Welbeck through other bodies, we notice almost all his clothes have been ripped off his body. Dr. Loomis replaces Barbara.

DR. LOOMIS All right, I'll take over.

The two nursing supervisors have been getting the max cart ready, snapping up the gateleg-footrest and attaching the I.V. tube to the oxygen jar, and that to the ambu bag.

BOCK Endotrachial tube.

DONOVAN *(rushing in background with others)* I'm sorry, Doctor, but we have another emergency in 823.

CHANDLER Endotrachial tube.

DR. LOOMIS Shall we get him up on the cart?

DR. MORSE Yeah.

Drs. Loomis, Bock and Morse struggle to lift the the nearly naked dead weight of Dr. Welbeck up from the floor and onto the max cart. Dr. Morse has picked up Drummond's chart from the bed where Welbeck had left it.

DR. MORSE All right, who is this patient? What's the story on this patient?

CLOSE-UP of Bock trying to hoist Welbeck and looking up slowly.

DR. MORSE Is this his chart, Dr. Bock?

Bock cocks his head to him.

DR. MORSE What's his name? Drummond?

Bock looks across to Barbara, now helping out at the max cart. She looks back at Bock. She shrugs. He shrugs. They exchange a smile.

BOCK Yes, his name's Drummond. That's his chart.

Straining under the effort, the three doctors get Welbeck off the floor.

DR. MORSE *(studying the chart)* Oh Christ, the poor son of a bitch just had a nephrectomy a week ago.

Mrs. Donovan exits into...

EIGHTH FLOOR, WEST CORRIDOR.

...as Mrs. Donovan comes out, Hitchcock turns to her.

HITCHCOCK Was it Drummond?

MRS. DONOVAN Who else would it be?

Hitchcock silently thanks God.

ROOM 806.

DR. MORSE *(off-screen)* Pick him up. Put him on it. Stop the massage.

Welbeck's body is finally on the max cart. Nurses and doctors converge on him. Dr. Loomis sets about intubating Welbeck, and the Nursing Supervisor begins clamping the metal bands of the E.K.G. machine on each of Welbeck's extremities.

While all this goes on, Bock and Barbara have picked up the remnants of Welbeck's jacket, trousers, shirt and underwear. Dr. Morse is squatting by the max-cart reading the E.K.G. script as it rolls slowly out of the cart.

DR. MORSE Ventricular fibrillation. Get me the paddles. Push another amp of bicarb.

The Nursing Supervisor starts applying electrode paste to the defibrillating paddles. Another nurse measures off an ampule of bicarbonate of soda which Dr. Loomis injects into the I.V. tube.

DR. MORSE Set it for two hundred.

Barbara unsnaps her father's valise and stuffs Welbeck's garments in it. Bock takes Welbeck's coat and piles Drummond's things on top of that.

The Nursing Supervisor hands Dr. Morse the defibrillating paddles to place on Welbeck's left breast.

NURSE   *(off-screen)*   That's two hundred.

DR. MORSE   Everybody back away.

All back away from the max-cart. Bock and Barbara are at the window, piled up with valise and coats; they look like they're off for Europe.

DR. MORSE   *(off-screen)*   One-two-three...

He pushes the defibrillating button, sending an electric shock through Welbeck's body so as to bounce it into the air.

Bock and Barbara remain at the window with heart-resuscitation team in background. Barbara slips into her own coat, in preparation for escape.

DR. MORSE   *(in background)*   Did he convert?

DR. LOOMIS   *(in background)*   No, he's still fibrillating.

DR. MORSE   *(in background)*   Let's go to four hundred.

BARBARA   *(sotto voce to Bock)*   What do we do now?

Bock is staring out the window. Barbara stares out with him.

THEIR P.O.V.: looking down onto the U-shaped drive of the entrance plaza of the hospital and First Avenue full of traffic. A band of some fifty black and Puerto Rican youths, including females and young white revolutionaries, most in Che Guevara garb, have broken past the security guards at the gates and spill across the drive. Some policemen and security guards move tentatively out of the hospital to intercept them.

The shouting can't be heard from up here. Off-screen we hear the activities of the resuscitation team.

NURSING SUPERVISOR *(off-screen)*   It's four hundred.

DR. MORSE   *(off-screen)* Everybody back One-two-three...

SOUND of the shock.

DR. MORSE   *(off-screen)* That didn't work either.

FIRST AVENUE. HIGH SHOT.

Low crowd noises. Bock looks out the window at the protesting mob below.

DR. MORSE   *(off-screen)* All right. Let me have a c.c. of Adrenaline and intercardiac needle.

CAMERA PANS SLOWLY UP over the melee in the plaza to the fence. Barbara and Bock stare down at the crowd.

DR. MORSE   *(off-screen)* Stop the massage. Ventricular fibrillation. Put another amp of bicarb. Two hundred.

ZOOM DOWN into the maelstrom to FULL SHOT of the Reverend Drummond dressed in Schaefer's white uniform, standing on the slim island separating the uptown traffic from the downtown traffic. Drummond is a private island of his own, hands stretched to the skies. He is prophesying.

DRUMMOND *(barely audible above the traffic rumbling heedlessly around him)* Let those who are in Judea flee to the mountains, for the age is closed, the season of the seventh seal is at hand!

ROOM 806.

Bock and Barbara slip through doctors and nurses, heading for the door.

DR. MORSE   Hang isopril, two in five hundred. Let's take one more crack with the paddles. Everybody back off the cart.

Bock, carrying two overcoats, and Barbara, wearing hers and carrying her father's valise, exit into...

EIGHTH FLOOR, WEST CORRIDOR.

...as Bock and Barbara come out, the activity is normal, with the exception of William Mead's bed along the wall. Hitchcock and two overcoated men are in the hallway, and Hitchcock hurries to Bock.

HITCHCOCK   Is he dead?

BOCK   They can't get him out of fib. I don't think he'll make it.

HITCHCOCK   Thank God. *(sighs, turns to the two detectives)*   This should close the case, Sergeant.

Bock and Barbara hurry toward the elevators.

THE HOSPITAL, HOLLY PAVILION, LOBBY.

The small army of militants and activists has broken through the security into the lobby. Their entrance is greeted by one small scream from a woman in the lobby. A LEADER of the invading troop calls out.

LEADER   Everybody take it easy! Nobody's going to be hurt! We just want the Director!

Others in the troop shout reassurances, but it doesn't really reassure anybody. The lady in the gift shop closes her door and locks up. People crowd in a solid block in the doorway to the coffee shop to see what's going on.

From the long tunnels of corridors, nurses, doctors, administrative personnel pause in their chores and errands and missions to watch the tide of events in the lobby.

HOLLY PAVILION, EXECUTIVE CORRIDOR.

The exit door is wrenched open, and Bock comes hurtling into the carpeted

executive corridor toward the lobby, and at that moment the troop of mili-
tants come rumbling in from the other end. Every door of the corridor fills
with secretaries and administrators unsure of what's happening.   Then,
Sundstrom elbows his way through the clutch of secretaries in his doorway
and comes into the corridor. He regards the militants moving down the cor-
ridor toward him.

SHOUTING CROWD   We want Sundstrom!   We want Sundstrom!
Community control!   Community control!   Hip-hip-Hippocrates!
Up with service! Down with fees!

SUNDSTROM You people want to see me?

FIRST MILITANT Yeah, baby, we want to see you...

SECOND MILITANT We're taking over this hospital, man...

SUNDSTROM   I've had it up to here.   I'm not dealing with this kind
of cheap blackmail!

LEADER Now look, man. Now wait a minute there!

FIRST MILITANT We're looking for a hostage!

LEADER Fourteen people just got arrested for doing...

In the background, one of their fellow revolutionaries speaks up...

MAN Lookit, man, where's the TV camera?

...but he's shut up by the Leader.

LEADER Would you be cool, man? *(now yelling)* Fourteen people got
arrested for doing nothing but living in their homes, which you people threw them out of.

CROWD Right on!

LEADER   So now we're going to arrest you.   We're going to hold you hostage and we ain't letting you go un...

Ambler, the medical student we met during Bock's teaching rounds, pushes in front of the Leader to face Sundstrom.

AMBLER   We, the members of the Doctors Liberation Committee indict this hospital for the criminal neglect of the community in which it is situated! We demand an immediate dissolution of the governing and executive boards.

SHOUT   What are you going to do about those fourteen ghetto people?

As the shouts continue, Sundstrom raises a hand to quiet the crowd.

SUNDSTROM   I am not going to do anything...about anything.

SHOUT   Yes, you are!

SUNDSTROM   By God, if you want to take over this hospital, you take it over!

SHOUTS   We will! Right on!

SUNDSTROM   You run it! I am finished! I quit! You run it! You pay the bills! You fight the city!

MILITANT   We will!

SUNDSTROM   You fight the state! You fight the unions. You fight the community! You...you think you can do a better job, you do it! Now I am finished! I quit! It's all yours!

Eyes filled with tears of rage, Sundstrom lowers his head and moves into the mass of militants, which parts for him to leave.

CROWD   Quit! Quit!

The mass engulfs Sundstrom, moving back out into the lobby with him, pushing him, shoving him, humiliating him.

REACTION SHOT of Bock watching it all from the far end of the corridor. He closes his eyes and the pain of watching all this shows on his face. He opens his eyes. The corridor is now silent and empty. He hurries to...

HOLLY PAVILION, THE LOBBY.

Bock rushes in, as the milling throng dissolves into the bystanders, security police and city cops. Common sense has settled in and the general tenor is to avoid any further trouble. We can hear the rhythmic patter of cops.

SHOUTS OF COPS All right, come on...come on—Let's clear the area. —Come on, let's clear this place...Keep cool. Everybody keep cool.

Bock elbows his way through the throng as it drifts toward the doors to...

THE HOSPITAL, ENTRANCE PLAZA. DAY.

...and goes through the gathering police. A mobile TV camera crew and a few reporters are hurrying up through the gates from First Avenue.

FIRST AVENUE. DAY.

The Reverend Drummond stands, a solitary human island, among the shrill ROAR of the city. The protesters protest endlessly, CHANTING, SHOUTING. Absolutely no one pays any attention to the gaunt, doctor-clad sixty-year-old man standing on an island.

Except, of course, for Bock, who must pause to wait for a red light. Bock hustles through the traffic to where Drummond stands.

DRUMMOND Let those who are in Judea flee to the mountains, for the age is closed, the season of the seventh seal is at hand! The age is closed! The season of the seventh se...

BOCK Dr. Welbeck is dead. They thought he was you.

DRUMMOND Yes, I know. We must arrange to have his body shipped to my Apache village where we will bury him with full tribal rites. In a day or two, somebody'll ask, "Whatever happened to Dr. Welbeck?" And it will be assumed he absconded to Brazil to join his partner, the eminent orthopedic surgeon, Dr. Noel Hogan. Welbeck, too, was mislaid, overlooked, forgotten to death, you see.

The ambulance pulls up and Barbara gets out of it.

BARBARA *(taking her father around to the back)* We have to hurry, Dad.

The light turns green. The traffic starts flowing around them, disjoined by the ambulance blocking one lane on each side of the dividing island. An ambulance attendant has opened the back doors to get Drummond in. Barbara hurries toward the front, climbs in, holds the door open for Bock. He stands a few paces back.

BOCK I'm not going. *(He moves to the ambulance, closes the door.)* The hospital's coming apart. I can't walk out on it when it's coming apart. Somebody has to be responsible, Barbara. Everybody's hitting the road, running to the hills, running away. Somebody's got to be responsible. *(across Barbara to the driver)* Kennedy Airport. You've got a two-thirty flight to make.

He turns, and the ambulance pulls away. Bock goes back to the sidewalk where he meets Sundstrom, now wearing his coat.

BOCK You going back in?

SUNDSTROM Yeah.

They make their way back toward...

THE HOSPITAL, ENTRANCE PLAZA.

The two physicians trudge across the U-drive.

SUNDSTROM *(matter-of-factly)* It's like pissing in the wind, right, Herb?

BOCK Right.

FADE OUT.

THE END

NETWORK

1976

*Original Story and Screenplay
by* **PADDY CHAYEFSKY**

Produced by **HOWARD GOTTFRIED**

Directed by **SIDNEY LUMET**

CAST CREDITS

MAX SCHUMACHER	William Holden
HOWARD BEALE	Peter Finch
DIANA CHRISTENSON	Faye Dunaway
FRANK HACKETT	Robert Duvall
NELSON CHANEY	Wesley Addy
ARTHUR JENSEN	Ned Beatty
LOUISE SCHUMACHER	Beatrice Straight
LAUREEN HOBBS	Marlene Warfield
GREAT AHMED KAHN	Arthur Burghardt
TV DIRECTOR	Bill Burrows
GEORGE BOSCH	John Carpenter
HARRY HUNTER	Jordan Charney
MARY ANN GIFFORD	Kathy Cronkite
JOE DONNELLY	Ed Crowley
WALTER AMUNDSEN	Jerome Dempsey
BARBARA SCHLESINGER	Conchata Ferrell
MILTON STEINMAN	Gene Gross
JACK SNOWDEN	Stanley Grover
CAROLINE SCHUMACHER	Cindy Grover
BILL HERRON	Darryl Hickman
ARTHUR ZANGWILL	Mitchell Jason
TV STAGE MANAGER	Paul Jenkins
MAX'S SECRETARY	Carolyn Krigbaum
ASSOCIATE PRODUCER	Kenneth Kimmins
TV PRODUCTION ASSISTANT	Lynn Klugman
AUDIO MAN	Zane Lasky
TOMMY PELLEGRINO	Michael Lipton
WILLIE STEIN	Michael Lombard
HERB THACKERAY	Pirie MacDonald
TV ASSOCIATE DIRECTOR	Russ Petranto
LOU	Bernard Pollock
SAM HAYWOOD	Roy Poole
EDWARD GEORGE RUDDY	William Prince
HELEN MIGGS	Sasha von Scherler
ROBERT MCDONOUGH	Lane Smith
WALTER GIANNINI	Theodore Sorel
MOSAIC FIGURE	Fred Stuthman
NARRATOR	Lee Richardson

FADE IN:

BLACK SCREEN

NARRATOR *(off-screen)* This story is about Howard Beale who was the network news anchorman on UBS-TV.

A BANK OF FOUR COLOR TELEVISION MONITORS

It is 7:14 P.M., Monday, September 22, 1975, and we are watching the news programs on CBS, NBC, ABC and UBS-TV—the network of our story. The AUDIO is OFF; and head shots of WALTER CRONKITE, JOHN CHANCELLOR, HOWARD K. SMITH and HARRY REASONER, and of course, the anchorman of our network, HOWARD BEALE, silently flicker across the four screens, interspersed with the news of the day— President Ford's new energy program, a hearing on Patty Hearst's bail, truce violations in Beirut; busing trouble in Boston.

NARRATOR *(off-screen)* In his time, Howard Beale had been a mandarin of television, the grand old man of news, with a HUT rating of 16 and a 28 audience share.

CAMERA MOVES IN to isolate Howard Beale, who is everything an anchorman should be—fifty-eight years old, silver-haired, magisterial, dignified to the point of divinity.

HOWARD Good evening. It is Monday, September the Twenty-Second, Nineteen Seventy-Five, and, today, a shot was fired at President Ford's motorcade in San Francisco. The President was unharmed. The incident happened late this afternoon, and we still do not have a filmed report. The shot was fired as Mr. Ford was leaving the St. Francis Hotel on his way to the San Francisco Airport. The President was shaking hands with people in front of the hotel when the shooting occurred. Secret Service agents rushed Mr. Ford into his car, and the motorcade went immediately to the airport. Police arrested a man with a six-shot revolver in his possession, although there is some confusion about this. Our last reports indicate the attempted assassination may have been made by a woman. In any event, this is the second attempt on the President's life in eighteen days, and we will have a comment to make about that later on in the program. Right now, though, we have a telephone report from Halsted Mayberry in San Francisco. Halsted, are you there?

NARRATOR *(off-screen)* In 1969, however, his fortunes began to decline. He fell to a 22 share. The following year, his wife died, and he was left a childless widower with an 8 rating and a 12 share. He became morose and isolated, began to drink heavily, and on September 22, 1975, he was fired, effective in two weeks. It was broken to him by Max Schumacher....

FIFTH AVENUE, SOUTH OF 57TH STREET. 11:30 P.M.

The area is deserted except for a few strollers window-shopping. Down near 55th Street, two roaring drunks, Howard Beale and MAX SCHU-MACHER, reel along.

NARRATOR *(off-screen)* ...who was President of the News Division at UBS. The two old friends got properly pissed.

CLOSER SHOT of Howard and Max, a craggy, lumbering, rough-hewn, 51-year-old man, thoroughly plastered and on a laughing jag.

HOWARD *(clutching the corner mailbox to keep from falling)* When was this?

MAX 1951...?

HOWARD   I was at CBS with Ed Murrow in 1951...didn't you join Murrow in 1951?

MAX   Must've been 1950 then. I was at NBC. Morning News. Associate producer. I was a kid, twenty-six years old... Anyway, they were building the lower level on the George Washington Bridge, and we were doing a remote there. Except nobody told me...!

For some reason, this knocks them out. Howard, wheezes with suppressed laughter. Max has to shout to get the rest of the story out.

MAX Ten after seven in the morning, I get a call. "Where the hell are you? You're supposed to be on the George Washington Bridge!" I jump out of bed...I throw my raincoat over my pajamas...I run down the stairs...I get out in the street...I flag a cab...I jump in. I say, "Take me to the middle of the George Washington Bridge!"

Both men dissolve into spasms of laughter.

MAX *(tears streaming down his cheeks)* The driver turns around. He says, "Don't do it buddy." *(so weak now he can barely talk)* He says, "You're a young man. You got your whole life ahead of you."

He stomps around on the sidewalk. Howard clutches the mailbox.

A BAR. 3:00 A.M.

Any bar. Mostly empty. Max and Howard in a booth, soddenly sober.

HOWARD I'm going to kill myself.

MAX Oh shit, Howard.

HOWARD I'm going to blow my brains out right on the air, right in the middle of the seven o'clock news.

MAX You'll get a hell of a rating, I'll tell you that. A fifty share easy.

HOWARD You think so?

MAX We could make a series out of it. Suicide of the Week. Hell, why limit ourselves? Execution of the Week—the Madame Defarge Show! Every Sunday night, bring your knitting and watch somebody get guillotined, hung, electrocuted, gassed. For a logo, we'll have some brute with a black hood over his head. Think of the spin-offs. Rape of the Week....

HOWARD *(getting caught up)* Terrorist of the Week?

MAX   I love it!   Suicides, assassinations, mad bombers, Mafia hit-men, murder in the barbershop, human sacrifices in witches' covens, automobile smashups. The Death Hour! A great Sunday night show for the whole family. We'll wipe that fucking Disney right off the air.

They snigger and snort. Howard lays his head down on the table.

HOWARD'S BEDROOM.   4:30 A.M., DARK.

Fully clothed, Howard sprawls asleep on his still-made bed in the dark bed-room. Suddenly, he bolts up, SCREAMING at unseen terrors.

HOWARD'S DOORSTEP. TUESDAY, 8:00 A.M.

Howard's HOUSEKEEPER, a middle-aged lady, lets herself into...

HOWARD'S APARTMENT, ENTRY FOYER.

The housekeeper, unbuttoning her coat, is greeted by a raucous clock ALARM, relentlessly BUZZING off-screen. She crosses into...

HOWARD'S LIVING ROOM.

...and opens the blinds, with an eruption of daylight. The shrill BUZZING gets louder, so she proceeds into...

HOWARD'S BACK FOYER.

...where the bedroom door is ajar. The BUZZING comes from here.

HOUSEKEEPER'S P.O.V.:   Howard Beale, still wearing last night's clothes, is curled in a position of fetal helplessness on the floor.

HOUSEKEEPER   *(after a moment)* Are you all right, Mr. Beale?

HOWARD   *(opens one blotto eye)* I'm fine, thank you, Mrs. Merryman.

He contrives to get to his feet as the Housekeeper crosses to the alarm clock and turns the BUZZING off.

CREDITS AND MUSIC ERUPT ONTO THE SCREEN—

N E T W O R K

Under and interspersed with CREDITS, a montage from a routine day.

HOWARD BEALE'S OFFICE, 5TH FLOOR. 9:20 A.M.

In his unpretentious office, cluttered with books, magazines, photographs and awards on the walls, Howard sits behind his desk, rattling away on his type-writer at his copy for that evening's broadcast. He pauses to pour himself a quick shot of scotch.

THE NIGHTLY NEWS, ROOM 517. 10:30 A.M.

This is a vast common room full of activity, bordered by individual produc-tion offices such as the one occupied by Howard and his team. It is packed with the desks of producers, associate producers, head writer and writers, pro-duction assistants, etc. The walls are festooned like bulletin boards. Two wire machines stand in a corner. Large blowups of Howard Beale are prominent-ly displayed.

There are small, shelved libraries of books, directories and magazines here and there.

The ever-present bank of four television monitors; and since it is 10:30 A.M., Tuesday, September 23, 1975, and since the AUDIO is OFF, the screens silently flicker with whatever was on that day at that time.

Howard comes out of his office through the HUM of informal industry and the occasional TYPEWRITER CLACKING and phones RINGING. Around him, the Nightly News personnel, all in their twenties and thirties, confer. Howard Beale makes for a ledge of reference books to check out some fact. He spreads the book out on an unoccupied desk. Someone tells him he's wanted on the phone. He nods, takes the call at that desk. Throughout, he belts back his glass of booze.

EXECUTIVE PRODUCER'S OFFICE. 1:00 P.M.

Another smallish office debouching off the main room like Howard's, jammed with NINE PEOPLE, standing or sitting wherever they can. The Executive Producer, HARRY HUNTER is in his early forties and behind the desk. Howard Beale sits on a Finnish modern couch, flanked by an ASSOCIATE PRODUCER and a MAN FROM THE GRAPHICS DEPARTMENT. Everybody else is in their twenties or thirties and is casually dressed. This is the daily run-down meeting when the schedule for that evening's broadcast is roughed out, and it sounds something like this.

HOWARD   *(reaches for the bottle of booze on Hunter's desk to refill his glass)* Let's do the Lennon deportation at the end of three.

HARRY HUNTER   That strong enough to bump?

HOWARD   *(sipping his booze)* In one minute I'll do a lead on Sarah Jane Moore to Mayberry in San Francisco.

ASSOCIATE PRODUCER   The film I saw was the Chief of Detectives.

GRAPHICS MAN   I think we got maybe ten seconds on the shooting itself.

PRODUCTION ASSISTANT   The whole thing is one-twenty-five.

HOWARD   How does that come out?

PRODUCTION ASSISTANT   About four-fifty...

ASSOCIATE PRODUCER   Are we using Squeaky Fromme?

HARRY HUNTER   Let's do that in two. Squeaky. Ford at the airport. Bump. Now, we using a map going into San Francisco?

GRAPHICS MAN   I prefer a news-pix.

Howard pours himself another shot of booze and sips it.

HOWARD   What've we got left?

PRODUCTION ASSISTANT   Gun control, Patty Hearst affidavit, guerillas in Chad, OPEC in Vienna....

4TH FLOOR CORRIDOR.   6:28 P.M.

In the small network-news make-up room Howard is getting a few last whisks from the MAKE-UP LADY. Finished, Howard pulls the Kleenex from his shirt collar, takes a last sip from his glass, gathers his papers, exits, turns and enters...

4TH FLOOR NETWORK NEWS STUDIO.

Typical newsroom studio full of cameras, cables, wall maps, flats and propping, etc. Howard nods, smiles to CAMERAMEN, ASSISTANT DIREC-TORS, ASSOCIATE PRODUCERS, as he makes his way to his desk facing Camera One. He sits, prepares his papers, looks up to the control room, and nods.

MUSIC ABRUPTLY OUT

END OF CREDITS.

4TH FLOOR CONTROL ROOM.

The wall clock reads 6:30. Typical control room with a double bank of television monitors including two color monitors, the show monitor and pre-set monitor. Before this array of TV screens sits the DIRECTOR, flanked by the PRODUCTION ASSISTANT who stop-watches the show, and by the TECHNICAL DIRECTOR, who operates a special board of buttons and knobs.

The monitor shows the network's Washington correspondent, JACK

SNOWDEN, doing a follow-up on the attempted assassination of President Ford in San Francisco.

In the back half of the control room, seated behind his shelf is Harry Hunter, now flirting with his Secretary, SHEILA.

SNOWDEN   *(on monitor)* The first attempt on President Ford's life was eighteen days ago, and again yesterday in San Francisco.

DIRECTOR   *(murmuring into his mike)* Lou, kick that little thing shut on ground level.

SNOWDEN   *(on monitor)* In spite of two attempts...

The show monitor screen has switched over to show film of President Ford arriving at the San Francisco airport.

The director and technical director turn in their seat to gossip with Harry Hunter and Sheila.

SNOWDEN   *(voice-over on monitor)* Mr. Ford says he will not become...

PRODUCTION ASSISTANT   Forty seconds.

SNOWDEN   *(on monitor)* ...a prisoner of the Oval Office—

DIRECTOR   ...headroll...rolling...

SNOWDEN   *(on monitor)* a hostage of would-be assassins...

TECHNICAL DIRECTOR   *(murmurs into mike)* twenty-five, twenty-six...

PRESIDENT FORD   *(on monitor)* ...the American People are good people...

HARRY HUNTER   *(to Sheila)* How the hell do you always get mixed up with married men?

PRESIDENT FORD *(on monitor)* ...Democrats, Independents, Republicans and others...

DIRECTOR *(leaning back to say to the secretary)* Sheila, if you're hot for married men, why go to strangers? What's wrong with me?

PRESIDENT FORD *(on monitor)* Under no circumstances will I capitulate...

PRODUCTION ASSISTANT ...ten seconds...

DIRECTOR *(into mike)* ten seconds coming to one...

PRESIDENT FORD *(on monitor)* ...to those who want to undercut all that's good in America...

PRODUCTION ASSISTANT ...forty seconds...

DIRECTOR *(into mike)* ...twenty seconds to one...one...

Howard Beale's image suddenly flips on-screen.

HOWARD *(on monitor)* Ladies and gentlemen, I would like at this moment to announce that I will be retiring from this program in two weeks' time because of poor ratings...

The director has whispered something to Sheila, which occasions sniggers from her and from Hunter. The technical director stands in order to get in on the joke.

ASSISTANT DIRECTOR *(to director)* What'd you say?

HOWARD *(on monitor)* ...and since this show was the only thing I had going for me in my life, I have decided to kill myself.

Sheila whispers something which causes Hunter to burst into laughter.

ASSISTANT DIRECTOR   *(to the director)* So what'd she say?

HOWARD   *(on monitor)* I'm going to blow my brains out right on this program a week from today.

PRODUCTION ASSISTANT   *(puzzled indeed by this diversion from the script)* Ten seconds to commercial.

HOWARD   *(on monitor)* So tune in next Tuesday. That'll give the public relations people a week to promote the show. That ought to get a hell of a rating, a fifty share easy.

A bewildered production assistant nudges the director, who wheels back to his mike.

DIRECTOR   *(into mike)* ...and...

PRODUCTION ASSISTANT   *(to the director)* Did you hear that?

DIRECTOR   Take VT A.

The monitor screen erupts into a commercial for catfood.

AUDIO MAN   *(leaning in from his glass cubicle)* What was that about?

PRODUCTION ASSISTANT   *(to the director)* Howard just said he was going to blow his brains out next Tuesday.

DIRECTOR   What're you talking about?

PRODUCTION ASSISTANT   Didn't you hear him? He just said...

HARRY HUNTER   What's wrong now?

PRODUCTION ASSISTANT   Howard just said he was going to kill himself next Tuesday.

HARRY HUNTER What do you mean Howard just said he was going to kill himself next Tuesday?

PRODUCTION ASSISTANT *(nervously riffling her script)* He was supposed to do a tag on Ron Nesson and go to commercial.

AUDIO MAN He said tune in next Tuesday, I'm going to shoot myself.

Everybody's attention is now on the double bank of black-and-white monitors showing agitated behavior all over the studio. Several screens show Howard at his desk in vehement discussion with a clearly startled FLOOR MANAGER with headset and a no less startled ASSOCIATE PRODUCER.

DIRECTOR *(on mike to Floor Manager)* What the hell's going on?

On the pre-set monitor screen, the Floor Manager looks up.

FLOOR MANAGER *(on screen, voice booming into the control room)* I don't know. He just said he was going to blow his brains out.

DIRECTOR *(into mike)* What the hell's this all about, Howard?

HOWARD *(on monitor, shouting at the floor personnel gathering around him)* Will you get the hell out of here? We'll be back on air in a couple of seconds!

HARRY HUNTER *(roaring into mike)* What the fuck's going on, Howard?

ASSOCIATE PRODUCER They want to know what the fuck is going on, Howard.

HOWARD *(on monitor)* I can't hear you.

DIRECTOR *(bawling at the Audio Man)* Put the studio mike on!

AUDIO MAN We're back on in eleven seconds.

PRODUCTION ASSISTANT   *(stop-watching)*   Ten seconds.

ASSISTANT DIRECTOR   Ready 2, Ready 2...

HARRY HUNTER   *(voice booming into the studio)*   Howard, what the hell are you doing? Have you flipped or what?!

ASSOCIATE PRODUCER   Harry, I think we better get him off.

HARRY HUNTER   *(roaring at Audio Man)*   Get him off!

AUDIO MAN   *(back in control room)*   What the hell's going on?

ASSOCIATE PRODUCER   *(battling Howard)*   Come on, Howard.   Let go of the fucking desk.   *(to Harry Hunter and everyone else)*   For Chrissakes. We're in fucking trouble down here! He won't let go of the fucking desk. Come on, give us a hand...

HARRY HUNTER   Turn the fucking sound off, you stupid son of a bitch! He's going out live!

PRODUCTION ASSISTANT   *(stop-watching)*   Three—two—one—

DIRECTOR   Take 2.

> *At which point, the Technical Director pushes a button; the jangling catfood commercial flips off the monitor, replaced by a scene of gathering bedlam around Howard's desk. The Audio Man flees to his cubicle to turn off the audio, but not before Harry Hunter can be heard.*

HARRY HUNTER   Chrissakes!   Black it out!   This is going out live to sixty-seven fucking affiliates! Shit!

5TH FLOOR, ELEVATOR AREA. 10:47 P.M.

> *FRANK HACKETT, Executive Senior Vice President of UBS, forty-one years old, of the new cool young breed of management/merchandising execu-*

ives, wearing a tuxedo—(He has been pulled out of a dinner party in Westchester by this unfortunate business.)—comes out of the elevator and turns briskly into...

5TH FLOOR CORRIDOR.

It is clotted with network EXECUTIVES of assorted sizes and ages. Hackett, en route to Room 509, the humming hub of activity here, pauses to comment.

HACKETT   Lou, can't we clear out that downstairs lobby? There must be a hundred people down there, every TV station and wire service in the city. I could barely get in.

LOU   How'm I going to clear them out, Frank?

ROOM 509, EXECUTIVE OFFICES OF THE NEWS DIVISION.

Hackett enters the common room, from which debouch the offices of President of News Max Schumacher, V.P. News Division ROBERT McDONOUGH, V.P. Public Relations News Division   MILTON STEINMAN, V.P. Legal Affairs News Division WALTER GIANNINI, V.P. Owned Stations News EMIL DUBROVNIK, V.P. Standards and Practices ARTHUR ZANG-WILL, General Manager News Radio MICHAEL SANDIES—and a number of other EXECUTIVES. The V.P. Sales, JOE DONNELLY, takes the phone from the V.P. News Sales, RICHARD KETTERING, seated at the desk of the secretary for V.P. Public Relations News Division.

DONNELLY   *(on phone)* How many spots were wiped out?

ZANGWILL   So far, over nine hundred fucking phone calls complaining about the foul language.

HACKETT   Shit.

P.R. MAN   *(in background on phone)* Come on, Mickey, what page are you putting it on?!

Hackett is already crossing into...

MAX'S OFFICE.

...which is jammed with NELSON CHANEY, President of UBS, fifty-two, a patrician, on the phone at Max's desk. He notes Hackett's arrival.

CHANEY   *(on phone)*   Frank Hackett just walked in.

Milton Steinman (whom we remember as V.P. Public Relations News Division), early fifties, a rumpled and ordinarily amiable man, stands by the desk on the phone.

STEINMAN   *(on phone)*   I can't release the tape, Marty. We're still studying it ourselves.

P.R. MAN   *(sticking his head in, to Steinman)*   ABC again, wants the tape...

STEINMAN   Tell him to go fuck himself. *(to phone)*   And that goes for you too, Marty.

HACKETT   *(to Howard Beale sitting on the couch)*   You're off the air as of now.

CHANEY   *(extending his phone to Hackett)*   He wants to talk to you.

HACKETT   *(to Max, leaning against a wall)*   Who's replacing Beale tomorrow?

MAX   We're flying up Snowden from Washington.

STEINMAN   *(turns up the volume knob on Max's desk)*   All right, everybody hold it. Let's see how the other networks handled this.

Three television monitors on the wall and one large office console of UBS-TV blurt out their respective pre-news commercials.

THACKERAY *(V.P. Stations Relations, from doorway)* The ten o'clock news opened with it.

HACKETT *(on phone)* Walter's drafted a statement. I haven't seen it yet. I just got here, John, I was at a dinner party.

Suddenly, the faces of OTHER NETWORK NEWSCASTERS and the UBS local news anchorman, TIM HALLOWAY, are on the screen.

CBS ANCHORMAN *(affably)* An unusual thing happened at one of our sister networks UBS this evening...

ABC ANCHORMAN *(almost simultaneously)* Howard Beale, one of television's most esteemed newscasters...

NBC ANCHORMAN Howard Beale interrupted his network news program tonight to announce...

HACKETT Shit. *(to Max)* How are we handling it?

MAX Halloway's going to make a brief statement at the end of the show to the effect Howard's been under great personal stress, et cetera...

Hackett clicks off the bank of monitor screens. They go black.

HACKETT *(on phone)* I'll call you back, John. *(returns the phone to its cradle, regards the gathering)* All right. We've got a stockholders' meeting tomorrow at which we're going to announce the restructuring of management plan, and I don't want this grotesque incident to interfere with that. I'll suggest Mr. Ruddy open with a short statement washing this whole thing off, and, you, Max, better have some answers in case some of those nuts that always come to stockholder's meetings...

MAX *(still leaning against the wall)* Mr. Beale has been under great personal and professional pressures.

HACKETT *(exploding)* I've got some goddam surprises for you too,

Schumacher! I've had it up to here with your cruddy division and its annual thirty-three million dollar deficit!

MAX   Keep your hands off my news division, Frank. We're responsible to corporate level, not you.

HACKETT   We'll goddam well see about that!

CHANEY   All right, take it easy. Right now, how're we going to get Beale out of here? I understand there's at least a hundred reporters and camera crews in the lobby.

MAX   We've got a limo waiting at the freight entrance. *(to Howard)* Howard, you're going to stay at my place tonight. There's bound to be press around yours.

AVENUE OF THE AMERICAS. WEDNESDAY, 10:00 A.M.

HIGH WIDE-ANGLE SHOT and/or SHOTS showing Television Row: that quarter mile of Sixth Avenue where the four television networks have their chrome, marble and glass buildings rearing futuristically into the sky— 30 Rock (NBC), Black Rock (CBS), and Hard Rock (ABC), and of course, the network of our story, UBS. It is a nice, sunny day.

UBS, 5TH FLOOR, MAX'S OFFICE. 10:00 A.M.

SUNLIGHT STREAMING in. Max sits at his desk in shirtsleeves.

MAX   *(on phone)* I want Snowden here by noon. Have Lester cover the C.I.A. hearings and give the White House to Doris.

Max's secretary sticks her head in.

SECRETARY   You're late for your screening, Max.

Max hangs up, stands, gathers his jacket off a chair and heads for the door.

MAX   If John Wheeler calls, switch him to Screening Room Seven.

He exits.

NINTH FLOOR, SCREENING ROOM 7.

A screening room of some 20 seats. Two people are already there: a whippet-like, casually-dressed man of thirty-six, BILL HERRON, and DIANA CHRISTENSON, dressed in slacks and blouse, thirty-four, tall, willowy, and with the best ass ever seen on a Vice President in Charge of Programming.

MAX *(entering)* I'm sorry, Bill. This Beale business...

HERRON It's all right.

MAX Sit down.

Max and Diana exchange nods and professionally polite greetings.

HERRON *(buzzing the projectionist)* Diana asked if she could sit in on this.

MAX Fine. *(sits, calls to Diana)* How's it going?

Diana shrugs, smiles.

HERRON I think you'll like this footage better than the stuff I showed you last time, Max.

The lights in the room go down. A shaft of light shoots out from the projection room. Max leans back, watches the documentary footage.

ON SCREEN, a handsome black woman in her early thirties is sitting in a typical panel discussion, flanked by three MEN and a WOMAN, two white and two black, all urban guerilla—fatigues, sunglasses and combat boots.

SUSSKIND *(on screen)* Laureen, what is the relationship of the Communist Party to these underground splinter groups?

LAUREEN HOBBS   *(on screen, calmly)*   The Communist Party believes that the most pressing political necessity today is the consolidation of the revolutionary, radical and democratic movements into a United front...

INSERT: (on screen) "Laureen Hobbs, U.S. Communist Party"

The PHONE BUZZES softly. Max picks it up.

MAX   *(into phone)*   Yeah?...Oh, goddammit, when, Louise?...Well, did he say anything?...All right, thanks.   *(hangs up, promptly picks up again)*   Four-eight-o-seven.

LAUREEN HOBBS   *(on screen, in background)*   Repression is the response of an increasingly desperate, imperialist ruling clique. Indeed, the entire apparatus of the bourgeois-democratic state especially its judicial systems and its prisons is disintegrating....

MAX   *(on phone)*   Harry, Howard Beale left my house about twenty minutes ago. Has he come in yet? Let me know when he arrives. *(hangs up)* Who's that? Laureen Hobbs?

HERRON   This is a David Susskind thing she did some time ago. I think we can use some of it.

LAUREEN HOBBS   *(on screen)*   The fascist thrust must be resisted in its seminal stages by the broadest possible coalition.

SCREENING ROOM 7. TWENTY MINUTES LATER.

Room still dark. NUMBERED WHITE LEADER is rolling on screen.

HERRON   What we're going to see now is something really sensational. The Flagstaff Independent Bank in Arizona was ripped off last week by a terrorist group called the Ecumenical Liberation Army, and they themselves actually took movies of the rip-off while they were ripping it off. Wait'll you see it.

The SCREEN suddenly erupts into film of the interior of a bank. THREE MEN, two of them black, and TWO WOMEN, one black and one white enter the bank and disperse to various parts as if on legitimate business.

DIANA   The Ecumenical Liberation Army—is that the one that kidnapped Patty Hearst?

HERRON   No, that's the Symbionese Liberation Army.   This is the Ecumenical Liberation Army. They're the ones who kidnapped Mary Ann Gifford three weeks ago.   There's a hell of a lot of liberation armies in the revolutionary underground and a lot of kidnapped heiresses. That's Mary Ann Gifford.

This last refers to the young white woman on screen lugging a shopping bag, as she gets in line at a teller's window.

DIANA   You mean, they actually shot this film while they were ripping off the bank?

HERRON   Yeah, wait'll you see it. I don't know whether to edit or leave it raw like this. That's the Great Ahmed Khan. He's the leader.

ON SCREEN, the film goes out of focus and bounces meaninglessly around the bank, settling on a large, powerful black man at one desk, presumably writing out a series of deposit slips.

DIANA   This is terrific stuff. Where did you get it?

HERRON   I got everything through Laureen Hobbs. She's my contact for all this stuff.

ON SCREEN, the CAMERA amateurishly WHOOSHES in and out of FOCUS to pick up MARY ANN GIFFORD, who bends over her shopping bag and pulls out a Czech service submachine gun 9 Parabellum that she points to the ceiling and fires. The FILM is SILENT, but the reactions of everyone around suggest something was fired. The FILM gets fragmented and panicky, as does the activity in the bank. The PHONE at Max's elbow

BUZZES. MAX picks up phone, while the bank hold-up proceeds in background.

HARRY HUNTER   *(on filter)* Max, I've got Howard on the other line.

MAX   All right. Put him on.

NIGHTLY NEWS, ROOM 517.

Harry Hunter is using an empty desk to phone. The background is full of the normal flow of news activity.

HARRY HUNTER   *(calls into Howard's office)* Howard. I've got Max on four. Would you pick up?

HOWARD'S OFFICE.

HOWARD   *(picks up phone)* Listen, Max, I'd like another shot.

SCREENING ROOM 7.

The silent footage of the frenetic bank robbery runs in the background.

MAX   *(on phone)* Oh, come on, Howard.

HOWARD'S OFFICE.

HOWARD   *(on phone)* I don't mean the whole show. I'd just like to come on, make some kind of brief farewell statement and then turn the show over to Jack Snowden. I have eleven years at this network, Max. I have some standing in this industry. I don't want to go out like a clown. It'll be simple and dignified. You and Harry can check the copy.

NIGHTLY NEWS ROOM.

ACROSS Harry Hunter on phone through the open door at Howard's office.

HARRY HUNTER   *(on phone)*   I think it'll take the strain off the show, Max.

HOWARD   *(on phone)*   Well, what do you think?

MAX   *(on phone)*   All right. And no booze today, Howard.

HOWARD'S OFFICE.

HOWARD   *(on phone)*   No booze.

SCREENING ROOM 7.

> *The film is over, lights are on. In the background, Diana and Herron stand, move for the door, wave goodbyes. Max waves slackly in return. He can't help noticing as Diana leaves that she has, indeed, the most beautiful ass ever seen on a V.P. Programming.*

UBS BUILDING, 14TH FLOOR, ELEVATOR AREA.

> *Diana and Herron come out of an elevator and turn left to the glass doors marked "DEPARTMENT OF PROGRAMMING." They continue into...*

PROGRAMMING DEPARTMENT, RECEPTION AREA.

> *There is no one at the receptionist's desk. They head down...*

PROGRAMMING DEPARTMENT, CORRIDOR.

> *Diana pauses en route to lean into one of the offices.*

DIANA   George, can you come in my office for a minute?

> *She and Herron continue on, turn into...*

PROGRAMMING DEPARTMENT, COMMON ROOM.

> *The SECRETARIES are slaving away, reading magazines and chatting. An occasional PHONE RINGS. BARBARA SCHLESINGER, chunky*

and in her late thirties, is instructing her SECRETARY in something. Diana hails Schlesinger.

DIANA   Barbara, is Tommy around anywhere?

BARBARA   I think so.

DIANA   I'd like to see the two of you for a moment.

She leads Herron now into...

DIANA'S SECRETARY'S OFFICE.

HELEN, the secretary, hands a sheaf of phone messages to Diana to take with her into...

DIANA'S OFFICE.

Followed by Herron, Diana enters and skims through her messages. The office is executive-size, windows looking out on the canyons of glass and stone skyscrapers on Sixth Avenue. Her desk is piled high with scripts. GEORGE BOSCH, V.P. Program Development East Coast, a slight, balding man of thirty-nine, enters the office, nods to Herron, takes a seat, followed by Barbara, who is Head of the Story Department, and TOMMY PELLE-GRINO, Assistant V.P. Programming, thirty-six, swarthy, coiffed with a moustache. They find seats on chairs, the couch. Herron stands.

DIANA   This is Bill Herron from our West Coast Special Programs Department—Barbara Schlesinger—George Bosch—Tommy Pellegrino. Look, I just saw some rough footage of a special Bill's doing on the revolutionary underground. Most of it's tedious stuff of Laureen Hobbs and four fatigue jackets muttering mutilated Marxism. But he's got about eight minutes of a bank robbery that is absolutely sensational. Authentic stuff. Actually shot while the robbery was going on. Remember the Mary Ann Gifford kidnapping? Well, it's that bunch of nuts. She's in the film shooting off machine guns. Really terrific footage. I think we can get a hell of a movie of the week out of it. Maybe even a series.

PELLEGRINO   A series out of what? What're we talking about?

DIANA   Look, we've got a bunch of hobgoblin radicals called the Ecumenical Liberation Army who go around taking home movies of themselves robbing banks. Maybe they'll take movies of themselves kidnapping heiresses, hijacking 747's, bombing bridges, assassinating ambassadors. We'd open each week's segment with that authentic footage, hire a couple of writers to write some story behind that footage, and we've got ourselves a series.

BOSCH   A series about a bunch of bank-robbing guerrillas?

SCHLESINGER   What're we going to call it? The Mao Tse Tung Hour?

DIANA   Why not? They've got "Strike Force," "Task Force," "SWAT"— why not Che Guevara and his own little mod squad? Listen, I sent you all a concept analysis report yesterday. Did any of you read it? *(apparently not)* Well, in a nutshell, it said the American people are turning sullen. They've been clobbered on all sides by Vietnam, Watergate, the inflation, the depression. They've turned off, shot up, and they've fucked themselves limp. And nothing helps. So—this concept analysis report concludes—the American people want somebody to articulate their rage for them. I've been telling you people since I took this job six months ago that I want angry shows. I don't want conventional programming on this network. I want counterculture. I want anti-establishment.

She closes the door.

DIANA   Now, I don't want to play butch boss with you people. But when I took over this department, it had the worst programming record in television history. This network hasn't one show in the top twenty. This network is an industry joke. We better start putting together one winner for next September. I want a show developed, based on the activities of a terrorist group. Joseph Stalin and his merry band of Bolsheviks. I want ideas from you people. And, by the way, the next time I send an audience research report around, you all better read it, or I'll sack the fucking lot of you. Is that clear? *(Apparently it is. She* *turns to Herron.)* I'll be out on the coast in four weeks. Can you set up a meeting with Laureen Hobbs for me?

HERRON   Sure.

N.Y. HILTON BANQUET ROOM. WEDNESDAY, 3:00 P.M.

LONG SHOT. A stockholders' meeting, standing room only, with some 200 STOCKHOLDERS seated in the audience and standing around the walls. On the rostrum, a phalanx of UBS CORPORATE EXECUTIVES, seated in three rows, including EDWARD RUDDY, Chairman of the Board, the PRESIDENTS and SENIOR VICE PRESIDENTS of the other divisions and other groups—the UBS Records Group, the UBS Publishing Group, the UBS Theater Chain, etc. Representing the network are Nelson Chaney and division heads GEORGE NICHOLS, President of the Radio Division, NORMAN MOLDANIAN, President Owned Stations, General Counsel WALTER AMUNDSEN, and of course, Max Schumacher, President of the News Division. Frank Hackett, Senior Executive Vice President UBS-TV, is at the lectern delivering the Annual Report.

HACKETT   *(droning)* But the business of management is management. And, at the same time CCA took control, the UBS-TV network was foundering with less than seven percent of national television revenues, most network programs being sold at station rates. I am therefore pleased to announce I am submitting to the Board of Directors a plan for the coordination of the main profit centers, and with the specific intention of making each division more responsive to management.

ANOTHER ANGLE SINGLING OUT MAX SCHUMACHER in the second row of the phalanx, bored and whispering to Nelson Chaney beside him. INCLUDE in frame the sixty-seven-year-old brahmin of television, Edward Ruddy in the front row, with Hackett in the background. It is some twenty minutes later.

HACKETT   *(still reading from his report)* Point Three. The division producing the lowest rate of return has been the News Division...

Max suddenly begins paying attention.

HACKETT   ...with its 98 million dollar budget and its average annual deficit of 32 million. I know that historically news divisions are expected to lose money. But, to our minds, this philosophy is a wanton fiscal affront to be resolutely resisted.

ANGLE on Hackett with a smoldering Max in background.

HACKETT   The new plan calls for local news to be transferred to Owned Stations Divisions.

Max stares angrily down toward Norman Moldanian, who studiously avoids his eye.

HACKETT   News-Radio would be transferred to the UBS Radio Division.

ACROSS Max turning in his seat to eye George Nichols behind him.

HACKETT   ...and, in effect, the News Division would be reduced...

Max leans forward to catch the eye of Edward Ruddy, staring sternly ahead.

HACKETT   ...from an independent division to a department accountable to network...

Max is on the verge of letting his temper erupt.

N.Y. HILTON BANQUET ROOM.   WEDNESDAY, 5:30 P.M.

The stockholders' meeting is over. A CRUSH of STOCKHOLDERS mingle with EXECUTIVES. Max Schumacher elbows his way through the crowded aisle to Edward Ruddy.

MAX   What was that all about, Ed?

RUDDY   *(urbane)* This is not the time, Max.

MAX   Why wasn't I told about this? Why was I led onto that podium and
      publicly humiliated in front of the stockholders? Goddammit, I spoke
      to John Wheeler this morning, and he assured me the News Division
      was safe. Are you trying to get me to resign? It's a hell of a way to do
      it.

RUDDY   *(silken voice)*   We'll talk about this tomorrow at our regular
      morning meeting.

Ruddy turns back to stockholders around him. Max wheels away enraged.

CONTROL ROOM, NETWORK NEWS SHOW.

*The wall CLOCK reads 6:28. The Director, Technical Director, Lighting
Director and Production Assistant are at their long shelf in front of the double bank of television monitors. The Audio Man is in his glass cube.*

*Harry Hunter and his secretary and the Unit Manager are on the raised
level in the back. Hunter is on the phone, looks up as the control room door
opens and Max, carrying his jacket, comes in. Hunter finishes his call, offers
his seat to Max, but Max stands in the back.*

PRODUCTION ASSISTANT   Five seconds...

LIGHTING DIRECTOR   Picture's too thick...

DIRECTOR   Coming to...and one—

*The show monitor flicks from its color patterns to show Howard Beale look-
ing up from the sheaf of papers on his desk.*

HOWARD   *(on monitor)*   Good evening. Today is Wednesday, September
      the Twenty-Fourth, and this is my last broadcast.   Yesterday, I
      announced on this program that I would commit public suicide,
      admittedly an act of madness. Well, I'll tell you what happened. I just
      ran out of bullshit...

HARRY HUNTER   All right, cut him off.

The monitor screen goes black.

MAX   *(from the back wall)*   Leave him on.

Howard's image promptly flicks back on.

HOWARD   *(on monitor, looking off-screen)*   Am I still on the air?

Everybody in the control room looks to Max.

MAX   If this is how he wants to go out, this is how he goes out.

HOWARD   *(on monitor)*   I don't know any other way to say it except I just ran out of bullshit.

The PHONE RINGS. Hunter picks it up. ANOTHER PHONE RINGS. Hunter's secretary picks it up.

HUNTER   *(on phone)*   Look, Mr. Schumacher's right here, do you want to talk to him?   *(offers phone to Max)*

HOWARD   *(on monitor)*   Bullshit is all the reasons we give for living, and, if we can't think up any reasons of our own, we always have the God bullshit.

HUNTER'S SECRETARY   Holy Mary Mother of Christ....

MAX   *(on phone)*   Yeah, what is it, Tom?

HOWARD   *(on monitor)*   We don't know why the hell we're going through all this pointless pain, humiliation and decay, so there better be some- one somewhere who does know. That's the God bullshit...

MAX   *(on phone)*   He's saying life is bullshit, and it is, so what're you screaming about?

He hangs up. The PHONE RINGS again. Hunter's secretary picks it up.

HOWARD   *(on monitor)* If you don't like the God bullshit, how about the
man bullshit? Man is a noble creature who can order his own world,
so who needs God?

HUNTER'S SECRETARY   *(to Max)* Mr. Amundsen for you, Mr. Schumacher.

MAX   I'm not taking calls.

HOWARD   *(on monitor)* Well, if there's anybody out there who can look
around this demented slaughterhouse of a world we live in and tell me
man is a noble creature, that man is full of bullshit.

DIRECTOR   *(staring in awe at the screen)* I know he's sober, so he's got to
be just plain nuts. *(starts to giggle)*

HARRY HUNTER   *(screaming)* What's so goddam funny?

DIRECTOR   I can't help it, Harry. It's funny.

HOWARD   *(on monitor)* I don't have any kids.

   A PHONE rings. Hunter's secretary picks it up.

HARRY HUNTER   Max, this is going out live to sixty-seven affiliates.

MAX   Leave him on.

HOWARD   *(on monitor)* ...and I was married for thirty-three years of shrill,
shrieking fraud...

   *A breathless and distraught YOUNG WOMAN bursts into the control
   room.*

YOUNG WOMAN   Mr. Hackett's trying to get through to you.

MAX   Tell Mr. Hackett to go fuck himself.

HOWARD *(on console)* I don't have any bullshit left. I just ran out of it, you see.

UBS BUILDING, LOBBY.

Patrician Edward Ruddy, Chairman of the Board, fastidious in a light top-coat, makes his way through the CRUSH of NEWSPAPER PEOPLE, WIRE SERVICE PEOPLE, CAMERA CREWS from CBS, NBC, ABC, from local stations, WPIX, WOR-TV, METROMEDIA, and from Channel 13. SECURITY GUARDS protect the elevators, and three more help Ruddy get through the GLARING CAMERA LIGHTS and the horde of mikes thrust at him.

RUDDY I'm sorry, I don't have all the facts yet. I'll make a statement later.

20TH FLOOR, LOBBY/LOUNGE/CORRIDOR.

Max stands by the deserted reception desk in the empty lounge. This is the top-management floor with posh-austere decor reflecting the eminence of those who work here. It is now a cathedral, hushed, echoing. At the far end, the double doors of the corner office open, and Nelson Chaney leans out to beckon Max.

MR. RUDDY'S OFFICE.

Large, regal with Impressionist originals on the walls and superb windows, through which the crepuscular grandeur of New York at night is seen. Ruddy sits behind his desk. JOHN WHEELER, fifty-nine, forceful but silent, lounges in a leather chair. The door opens and Nelson Chaney and Max Schumacher come in. They all nod at each other. Max slumps into a leather chair.

RUDDY *(to Chaney)* I'll want to see Mr. Beale after this.

Chaney promptly picks up a corner phone and calls the 14th Floor.

RUDDY The way I hear it, Max, you're primarily responsible for this colossally stupid prank. Is that the fact, Max?

MAX   That's the fact.

RUDDY   It was unconscionable. There doesn't seem to be anything more
to say.

MAX   I have something to say, Ed. I'd like to know why that whole
debasement of the News Division announced at the stockholders'
meeting today was kept secret from me. You and I go back twenty
years, Ed. I took this job with your personal assurance that you would
back my autonomy against any encroachment. But ever since CCA
acquired control of the UBS Systems ten months ago, Hackett's been
taking over everything. Who the hell's running this network, you or
some conglomerate called CCA? I mean, you're the Chairman of the
Systems Group, and Frank Hackett's just CCA's hatchet man. Nelson
here—for Pete's sake, he's the president of the network—he hasn't got
anything to say about anything anymore.

RUDDY   I told you at the stockholders' meeting, Max, that we would dis-
cuss all that at our regular meeting tomorrow morning. If you had
been patient, I would've explained to you that I too thought Frank
Hackett precipitate and that the reorganization of the News Division
would not be executed until everyone, specifically you, Max, had been
consulted and satisfied. Instead, you sulked off like a child and
engaged this network in a shocking and disgraceful episode. Your
position here is no longer tenable regardless of how management is
restructured. I'll expect your resignation at ten o'clock tomorrow
morning, and we will coordinate our statements to the least detriment
of everyone. *(to Wheeler)* Bob McDonough will take over the News
Division till we sort all this out. *(Wheeler nods. Ruddy turns to Chaney
still on the phone.)* I'd like to see Mr. Beale now.

CHANEY   *(on phone)* They're looking for him, Ed. They don't know
where he is.

UBS BUILDING, LOBBY.

Howard Beale, bleached white by the GLARE of the CAMERA LIGHTS, is obscured by the CRUSH of cameras, REPORTERS, SECURITY GUARDS.

HOWARD   Every day, five days a week, for fifteen years, I've been sitting behind that desk. The dispassionate pundit...

DIANA'S APARTMENT, BEDROOM.

Diana, naked on the edge of her bed in a dark room, watches Howard Beale's impromptu press conference on television.

HOWARD   *(on TV screen)*   ...reporting with seemly detachment the daily parade of lunacies that constitute the news...and...

Also on the bed is a naked STUD, who isn't really interested in the news. He is fondling, fingering, noodling and nuzzling Diana with the clear intention of mounting her.

HOWARD   *(on TV screen)*   ...just once I wanted to say what I really felt.

The young stud is getting around to nibbling Diana's breasts.

DIANA   *(watching the TV set with single-minded intensity)*   Knock it off, Arthur.

UBS BUILDING. THURSDAY, SEPTEMBER 25, 9:00 A.M.

Bright morning sunshine. Diana enters the building wearing a pantsuit and carrying a half dozen scripts.

UBS BUILDING, LOBBY.

Diana pauses at the newsstand to pick up the morning papers; she reads en route to the elevators.

UBS BUILDING, 14TH FLOOR. 9:15 A.M.

Diana whisks through the door of DEPARTMENT OF PROGRAMMING.

PROGRAMMING DEPARTMENT, COMMON ROOM.

THREE SECRETARIES are abuzz about last night's Howard Beale show, as Diana crosses to her own office. Diana's secretary, Helen, scurries after her, as Barbara Schlesinger comes out of her office carrying four scripts.

DIANA'S OUTER OFFICE.

Diana rummages among papers on top of Helen's desk as Helen enters.

DIANA   Did the overnight ratings come in yet?

HELEN   They're on your desk.

DIANA   Have you still got yesterday's overnights around?

HELEN   Shall I bring them in?

DIANA   Yeah.

DIANA'S OFFICE.

Sunlight blasts in, as Diana moves to her own desk, scanning the front pages of the newspapers piled on her desk. She sits to study the ratings. Helen enters and hands the previous overnights to Diana. Helen exits as Schlesinger enters and sinks onto a chair with a sigh.

SCHLESINGER   These are those four outlines submitted by Universal for an hour series. You needn't bother to read them. I'll tell them to you. The first one is set in a large eastern law school, presumably Harvard. The series is irresistibly entitled "The New Lawyers." The running characters are a crusty but benign ex-Supreme Court Justice, presumably Oliver Wendell Holmes by way of Dr. Zorba. There is a beautiful girl graduate student and the local district attorney who is brilliant and sometimes cuts corners...

DIANA   *(studying the overnights)* Next one...

SCHLESINGER   The second one is called "The Amazon Squad."

DIANA   *(studying the overnights)* Lady cops?

SCHLESINGER   The running characters are a crusty but benign police lieutenant who's always getting heat from the Commissioner, a hard-nosed, hard-drinking detective who thinks women belong in the kitchen, and a brilliant and beautiful young girl cop fighting the feminist battle on the force...

DIANA   *(now studying the front page of the* Daily News*)* We're up to our ears in lady cop shows.

SCHLESINGER   The next one is another investigative reporter show. A crusty but benign managing editor who's always getting heat from the publisher...

DIANA   The Arabs have decided to jack up the price of oil another twenty percent, and the CIA has been caught opening Senator Humphrey's mail, there's a civil war in Angola, another one in Beirut, New York City's facing default, they've finally caught up with Patricia Hearst and... *(She flips the* Daily News *over so Barbara can read it.)* ...the whole front page of the *Daily News* is Howard Beale.

ACROSS Barbara Schlesinger, half-standing to read the front page, which consists of a three-quarter-page blow-up of Howard Beale topped by a fifty-two point black banner headline: BEALE FIRED.

DIANA   It was also a two-column story on page one of the *Times.* *(calls to the outer office)* Helen, call Mr. Hackett's office. See if he can give me a few minutes this morning.

UBS BUILDING, 15TH FLOOR. 10:00 A.M.

Diana turning into...

HACKETT'S OUTER OFFICE.

The secretary waves Diana straight into...

HACKETT'S OFFICE.

Hackett sits unhappily at his desk poring over memos from his Stations Relations Department and reports from his Sales Department.

HACKETT   *(not bothering to look up)* KTNS Kansas City refuses to carry our network news anymore unless Beale is taken off the air.

DIANA   *(dropping the sheet of paper on his desk)* Did you see the overnights on the Network News? It has an 8 in New York and a 9 in L.A. and a 27 share in both cities. Last night, Howard Beale went on the air and yelled bullshit for two minutes, and I can tell you right now that tonight's show will get a 30 share at least. I think we've lucked into something.

HACKETT   Oh, for God's sake, are you suggesting we put that lunatic back on the air yelling bullshit?

DIANA   Yes, I think we should put Beale back on the air tonight and keep him on. Did you see the *Times* this morning? Did you see the *News*? We've got press coverage on this you couldn't buy for a million dollars. Frank, that dumb show jumped five rating points in one night! Tonight's show has got to be at least fifteen! We just increased our audience by twenty or thirty million people in one night. You're not going to get something like this dumped in your lap for the rest of your days, and you just can't piss it away! Howard Beale got up there last night and said what every American feels—that's he's tired of all the bullshit. He's articulating the popular rage. I want that show, Frank. I can turn that show into the biggest smash in television.

HACKETT   What do you mean, you want that show? It's a news show. It's not your department.

DIANA   I see Howard Beale as a latter-day prophet, a magnificent messianic figure, inveighing against the hypocracies of our times, a strip Savonarola, Monday through Friday. I tell you, Frank, that could just go through the roof. And I'm talking about a six dollar cost per thousand show! I'm talking about a hundred, a hundred thirty thousand dollar minutes! Do you want to figure out the revenues of a strip show that sells for a hundred thousand bucks a minute? One show like that could pull this whole network right out of the hole. Now, Frank, it's being handed to us on a plate; let's not blow it.

Hackett's intercom BUZZES.

HACKETT   *(on intercom)* Yes?...Tell him I'll be a few minutes. *(clicks off, regards Diana)* Let me think it over.

DIANA   Frank, let's not go to committee about this. It's twenty after ten, and we want Beale in that studio by half past six. We don't want to lose the momentum.

HACKETT   For God's sake, Diana, we're talking about putting a manifestly irresponsible man on national television. I'd like to talk to Legal Affairs at least. And Herb Thackeray and certainly Joe Donnelly and Standards and Practices. And you know I'm going to be eyeball to eyeball with Mr. Ruddy on this. If I'm going to the mat with Ruddy, I want to make sure of some of my ground. I'm the one whose ass is going on the line. I'll get back to you, Diana.

EXECUTIVE DINING ROOM. 12:20 P.M.

In a large, empty room of WHITE-LINENED TABLES sit five men at a table with a spectacular view of midtown Manhattan. The five are Frank Hackett, Nelson Chaney, General Counsel Walter Amundsen, Standards and Practices' Arthur Zangwill, and Joe Donnelly of Sales.

CHANEY   *(rising)* I don't believe this! I don't believe the top brass of a national television network are sitting around their Caesar salads...

HACKETT   The top brass of a *bankrupt* national television network, with projected losses of close to a hundred and fifty million dollars this year.

CHANEY   I don't care how bankrupt!   You can't seriously be proposing—and the rest of us seriously considering—putting on a pornographic network news show! The F.C.C. will kill us!

HACKETT   Sit down, Nelson. The F.C.C. can't do anything except rap our knuckles.

Chaney sits.

AMUNDSEN   I don't even want to think about the litigious possibilities, Frank. We could be up to our ears in lawsuits.

CHANEY   The affiliates won't carry it.

HACKETT   The affiliates will kiss your ass if you can hand them a hit show.

CHANEY   The popular reaction...

HACKETT   We don't know the popular reaction. That's what we have to find out.

CHANEY   *The New York Times*...

HACKETT   *The New York Times* doesn't advertise on our network.

CHANEY   *(stands)* All I know is that this violates every canon of respectable broadcasting.

HACKETT   We're not a respectable network. We're a whorehouse network, and we have to take whatever we can get.

CHANEY   Well, I don't want any part of it. I don't fancy myself the president of a whorehouse.

HACKETT   That's very commendable of you, Nelson. Now, sit down. Your indignation has been duly recorded, you can always resign tomorrow.

Chaney sits.

HACKETT   Look, what in substance are we proposing? Merely to add editorial comment to our network news show. Brinkley, Sevareid, and Reasoner all have their comments. So now Howard Beale will have his. I think we ought to give it a shot. Let's see what happens tonight.

DONNELLY   Well, I don't want to be the Babylonian messenger who has to tell Max Schumacher about this.

HACKETT   *(flagging a waiter)* Max Schumacher doesn't work at this network anymore. Mr. Ruddy fired him last night. *(to the waiter)* A telephone, please. *(to his colleagues)* Bob McDonough's running the News Division now.

A phone is put before Hackett, who picks it up and murmurs.

HACKETT   Bob McDonough in News, please.

MAX'S OFFICE. 1:40 P.M.

Max is on the phone and cleaning out his desk and office. He piles his files into empty cartons everywhere. He skims through papers, talking.

MAX   I don't know, Dick. I might teach, I might write a book, whatever the hell one does when one approaches the autumn of one's years.

Howard Beale walks in carrying an 8 x 12 photo.

MAX   *(studying the photo)* My God, is that me? Was I ever that young? *(on phone)* Howard just showed me a picture of the whole Ed Murrow gang when I was at CBS. My God, Bob Trout, Harry Reasoner,

Cronkite, Hollenbeck, and that's you, Howard, right?...I'll see you, Dick. *(hangs up)*

HOWARD *(points at photo)* You remember this kid? He's the kid I think you once sent out to interview Cleveland Amory on vivisection.

MAX *(laughs)* That's him. That's him!

They both laugh. Milton Steinman pokes his head in.

STEINMAN What the hell's so funny?

NEWS DIVISION, EXECUTIVE OFFICES, ROOM 509.

Bob McDonough, V.P. Network News and interim head of the division, enters. He looks distressed. PEOPLE, as well as LAUGHTER and SHOUTING, spill out of Max's office. Even secretaries share in the fun. McDonough wonders what the hell it's about and makes his way through the CRUSH into...

MAX'S OFFICE.

The room is full of News Executives—Max, Howard, Harry Hunter, Walter Gianini, Michael Sandies, Milton Steinman and young producers delighted to hear memories of maverick TV days.

MAX I jump out of bed in my pajamas! I grab my raincoat, run down the stairs, run out into the middle of the street, flag a cab. I jump in, I yell: "Take me to the middle of the George Washington Bridge!"

HOWLS of laughter.

MAX The driver turns around, he says, "Don't do it, kid, you got your whole life ahead of you!"

The room ROCKS. Bob McDonough appears in the doorway.

McDONOUGH Well, if you think that's funny, wait'll you hear this. I've just come down from Frank Hackett's office, and he wants to put Howard back on the air tonight. Apparently, the ratings jumped five points last night, and he wants Howard to go back on and do his angry-man thing.

STEINMAN What're you talking about?

McDONOUGH I'm telling you. They want Howard to go on yelling bull-shit. They want Howard to go on spontaneously letting out his anger, a latter-day prophet, denouncing the hypocrisies of our times.

HOWARD Hey, that sounds pretty good.

MAX Who's this they?

McDONOUGH Hackett. Chaney was there, the Legal Affairs guy, and that girl from Programming.

MAX Christenson? What's she got to do with it?

GIANINI (in background) You're kidding, aren't you, Bob?

McDONOUGH I'm not kidding. I told them, "We're running a news department down there, not a circus. And Howard Beale isn't a beard-ed lady. And if you think I'll go along with this bastardization of the news, you can have my resignation along with Max Schumacher's right now. And I think I'm speaking for Howard Beale and everybody else down there in News."

HOWARD Hold it, McDonough, that's my job you're turning down. I'll go nuts without some kind of work. What's wrong with being an angry prophet denouncing the hypocrisies of our times? What do you think, Max?

MAX Do you want to be an angry prophet denouncing the hypocrisies of our times?

HOWARD   Yeah, I think I'd like to be an angry prophet denouncing the hypocrisies of our times.

MAX   Then grab it.

5TH FLOOR CORRIDOR. 3:00 P.M.

Mr. Ruddy comes down the corridor toward Room 509. A VIDEOTAPE MAN, popping out of a room, quickly halts.

VIDEOTAPE MAN   *(respectfully)* Afternoon, Mr. Ruddy.

RUDDY   Good afternoon.

He passes on towards...

ROOM 509.

Ruddy enters, as SIX SECRETARIES, pecking away at typewriters, all pause in awe.

SECRETARIES   Good afternoon, Mr. Ruddy. Good afternoon, Mr. Ruddy.

Ruddy passes through to...

MAX'S OUTER OFFICE.

MITZI, Max's secretary, hums an acknowledgement.

MITZI   He's waiting for you, Mr. Ruddy.

RUDDY   Thank you.

He goes into...

MAX'S OFFICE.

He closes the door.

RUDDY   Nelson Chaney tells me Beale may actually go on the air this evening.

MAX   As far as I know, Howard's going to do it. Are you going to sit still for this, Ed?

RUDDY   *(takes a folded paper from an inside pocket)*   Yes. I think Hackett's overstepped himself. There's some kind of corporate maneuvering going on, Max. Hackett is clearly forcing a confrontation. That would account for his behavior at the stockholders' meeting. However, I think he's making a serious mistake with this Beale business. I suspect CCA will be upset by Hackett's presumptuousness, certainly Mr. Jensen will. So I'm going to let Hackett have his head for awhile. He just might lose it over this Beale business. *(places the paper on Max's desk)*   I'd like you to reconsider your resignation. *(moves to the couch, sits, crosses his legs)*   I have to assume Hackett wouldn't take such steps without some support on the CCA Board. I'll have to go directly to Mr. Jensen. When that happens, I'm going to need every friend I've got. And I certainly don't want Hackett's people in all the divisional positions. So I'd like you to stay on, Max.

MAX   Of course, Ed.

RUDDY   *(stands)*   Thank you, Max.

He opens the door and leaves.

MAX'S OFFICE. WEDNESDAY, OCTOBER 1, 7:00 P.M.

Max sits in an office lit only by his desk lamp watching "The Network News Show" starring Howard Beale on a console.

NARRATOR   The initial response to the new Howard Beale was not auspicatory. The press was without exception hostile and the industry reaction negative. The ratings for the Thursday and Friday show were both 14 and with a 37 share, but Monday's rating dropped two points, clearly suggesting the novelty had worn off.

On the office console, the show comes to an end with the THEME MUSIC engulfing the sound, as credits roll. Max clicks it off and sits glumly. He becomes aware of another presence in the room. Diana Christenson stands in the doorway in a white blouse and dark slacks, carrying her jacket and bag. Just in case we haven't noticed her beauty, we do now, as she stands framed in the doorway, backlit, suddenly sensuous, even voluptuous.

DIANA   *(enters)* Did you know there are a number of psychics working as licensed brokers on Wall Street? *(She sits, fishes a cigarette out of her purse.)* Some of them counsel their clients by use of Tarot cards. They're all pretty successful, even in a bear market and selling short. I met one of them a couple of weeks ago and thought of doing a show around her. "The Wayward Witch of Wall Street," something like that. But, of course, if her tips were any good, she could wreck the market. So I called her this morning and asked her how she was on predicting the future. She said she was occasionally prescient. "For example," she said, "I just had a fleeting vision of you sitting in an office with a craggy middle-aged man with whom you are or will be emotionally involved." So here I am.

MAX   She does all this with Tarot cards?

DIANA   No, this one operates on parapsychology. She has trance-like episodes and feels things in her energy field. I think this lady can be very useful to you, Max.

MAX   In what way?

DIANA   Well, you put on news shows, and here's someone who can predict tomorrow's news for you. Her name, aptly enough, is Sybil. Sybil the Soothsayer. You could give her two minutes of trance at the end of a Howard Beale show, say once a week, Friday, which is suggestively occult, and she could oraculate. Then next week, everyone tunes in to see how good her predictions were.

MAX   Maybe she could do the weather.

DIANA *(smiles)* Your network news show is going to need some help, Max, if it's going to hold. Beale doesn't do the angry man thing well at all. He's too kvetchy. He's being irascible. We want a prophet, not a curmudgeon. He should do more apocalyptic doom. I think you should take on a couple of writers to write some jeremiads for him. I see you don't fancy my suggestions.

MAX Hell, you're not being serious, are you?

DIANA Oh, I'm serious. The fact is, I could make your Beale show the highest-rated news show in television, if you'd let me have a crack at it.

MAX What do you mean, have a crack at it?

DIANA I'd like to program it for you, develop it. I wouldn't interfere with the actual news. But teevee is show biz, Max, and even the News has to have a little showmanship.

MAX My God, you are serious.

DIANA I watched your six o'clock news today. It's straight tabloid. You had a minute and a half on that lady riding a bike naked in Central Park. On the other hand, you had less than a minute of hard national and international news. It was all sex, scandal, brutal crimes, sports, children with incurable diseases and lost puppies. So I don't think I'll listen to any protestations of high standards of journalism. You're right down in the street soliciting audiences like the rest of us. All I'm saying is, if you're going to hustle, at least do it right. I'm going to bring this up at tomorrow's network meeting, but I don't like network hassles, and I was hoping you and I could work this out between us. That's why I'm here right now.

MAX *(sighs)* And I was hoping you were looking for an emotional involvement with a craggy middle-aged man.

DIANA I wouldn't rule that out entirely.

They appraise each other for the possibilities of something more than a professional relationship. They're there.

MAX   Well, Diana, you bring all your ideas up at the meeting tomorrow. Because, if you don't, I will. I think Howard is making a goddam fool of himself, and so does everybody Howard and I know in this industry. It was a fluke. It didn't work. Tomorrow, Howard goes back to the old format and this gutter depravity comes to an end.

DIANA   *(smiles, stands)* Okay.

She leans to flick her ash into Max's ashtray. By the cone of light issuing from the desk lamp, it is nipple-clear that she is bra-less. Max notes the assertive swells of her body. Diana moves languidly to the door to leave but Max suddenly speaks.

MAX   I don't get it, Diana. You hung around till half past seven and came all the way down here just to pitch a couple of looney show biz ideas when you knew goddam well I'd laugh you out of this office. I don't get it. What's your scam in this anyway?

Diana moves back to the desk and crushes her cigarette in the tray.

DIANA   Max, my little visit here tonight was just a courtesy made out of respect for your stature in the industry and because I've personally admired you ever since I was a kid majoring in speech at the University of Missouri. But sooner or later, with or without you, I'm going to take over your network news show, and I figured I might as well start tonight.

MAX   I think I once gave a lecture at the University of Missouri.

DIANA   I was in the audience. I had a terrible schoolgirl crush on you for a couple of months.

She glides back to the doorway again.

MAX   Listen, if we can get back for a moment to that gypsy who predicted all that about emotional involvements and middle-aged men...what're you doing for dinner tonight?

Diana pauses in the doorway, then moves back to the telephone on the desk, taps out a number, waits for a moment.

DIANA *(into phone)*   I can't make it tonight, Luv, call me tomorrow.

She returns the receiver to its cradle, looks at Max. Their eyes lock.

MAX   Do you have any favorite restaurant?

DIANA   I eat anything.

MAX   Son of a bitch, I get the feeling I'm being made.

DIANA   You sure are.

MAX   I better warn you, I don't do anything on the first date.

DIANA   We'll see.

She moves for the dou.   Max stares down at his desk, then stands.

MAX *(to himself)*   Schmuck. What are you getting into?

He sighs and flicks off his desk lamp.

A RESTAURANT.

Max and Diana are finishing dinner. Max orders two coffees, black.

DIANA   *(plying away at ice cream)*   I was married for four years and pretended to be happy and had six years of analysis and pretended to be sane. My husband ran off with his boyfriend, and I had an affair with my analyst. He told me I was the worst lay he had ever had. I can't tell you how many men have told me what a lousy lay I am. I apparently have a masculine temperament. I arouse quickly, consummate prematurely, and can't wait to get my clothes back on and get out of that bedroom. I seem to be inept at everything except my work. I'm goddam good at my work and so I confine myself to that. All I want out of life is a 30 share and a 20 rating. You're married surely.

MAX Twenty-five years. I have a married daughter in Seattle who's six months pregnant, and a younger girl who starts at Northwestern in January.

DIANA Well, Max here we are. Middle-aged man reaffirming his middle-aged manhood and a terrified young woman with a father complex. What sort of script do you think we can make out of this?

MAX Terrified, are you?

DIANA *(pushes her ice cream away, regards him affably)* Terrified out of my skull, man. I'm the hip generation, man, right on, cool, groovy, the greening of America, man, remember all that? God, what humbugs we were. In my first year at college, I lived in a commune, dropped acid daily, joined four radical groups and fucked myself silly on a bare wooden floor while somebody chanted sufi suras. I lost six weeks of my sophomore year, because they put me away for trying to jump off the top floor of the Administration Building. I've been on the top floor ever since. Don't open any windows around me, because I just might jump out. Am I scaring you off?

A WAITER brings the coffee.

MAX No. The corridor gossip says you're Frank Hackett's backstage girl.

DIANA *(sipping coffee, smiles)* I'm not. Frank's a corporation man, body and soul. He has no loves, lusts or allegiances that are not consummately directed towards becoming a CCA Board Member. So why should he bother with me? I'm not even a stockholder.

MAX How about *your* loves, lusts and allegiances?

They smile at each other.

DIANA   Is your wife in town?

MAX   Yes.

DIANA   Well, then, we better go to my place.

HOWARD BEALE'S BEDROOM.

Howard is fast asleep in his empty, hushed room.

HOWARD   *(suddenly)*   I can't hear you. You'll have to speak a little louder.

He gets up on one elbow, eyes still closed, cocks his head as if he were listening to someone.

HOWARD   *(whispers with dread, his eyes open)*   Yes, I hear you...Yes, yes.

CAMERA DOLLIES inexorably down to TIGHT PORTRAIT CLOSE-UP of Howard Beale in a state of beatitude.

HOWARD   *(almost inaudible awe)*   Why me?   *(louder)*   I said, why me?

TIGHT CLOSE-UP of Howard Beale.

HOWARD   *(with beatitude and serenity)*   Okay...

NIGHTLY NEWS, ROOM 517.

Max enters into the morning hum of activity. PHONES RING. Harry Hunter, going over some wire releases with his HEAD WRITER, looks up.

MAX   Howard in his office?   *(Hunter nods.)*   Harry, I'm killing this whole screwball angry prophet thing. We're going back to straight news as of tonight's show.

HUNTER   Okay.

Max veers off for...

NETWORK NEWS CONTROL ROOM.

The CLOCK says 6:29, and the control room staff are at their posts. Harry Hunter is on the phone.

HUNTER *(muttering into phone)* Max, I'm telling you he's fine. He's been sharp all day, he's been funny as hell. He had everybody cracking up at the rundown meeting....I told him, I told him....

On the SHOW MONITOR, Howard Beale at his desk, awaiting his cue as he fingers his papers. The CLOCK CLICKS TO 6:30, the director murmurs into his mike. Howard looks out from the screen to his vast audience.

HOWARD *(on monitor)* Last night, I was awakened from a fitful sleep shortly after two o'clock in the morning by a shrill, sibilant, faceless voice that was sitting in my rocking chair. I couldn't make it out at first in the dark bedroom. I said, "I'm sorry, you'll have to talk a little louder." And the Voice said to me, "I want you to tell the people the truth, not an easy thing to do, because the people don't want to know the truth." I said, "You're kidding. How the hell would I know what the truth is?" But the Voice said to me, "Don't worry about the truth. I'll put the words in your mouth." And I said, "What is this, the burning bush? For God's sake, I'm not Moses." And the Voice said to me, "And I'm not God, what's that got to do with it..."

NETWORK NEWS CONTROL ROOM.

Harry Hunter remains on phone, as the control room staff sit staring at the monitor.

HUNTER *(on phone)* What do you want me to do?

MAX'S OFFICE.

At his desk, his chin cupped in his right hand, Max stares at Howard on his office console.

MAX *(sighing his resignation into the phone)* Nothing.

HOWARD (*on console*) And the Voice said to me, "We're not talking about eternal truth or absolute truth or ultimate truth! We're talking about impermanent, transient, human truth! I don't expect you people to be capable of truth! But, goddammit, you're at least capable of self-preservation! That's good enough! I want you to go out and tell the people to preserve themselves."

MAX   (*on phone*) Right now, I'm trying to remember the name of that psychiatrist that took care of him when his wife died.

NETWORK NEWS STUDIO.

TIGHT SHOT of Howard, his voice rising, his eyes glowing with fervor.

HOWARD   And I said to the Voice, "Why me?" And the Voice said, "Because you're on television, dummy!"

DIANA'S OFFICE.

Diana watches Howard on her console.

DIANA Beautiful.

HOWARD (*on console*) "You have forty million Americans listening to you. After tonight's show, you could have fifty million. For Pete's sake, I don't expect you to walk the land in sackcloth and ashes preaching the Armageddon. You're on teevee, man!"

MAX'S OFFICE.

Max is no longer on the phone but leafing through an address book.

HOWARD (*on console*) So I thought about it for a moment.

Max punches in a phone number on his private line.

HOWARD (*live*) And then I said, "Okay."

5TH FLOOR CORRIDOR.

Howard and Harry Hunter are followed by the rest of the control room staff, as they march out of the stairway, down the corridor to...

NIGHTLY NEWS, ROOM 517.

...and toward Howard's office while the crew disperse to their own desks to exchange comments with the Nightly News personnel still there. Howard walks straight as a ramrod, eyes uplifted, serene to the point of transcendence. He and Hunter go into...

HOWARD'S OFFICE.

Max is waiting on the couch. He stands.

MAX   Close the door, Harry.

Hunter does so.

MAX   Howard, I'm taking you off the air. I called your psychiatrist. I think you're having a breakdown, require treatment, and Dr. Sindell agrees.

HOWARD   This is not a psychotic episode. It is a cleansing moment of clarity. I am imbued, Max. I am imbued with some special spirit. It's not a religious feeling at all. It is a shocking eruption of great electrical energy! I feel vivid and flashing as if suddenly I had been plugged into some great cosmic electromagnetic field. I feel connected to all living things, to flowers, birds, to all the animals of the world and even to some great unseen living force, what I think the Hindus call Prana. *(He stands rigid, his eyes staring mindlessly out, revealing the anguish of so transcendental a state.)* It is not a breakdown. I have never felt so orderly in my life! It is a shattering and beautiful sensation. It is the exalted flow of the space-time continuum, save that it is spaceless and timeless and of such loveliness! I feel on the verge of some great ultimate truth! *(He stares haggardly at Max; his breath comes with difficulty as he begins to shout.)* You will not take me off the air for now or for any other spaceless time!

Howard promptly falls onto the floor, into a dead swoon.

MAX   *(hurrying to his prostrate friend)* Oh boy!

HUNTER   Is he okay?

MAX   *(bent over Howard)* He's just fainted. I better get him back to my house again for the night. Help me get him up.

A CRASH OF THUNDER.

MAX'S APARTMENT, BEDROOM. NIGHT.

THUNDER CRASHES outside. RAIN pelts against the windows of the dark room. Max and his wife, LOUISE, are fast asleep. CAMERA PANS, DOLLIES out of their bedroom and into...

LIVING ROOM.

Howard sleeps on the living room sofa. Now he slowly sits up, then stands in his borrowed pajamas, goes to the hall closet, fetches a raincoat, unchains, unbolts and unlocks the front door, and goes out.

N.Y., THE EAST 60's. WEDNESDAY, OCTOBER 3, 7:30 A.M.

Another CRASH and RUMBLE of thunder. Rain pelts the streets.

MAX'S APARTMENT, BEDROOM.

ALARM CLOCK BUZZING. Mrs. Louise Schumacher, a handsome matron of fifty, clicks it off and gets out of bed. Max turns over, sleeps on. Louise starts into the bathroom, then goes out into...

BACK HALLWAY.

...where she continues into...

LIVING ROOM.

She looks concerned. The couch had been made up for a bed and is now rumpled but empty. She looks back up the hallway to the guest bathroom. The door is open but nobody is there. She pads across the living room/dining room area, poking her head into the kitchen. She pauses outside her daughter's closed bedroom door, opens it, looks in, closes it, then returns to...

THE BEDROOM.

Louise sits on Max's side of the bed and shakes him.

LOUISE   Wake up, Max, because Howard's gone. I'll make you some coffee.

MAX   Shit.

She moves off, as he slowly sits up.

FRANK HACKETT'S OFFICE.

Hackett rages at Max, slumped in a chair. Diana and Herb Thackeray are also there.

HACKETT   What do you mean, you don't know where he is? The son of a bitch is a hit, goddammit. Over two thousand phone calls! Go down to the mailroom! As of this minute, over fourteen thousand telegrams! The response is sensational! Herb, tell him! *(Thackeray starts to tell him, but Hackett roars over him.)* Herb's phone hasn't stopped ringing. Every goddam affiliate from Albuquerque to Sandusky! The response is sensational! *(The PHONE RINGS, Hackett seizes it.)* What?...All right...(He hangs up, snaps at Thackeray.) It's your office, Herb. You better get back there.

Thackeray exits. Hackett roars on.

HACKETT   Moldanian called me! Joe Donnelly called me! We've got a goddam hit, goddam it! Diana, show him the *Times*! We even got an editorial in the holy goddam *New York Times*. "A Call to Morality!" That crazy son of a bitch, Beale, has caught on! So don't tell me you don't know where he is!

MAX   *(roaring back)* I don't know where he is. He may be jumping off a roof for all I know. The man is insane. He's no longer responsible for himself. He needs care and treatment. And all you graverobbers care about is he's a hit.

DIANA   You know, Max, it's just possible that he isn't insane, that he is, in fact, imbued with some special spirit.

MAX   My God, I'm supposed to be the romantic. You're supposed to be the hard-bitten realist!

DIANA   All right. Howard Beale obviously fills a void. The audience out there obviously wants a prophet, even a manufactured one, even if he's as mad as Moses. By tomorrow, he'll have a fifty share, maybe even a sixty share. Howard Beale is processed instant God, and right now it looks like he may just go over bigger than Mary Tyler Moore.

MAX   I'm not putting Howard back on the air.

DIANA   It's not your show anymore, Max. It's mine.

MAX   You're nuts. You're nuttier than Howard!

HACKETT   I gave her the show, Schumacher. I'm putting the network news show under programming. Mr. Ruddy has had a mild heart attack and is not taking calls. In his absence, I'm making all network decisions, including one I've been wanting to make a long time. You're fired. I want you out of this building by noon. I'll leave word with the security guards to throw you out if you're still here.

MAX   Well, let's just say, fuck you, Hackett. You want me out, you're going to have to drag me out kicking and screaming. And the whole news division will walk out kicking and screaming with me.

HACKETT   You think they're going to quit their jobs for you? Not in this recession, buddy.

MAX   When Ruddy gets back, he'll have your ass.

HACKETT   I got a hit, Schumacher, and Ruddy doesn't count anymore. He was hoping I'd fall on my face with this Beale show, but I didn't. It's a big, fat, big-titted hit, and I don't have to waffle around with Ruddy anymore. If he wants to take me up before the CCA Board, let him. And do you think Ruddy's stupid enough to go to the CCA Board and say, "I'm taking our one hit show off the air?" And comes November Fourteen, I'm going to be standing up there at the annual CCA management review meeting, and I'm going to announce projected earnings for this network for the first time in five years. And, believe me, Mr. Jensen will be sitting there rocking back and forth in his little chair, and he's going to say, "That's very good, Frank, keep it up." So don't have any illusions about who's running this network from now on. You're fired. I want you out of your office before noon. Or I'll have you thrown out.

MAX   *(to Diana)* And you go along with this?

DIANA   Well, Max, I told you I didn't want a network hassle over this. I told you I'd much rather work the Beale show out just between the two of us.

MAX   *(stands)* Well, let's just say, fuck you too, honey. *(to Hackett)* Howard Beale may be my best friend! I'll go to court. I'll put him in a hospital before I let you exploit him like a carnival freak.

HACKETT   You get your psychiatrists, and I'll get mine.

MAX   *(heading for the door)* I'm going to spread this whole reeking business in every paper and on every network, independent, group, and affiliated station in this country. I'm going to make a lot of noise about this.

HACKETT   Great! We need all the press we can get.

Max exits. Hackett clicks his intercom.

HACKETT   *(on intercom)* Get me Mr. Cabell. *(to Diana)* Something going on between you and Schumacher?

DIANA   *(sighs)* Not anymore.

SIXTH AVENUE. 6:40 P.M., NIGHT.

THUNDER CRASHES—RAIN lashes the street. PEDESTRIANS struggle against the slashing rain. The streets gleam wetly, the heavy TRAFFIC heading uptown crushes and HONKS along, erratic enfilades of headlights in the shiny black streets.

The entrance to the UBS Building. Howard Beale, wearing a coat over his pajamas, drenched to the skin, his gray mop plastered in streaks to his brow, hunched against the rain, climbs the steps and pushes the glass door at the entrance and goes into...

UBS BUILDING, LOBBY.

TWO SECURITY GUARDS at the desk watch Howard pass.

SECURITY GUARD   How do you do, Mr. Beale?

Howard stops, turns, stares haggardly at the Security Guard.

HOWARD   *(mad as a loon)* I have to make my witness.

SECURITY GUARD   *(agreeably)* Sure thing, Mr. Beale.

Howard plods off to the elevators.

NETWORK NEWS CONTROL ROOM.

Behind the usual efficient activity stands Diana in the shadows. On the SHOW MONITOR, Jack Snowden, Beale's replacement, has been doing the news straight.

SNOWDEN *(on monitor)* ...Oil ministers of the OPEC nations meeting in Vienna still haven't decided how much more to increase the price of oil next Wednesday. Iran and some of the Arab states want to jack up the price by as much as 20 percent...

PRODUCTION ASSISTANT Five seconds...

TECHNICAL DIRECTOR Twenty-five in Vienna...

DIRECTOR And...two...

SNOWDEN *(on monitor)* The Saudi Arabians are being more cautious. They just want a 10 percent increase. More on that story from Edward Fletcher in Vienna.

All this overlaps and is under a BUZZ on Harry Hunter's phone.

HUNTER *(on phone)* Yeah?...Okay. *(hangs up, to Diana)* He came in the building about five minutes ago.

PRODUCTION ASSISTANT Ten seconds coming to one...

DIANA Make sure he gets here. Tell Snowden when he comes in the studio to let him go on.

HUNTER *(to the stage manager)* Did you get that, Paul?

The STAGE MANAGER nods, passes on the instruction to his A.D. On the SHOW MONITOR, we see footage of the OPEC Vienna meeting, lots of Arab headdresses and bearded Levantine faces at conference tables, and we are hearing the VOICE of EDWARD FLETCHER in Vienna.

FLETCHER *(on monitor)* This has probably been the most divisive meeting the oil-producing states have ever had. The thirteen nations of OPEC have still not been able to decide by how much to increase the price of oil....

On the SHOW MONITOR the footage flicks to Sheikh Zaki Yamani being interviewed by a corps of correspondents.

FLETCHER *(voice-off)* Saudi Arabian oil minister Sheikh Zaki Yamani flew to London yesterday for further consultations with his government. He returned to the Vienna meetings today....

Nobody in the control room is paying attention to Yamani. They are watching the double bank of black-and-white monitors showing Howard Beale entering the studio, drenched, hunched, staring into his own space, and moving with single-minded purpose across the studio past cameras and CREW to his desk, which is being vacated for him by Jack Snowden. The film clips of Yamani ends.

ASSISTANT DIRECTOR Ready...two...

DIRECTOR Take two.

And suddenly the obsessed face of Howard Beale with unworldly fervor and red eyes, manifestly mad, fills the MONITOR SCREEN.

HOWARD *(on monitor)* I don't have to tell you things are bad. Everybody knows things are bad. It's a depression. Everybody's out of work or scared of losing their job, the dollar buys a nickel's worth, banks are going bust, shopkeepers keep a gun under the counter, punks are running wild in the streets, and there's nobody anywhere who seems to know what to do, and there's no end to it. We know the air's unfit to breathe and our food is unfit to eat, and we sit and watch our teevees while some local newscaster tells us today we had fifteen homicides and sixty-three violent crimes, as if that's the way it's supposed to be. We all know things are bad. Worse than bad. They're crazy. It's like everything's going crazy. So we don't go out anymore. We sit in the house, and slowly the world we live in gets smaller, and all we ask is, please, at least leave us alone in our own living rooms. Let me have my toaster and my teevee and my hair dryer and my steel-belted radials, and I won't say anything, just leave us alone. Well, I'm not going to leave you alone. I want you to get mad.

ANOTHER ANGLE showing the rapt attention of the PEOPLE in the control room, especially of Diana.

HOWARD   I don't want you to protest. I don't want you to riot. I don't want you to write your congressmen. Because I wouldn't know what to tell you to write. I don't know what to do about the depression and the inflation and the defense budget and the Russians and crime in the street. All I know is first you've got to get mad. You've got to say, "I'm a human being, goddammit. My life has value." So I want you to get up now. I want you to get out of your chairs and go to the window. Right now. I want you to go to the window, open it, and stick your head out and yell. I want you to yell, "I'm mad as hell, and I'm not going to take this any more!"

DIANA   *(grabs Hunter's shoulder)* How many stations does this go out live to?

HUNTER   Sixty-seven. I know it goes to Louisville and Atlanta, I think...

HOWARD   *(on monitor)* Get up from your chairs. Go to the window. Open it. Stick your head out and yell and keep yelling.

Diana has already left the control room.

HOWARD   *(on monitor)* First, you've got to get mad. When you're mad enough we'll figure out what to do about the depression.

15TH FLOOR, ELEVATOR AREA.

Diana bursts out of the elevator and strides down to a clot of EXECUTIVES and PERSONNEL blocking an open doorway. She pushes into...

THACKERAY'S OFFICE/ STATIONS RELATIONS.

Herb Thackeray is on the phone, staring at Howard Beale on his wall monitor. His STAFF fill his and his secretary's offices. The Assistant V.P. Stations Relations, a thirty-two-year-old fellow named RAY PITOFSKY is also on the phone. Another ASSISTANT V.P. is on another phone.

DIANA *(shouting to Thackeray)* Whom are you talking to?

THACKERAY WCGG, Atlanta.

DIANA Are they yelling in Atlanta, Herb?

THACKERAY *(on phone)* Are they yelling in Atlanta, Ted?

HOWARD *(on console)* ...and the inflation and the oil crisis...

PITOFSKY *(holding phone)* They're yelling in Baton Rouge.

Diana grabs the phone from him.

DIANA *(handing phone back, exulting)* Son of a bitch! We struck the motherlode!

MAX'S APARTMENT, LIVING ROOM.

Max, Louise, and their seventeen-year-old daughter, CAROLINE, watch "The Network News Show."

HOWARD *(on the set)* Stick your head out and yell. I want you to yell, "I'm mad as hell, and I'm not going to take this anymore!"

Caroline gets up and heads for the window.

LOUISE Where are you going?

CAROLINE I want to see if anybody's yelling.

HOWARD *(on TV set)* Right now. Get up. Go to your window...

Caroline opens the window and looks out the rain-swept streets of the Upper East Side, the bulking, anonymous apartment houses and occasional brownstones. It is thunder dark; a distant clap of THUNDER CRASHES somewhere off and LIGHTNING shatters the dank darkness. In the sudden HUSH following the thunder, a thin voice can be heard down the block.

THIN VOICE *(off-screen)* I'm mad as hell, and I'm not going to take this anymore!

HOWARD *(on TV set)* ...open your window...

Max joins his daughter at the window. RAIN sprays against his face.

MAX'S P.O.V.: He sees occasional windows open. Across from his apartment house, a MAN opens the front door of a brownstone.

MAN *(shouting)* I'm mad as hell, and I'm not going to take this anymore!

OTHER SHOUTS are heard. From the twenty-third floor Max sees the erratic landscape of Manhattan. Silhouetted HEADS in windows—here, there, and then out of nowhere everywhere, SHOUTING out into the slashing black RAIN.

VOICES I'm mad as hell, and I'm not going to take this anymore!

A terrifying THUNDERCLAP, followed by a FULGURATION of LIGHTNING, punctuates the gathering CHORUS coming from the huddled, black border of the city's SCREAMING people, an indistinguishable tidal roar of human RAGE, as formidable as the THUNDER RUMBLING above. It sounds like the Nuremberg rally.

Max stands with Caroline at the open terrace window, listening to the stupefying ROARS and THUNDER all around him. He closes his eyes, sighs, and there's nothing he can do about it anymore. It's out of his hands.

LOS ANGELES AIRPORT. WEDNESDAY, OCTOBER 16.

A jumbo 747 touches down at L.A. Airport.

NARRATOR   By mid-October, the Howard Beale show had settled in at a 42 share, more than equalling all the other network news shows combined.

Diana and Barbara Schlesinger, carrying attaché cases, scripts, hand baggage, deplane.

NARRATOR   In the Neilsen Ratings, the Howard Beale show was listed as the fourth highest-rated show of the month, surpassed only by "The Six Million Dollar Man," "All in the Family," and "Phyllis," a phenomenal state of affairs for a news show.

WEST COAST UBS BUILDING. DAY.

A towering glass building on Santa Monica Boulevard.

NARRATOR   And, on October the Fifteenth, Diana Christenson flew to Los Angeles...

WEST COAST UBS BUILDING, CONFERENCE ROOM.

Diana eats sandwiches at a luncheon meeting with her West Coast Programming Department.

NARRATOR   ...for what the trade calls pow-wows and confabs with her West Coast programming execs.

GLENN KOSSOFF and Barbara Schlesinger, and THREE OTHER MEN, the Assistant V.P. Program Development West Coast, Head of the Story Department West Coast, and a man from Audience Research, plus another WOMAN in Daytime Programming West Coast all sit around a room-length, mod-shaped conference table. Diana is at a large display board at the far end. This is an improvised Programming Board. It shows what all four networks have on by the half hour for all seven days of the week.

UBS BUILDING WEST COAST. DIANA'S OFFICE.

Diana is behind the desk, with Schlesinger on the couch. Glenn Kossoff ushers in Bill Herron, Laureen Hobbs in an Afro and dashiki. With them is SAM HAYWOOD, a shaggy lawyer in the Clarence Darrow tradition with a string tie and folksy drawl, a younger Harvard-intellectual lawyer, MEL GRANT, and THREE AGENTS from William Morris named LENNIE, WALLIE and ED—who are fairly indistinguishable.

Diana rises to greet them, extending her hand to Laureen.

DIANA   Christ, you brought half the William Morris West Coast office with you. I'm Diana Christenson, a racist lackey of the imperialist ruling circles.

LAUREEN   I'm Laureen Hobbs, a bad-ass Commie nigger.

DIANA   Sounds like the basis of a firm friendship. *(to Kossoff)* We're going to need more chairs.

In the background Schlesinger is exchanging hellos with the agents, one of whom proffers her baby pictures. It's all jolly as hell.

SCHLESINGER   Anybody want coffee?

LENNIE   Black with Sucaryl.

Kossoff and a secretary are hauling in chairs.

LAUREEN   This is my lawyer, Sam Haywood, and his associate Mel Grant.

Handshakes, nods, as they sit and give coffee orders to the secretary.

HAYWOOD   *(an old union lawyer, given to peroration)* Well, Ms. Christenson, just what the hell's this all about? Because when a national television network in the person of bubby here *(indicates Herron)* comes to me and says he wants to put the on-going struggle of the oppressed masses on prime-time television, I have to regard this askance...

Diana would answer Haywood, but he's just hitting his stride, and chairs are brought in.

HAYWOOD   I have to figure this as an antithetical distraction. The thesis here, if you follow me, is that the capitalist state is in a terminal condition now, and the antithesis is the maturation of the fascist state, and when the correlative appendages of the fascist state come and say to me they want to give the revolution a weekly hour of prime-time television, I've got to figure this is preventive co-optation, right?

There are enough chairs now for all to sit. The secretary goes for coffee. A hush follows Haywood's Hegelian instruction, and Diana would again answer, but Haywood is center-stage, in the full swell of rhetoric.

HAYWOOD   The ruling classes are running scared, right? You turned the full force of your cossack cops and paramilitary organs of repression against us. But now the slave masters hear the rumble of revolution in their ears. So you have no alternative but to co-opt us. Put us on teevee and pull our fangs. And we're supposed to sell out, right? For your gangster gold? Well, we're not going to sell out, baby! You can take your fascist teevee and shove it right up your paramilitary ass! I'm here to tell you, we don't sell out! We don't want your gold! We're not going on your teevee!

A hush descends as everybody digests this opening statement.

DIANA   Oh, shit, Mr. Haywood, if you're not interested in my offer, why the hell did you bring two lawyers and three agents from the William Morris office along?

GRANT   What Mr. Haywood was saying, Ms. Christenson, was that our client, Ms. Hobbs, wants it up front that the political content of the show has to be entirely in her control.

DIANA   She can have it. I don't give a damn about the political content.

LAUREEN What kind of show'd you have in mind, Diana?

DIANA We're interested in doing a weekly dramatic series based on the Ecumenical Liberation Army, and I'll tell you what the first show has to be: a two-hour special on Mary Ann Gifford. I'll tell you what I want. I want a lot more film like the bank rip-off the Ecumenicals sent in. The way I see this series is every week we open with the authentic footage of an act of political terrorism, taken on the spot and in the actual moment; then we go into the drama behind the opening film footage. That's your job, Ms. Hobbs. You've got to get the Ecumenicals to bring in that film for us. The network can't deal with them directly. They are, after all, wanted criminals.

LAUREEN The Ecumenical Liberation Army is an ultra-left sect creating political confusion with wildcat violence and pseudo-insurrectionary acts, which the Communist Party does not endorse. The American masses are not yet ready for open revolt. We would not want to produce a television show celebrating historically deviational terrorism.

DIANA Ms. Hobbs, I'm offering you an hour of prime-time television every week into which you can stick whatever propaganda you want.

LAUREEN The Ecumenicals are an undisciplined ultra-left gang, and the leader is an eccentric to say the least. He calls himself the Great Ahmed Khan and wears a hussar's shako.

DIANA Ms. Hobbs, we're talking about thirty to fifty million people a shot. That's a lot better than handing out mimeographed pamphlets on ghetto street corners.

LAUREEN I'll have to take this matter to the Central Committee, and I'd better check this out with the Great Ahmed Khan.

DIANA I'll be in L.A. until Saturday, and I'd like to get this thing rolling.

AN ISOLATED FARMHOUSE IN ENCINO. NIGHT.

Laureen Hobbs sits on the stoop, talking to another member of the Central

Committee, a middle-aged white man named WITHERSPOON. The door behind them opens and DOWLING, a young white man wearing a fatigue jacket and torn levis and sunglasses pokes his head out.

DOWLING Okay.

Laureen and Witherspoon rise and follow Dowling into...

THE ECUMENICALS' HEADQUARTERS, FOYER.

Darkness shrouds the shambles of cartons, crates, scraps of food and litter. WATKINS, a young black man in his thirties, stands on the stairway holding an army rifle and follows Laureen and Witherspoon into...

THE DINING ROOM.

...or what had once served as a dining room. A naked bulb provides light. On a wooden folding chair sits the GREAT AHMED KHAN, a brooding black man in his thirties. He wears a hussar's shako and the crescent moon of the Midianites hangs around his neck. His chair is the only furniture visible in the room.

Tattered sleeping bags and newspapers cover the floor, and the walls are bare except for various militant posters of the likes of Mao and Marlon Brando. Boxes of ammunition and grenades and mortar shells are stacked up.

In attendance are a young black women in her early twenties and a young white woman, MARY ANN GIFFORD, who is a fire-eating militant with a bandolier of cartridges across her torn shirt. Laureen pulls up an empty crate.

LAUREEN Well, Ahmed, you ain't going to believe this, but I'm going to make a teevee star out of you. Just like Archie Bunker. You're going to be a household word.

AHMED What the fuck are you talking about?

A rataplan of kettledrums and a tarantara of trumpets alerts us to an event.

UBS CONTROL ROOM. MONDAY, JANUARY 27, 1976.

DIRECTOR   ...and one...
The show monitor cuts to a beaming ANNOUNCER.

ANNOUNCER Ladies and gentlemen, let's hear it! How do you feel....?

The monitor shows the packed AUDIENCE roaring happily.

AUDIENCE   We're mad as hell, and we're not going to take this anymore!

THE STUDIO.

ANNOUNCER   *(in front of a curtain)*   Ladies and Gentlemen! "The Network News Hour"!

CUT to the announcer on the Control Room show monitor.

ANNOUNCER ...with Sybil the Soothsayer, Jim Webbing and his It's-the-Emmes-Truth Department, Miss Mata Hari and her Skeletons in the Closet, tonight another segment of Vox Populi, and starring...

MUSIC: a flourish of drums!

ANNOUNCER ...the mad prophet of the airways, Howard Beale!!

MUSIC: a full symphony orchestra soars into an imperial crescendo!

The houselights go to black. The curtain slowly rises. A SHAFT OF LIGHT emanating from on high shoots down onto the bare stage, where only one stained glass window hangs, suspended by wires. Howard Beale struggles on from the wings, looking austere in a black suit and tie. He finds the spotlight and stands shielding his eyes from the blinding light.

The audience greets him with TUMULTUOUS APPLAUSE.

HOWARD   *(erupts into a Savanarola-style tirade)*   Edward George Ruddy

died today! Edward George Ruddy was the Chairman of the Board of
the Union Broadcasting Systems. And he died at eleven o'clock this
morning of a heart condition. And woe is us, we're in a lot of trouble!
So a rich little man with white hair died, what's that got to do with the
price of rice, right? Why is that woe to us? Because you and sixty-
two million other Americans are watching me right now, that's why!
Because less than three percent of you people read books. Because
less than fifteen percent of you read newspapers. Because the only
truth you know is what you get over this tube! There is a whole and
entire generation right now who never knew anything that didn't
come out of this tube. This tube is the gospel. This tube is the ultimate revelation. This tube can make or break presidents, popes and
prime ministers. This tube is the most awesome goddam force in the
whole godless world! And woe is us if it ever falls in the hands of the
wrong people. And that's why woe is us that Edward George Ruddy
died.   Because this network is now in the hands of CCA, the
Communications Corporation of America.   We've got a new
Chairman of the Board, a man named Frank Hackett now sitting in
Mr. Ruddy's office on the twentieth floor. And when the twelfth
largest company in the world controls the most awesome goddam
propaganda force in the whole godless world, who knows what shit
will be peddled for truth on this tube? So, listen to me! Television is
not the truth! Television is a goddamned amusement park. Television
is a circus, a carnival, a travelling troupe of acrobats and story-tellers,
singers and dancers, jugglers, sideshow freaks, lion-tamers and foot-
ball players. We're in the boredom-killing business! If you want truth
go to God, go to your guru, go to yourself because that's the only place
you'll ever find any real truth. But man, you're never going to get any
truth from us. We'll tell you anything you want to hear. We lie like
hell! We'll tell you Kojack always gets the killer, and nobody ever gets
cancer in Archie Bunker's house. And no matter how much trouble
the hero is in, don't worry. Just look at your watch. At the end of the
hour, he's going to win. We'll tell you any shit you want to hear! We
deal in illusion, man! None of it's true. But you people sit there—all
of you—day after day, night after night, all ages, colors, creeds. We're
all you know. You're beginning to believe this illusion we're spinning
here. You're beginning to think the tube is reality and your own lives
are unreal. You do whatever the tube tells you. You dress like the

tube, you eat like the tube, you raise your children like the tube, you think like the tube. This is mass madness, you maniacs! In God's name, you people are the real thing! We're the illusions. So turn off this goddam set! Turn it off right now. Turn it off and leave it off. Turn it off right now, right in the middle of this very sentence I'm speaking now....

At which point, Howard Beale's red-eyed rage of prophesy causes him to swoon. He falls.

CCA CONFERENCE ROOM. MONDAY, JANUARY 27.

A Valhalla of a room on the 43rd and 44th floors of the CCA Building is theatrically dark, with the lighting at the moment issuing from a slide projector at the back of the room where Frank Hackett, dressed in banker's grays, delivers his Annual Report. On the screen, we see charts of figures, and a little red ARROW darts from one to another, accompanying Hackett's droning. Seated in a semi-circular arrangement like a miniature United Nations are the 214 SENIOR EXECUTIVES. Each has his own desk, swivel chair, pin spotlight, bound company reports, and a nameplate.

NOTE in dead center of the first row, one specific CHAIR shielding its occupant from visibility swivels back and forth, back and forth....

HACKETT   *(on podium)* UBS was running at a cash-flow break-even point after taking into account one hundred and ten million dollars of negative cash-flow from the network. It was clear the fat on the network had to be flitched off.

Another CLOSER ANGLE on the chair swivelling back and forth.

HACKETT   Please note an increase in projected initial programming revenues in the amount of twenty-one million dollars, due to the phenomenal success of "The Howard Beale Show." I expect a positive cash-flow for the entire complex of forty-five million achievable in this fiscal year, a year, in short, ahead of schedule.

ANOTHER ANGLE EVEN CLOSER on the swivelling chair, still not revealing its occupant.

HACKETT   I go beyond that. This network may well be the most significant profit center of the communications complex...

A FULL SHOT of Hackett barely concealing his pride.

HACKETT   ...and, based upon the projected rate of return on invested capital, and if merger is eventually accomplished, the communications complex may well become the towering and most profitable center in the entire CCA empire. I await your questions and comments. Mr. Jensen?

CAMERA PANS ACROSS the huge span of tiered seats to the SWIVEL-LING CHAIR, revealing a bald, bespectacled man with a Grant Woods face. This is ARTHUR JENSEN, the President and Chairman of the Board of CCA.

JENSEN   Very good, Frank. Exemplary. Keep it up.

TIGHT SHOT of Hackett, basking in this praise, suffused with pride.

N.Y., TEMPLE EMANUEL. TUESDAY, JANUARY 28, 10:30 A.M.

Edward George Ruddy lying in state. Beneath the vaulted reaches of the Temple the white yarmalka-ed RABBI officiates in background. There's standing room only, and UBS NETWORK BRASS are scattered throughout the congregation.

Max is among the consolers, following his eyes to several rows of pews down on the other side of the aisle where Diana is sitting. Aware of Max's eyes on her, she turns her face a bit so that their eyes meet briefly. She smiles, turns back to the Rabbi's eulogy.

65TH STREET, MAIN ENTRANCE TO TEMPLE EMANUEL.

SNOW drifts down over a CROWD of condolers on the sidewalk. A cortege of black limousines line up in front of the temple as FUNERAL DIREC-TORS guide them into their respective limousines. A curious crowd of PASSERSBY watch. Max Schumacher threads his way through the CRUSH to where Diana Christenson stands with Nelson Chaney and Walter Amundsen, all bundled up in winter coats. "Hello, Max, how are you" and "How's everything, Walter," get muttered in the cold.

MAX *(to Diana)* Buy you a cup of coffee?

DIANA Hell, yes.

After goodbyes all around, CAMERA DOLLIES as Max and Diana move away from the CRUSH on the sidewalk. They turn the corner onto...

FIFTH AVENUE. DAY.

They walk silently downtown. SNOW drifts down on them.

MAX Do you have to get back to the office?

DIANA Nothing that can't wait.

They continue walking silently.

DIANA I drop down to the news studios every now and then and ask Howard Beale about you. He says you're doing fine. Are you?

MAX No.

DIANA Are you keeping busy?

MAX After a fashion. This is the third funeral I've been to in two weeks. I have two other friends in hospital who I visit regularly. I've been to a couple of christenings. All my friends seem to be dying or having grandchildren.

DIANA You should be a grandfather about now. You have a pregnant daughter in Seattle, don't you?

MAX Any day now. My wife's out there for the occasion. I've thought many times of calling you.

DIANA I wish you had.

They both suddenly stop on Fifth Avenue between 64th and 65th Streets and regard each other. An occasional snowflake moistens their cheeks, wets their hair.

DIANA I bumped into Sybil the Soothsayer in the elevator last week. I said, "You know, Sybil, about four months ago, you predicted I would get involved with a craggy, middle-aged man, and, so far, all that's happened is one many-splendored night. I don't call that getting involved." And she said, "Don't worry. You will." It was a many-splendored night, wasn't it, Max?

MAX Yes, it was.

DIANA Are we going to get involved, Max?

MAX Yes. I need to get involved very much. How about you?

DIANA I've reached for the phone to call you a hundred times, but I was sure you hated me for my part in taking your news show away.

MAX I probably did. I don't know any more. All I know is I can't keep you out of my mind.

They stare at each other, bemused by the abrupt but fragile explosion of their feelings. The SNOW drifts down. PEDESTRIANS move back and forth around them. The Fifth Avenue downtown traffic grinds along noisily.

DIANA My God, she's uncanny.

MAX   Who?

DIANA   Sybil the Soothsayer. We've got a modern-day Greek drama here, Max. Two star-crossed lovers ordained to fall disastrously in love by the gods. A December-May story. Happily married middle-aged man meets desperately lonely young career woman, let's say a violinist. They both know their illicit love can only end in tragedy, but they are cursed by the gods and plunge dementedly in love. For a few brief moments, they are happy. He abandons devoted wife and loving children, and she throws away her concert career. The soothsayer appears again and warns the girl she will die if she persists in this heedless love affair. She defies the soothsayer. But now one of the man's children is rushed to the hospital with a mysterious disease. He rushes back to his family, and she is left to throw herself on the railroad tracks. Give me a two-page outline on it, Max. I might be able to sell it to Xerox.

MAX   A bit too austere for teevee, I think. Why don't we just wing it?

She laughs, then he. A PASSERBY darts them a curious glance.

UBS BUILDING, DIANA'S OFFICE. FRIDAY, FEBRUARY 28.

Diana is ebullient as she puts last-minute things into a weekend bag and argues with the squawk box of her speaker phone.

DIANA   I know what NBC offered them, Marty, so I'm saying go to three point five, and I want an option for a third run on all of them...Marty, I'm in a big hurry, and you and Charlie are supposed to be negotiating this, so goodby and good luck, and I'll see you Monday.

She snaps her bag shut, whisks her sheepskin-lined coat out of the closet and strides out into..

DIANA'S SECRETARY'S OFFICE.

...where there is no one sitting and continues out into...

PROGRAMMING DEPARTMENT, COMMON ROOM.

...where a few SECRETARIES are still at their desks. Tommy Pellegrino is just coming out of his office.

PELLEGRINO *(calls to Diana)* Jimmy Caan's agent just called and says absolutely nix.

DIANA You can't win them all.

PELLEGRINO Where can I reach you later today?

DIANA *(exiting)* You can't. I'll be gone all weekend.

UBS BUILDING, SIXTH AVENUE. AFTERNOON.

Diana, now in her coat and carrying her weekend bag, comes happily out through the entrance doors, heads for 55th Street, spots a double-parked car and, heedless of traffic, heads across the street to...

55TH STREET.

Max Schumacher in a rented Chevy, leans across to open the door for her. She slips into the front seat, slams the door, nestles her head on Max's over-coated shoulder, as he starts the ignition.

DIANA *(happy and in love)* NBC's offering three point two and a half mil per for a package of five James Bond pictures, and I think I'm going to steal them for three point five with a third run...

They move out into the heavy traffic of Sixth Avenue.

DESERTED BEACH IN THE HAMPTONS. DUSK.

Traditional lyric love scene. The two mackinawed lovers walk hand-in-hand on a lovely stretch of deserted winter beach. The tide is coming in...

DIANA *(bubbling)* The Vigilante show is sold firm. Ford took a complete position at, so help me, fifty-five CPM. In fact, I'm moving the Vigilante show to nine, and I'm going to stick "The Mao Tse Tung Hour" in at eight, because we're having a lot of trouble selling "The Mao Tse Tung Hour." This way we give it a terrific lead-in from "The Howard Beale Show," and we'll back into "The Vigilantes," and it certainly ought to carry its own time slot.

ROMANTIC LITTLE ITALIAN RESTAURANT.

The obligatory checkered tablecloth, candles, wine. Diana and Max are at dinner and utterly rapt in each other.

DIANA *(pouring out her heart)* That Mao Tse Tung Hour is turning into one big pain in the ass. We're having heavy legal problems with the federal government right now. Two FBI guys turned up in Hackett's office last week and served us with a subpoena. They heard about our Flagstaff bank ripoff film, and they want it. We're getting around that by doing the show in collaboration with the News Division, so Hackett told the FBI to fuck off. We're standing on the First Amendment: freedom of the press and the right to protect our sources...

MOTOR COURT. NIGHT.

Diana and Max get out of their car and head for a ground-level room. Max unlocks the door.

DIANA *(chirping merrily along)* ...Walter thinks we can knock out the misprision of felony charge...

They go into...

MOTOR COURT, THEIR ROOM.

Max flicks the light on, kicks the door shut, and they are instantly into each other's arms in a passionate embrace.

DIANA ...but he says absolutely nix on going to series. They'll hit us with inducement and conspiracy to commit a crime...

She busily removes her shoes, unbuttons her blouse, whisks out of her slacks, down to her bikini panties. She is now scouring the walls for a thermostat.

DIANA ...Christ, it's cold in here...*(She turns up the heat.)* You see we're paying these nuts from the Ecumenical Liberation Army ten thousand bucks a week to bring in authentic film footage on their revolutionary activities, and that constitutes inducement to commit a crime. And Walter says we'll all wind up in federal prison...

Nubile and nearly naked, she entwines herself around Max, who by now has stripped down to his trousers. The two hungering bodies slide down onto the bed where they commence an affable moment of amative foreplay.

DIANA *(efficiently unbuckling and unzippering Max's trousers)* ...I said, "Walter, let the government sue us! We'll take them to the Supreme Court! We'll be front page for months! *The Washington Post* and *The New York Times* will be doing two editorials a week about us! We'll have more press than Watergate!"

Groping, grasping, gasping and fondling, they contrive to denude each other, and in a fever of sexual hunger, Diana mounts Max. The screen is filled with the voluptuous writhings of love. Diana cries out with increasing exultancy...

DIANA *(in the throes of passion)* ...All I need...is six weeks of federal litigation...and "The Mao Tse Tung Hour"...can start carrying its own time slot!

She screams in consummation, sighs a long, deliciously shuddering sigh, and sinks softly down into Max's embrace. For a moment, she rests her head on Max's chest, eyes closed in feline contentment.

DIANA *(after a moment, begins purring)* What's really bugging me now is my daytime programming. NBC's got a lock on daytime with their lousy game shows, and I'd like to bust them. I'm thinking of doing a homosexual soap opera—"The Dykes"—the heart-rending saga of a woman helplessly in love with her husband's mistress. What do you think?

MAX'S LIVING ROOM. MONDAY, FEBRUARY 25.

Max and Louise are in the middle of an ugly domestic scene. Louise sits erect on an overstuffed chair, her eyes wet with imminent tears. Max, under stress, strides around the room.

LOUISE *(shrilly)* How long has it been going on?

MAX *(prowling around the room)* A month. I thought at first it might be a transient thing and blow over in a week. I still hope to God it's just a menopausal infatuation. But it *is* an infatuation, Louise. There's no sense my saying I won't see her again, because I will. Do you want me to clear out, go to a hotel?

LOUISE Do you love her?

MAX I don't know how I feel. I'm grateful I still feel anything. I know I'm obsessed with her.

LOUISE Then say it! Don't keep telling me you're obsessed, you're infatuated—say you're in love with her!

MAX I'm in love with her.

LOUISE Then get out, go to a hotel, go anywhere you want, go live with her, but don't come back! Because after twenty-five years of building a home and raising a family and all the senseless pain we've inflicted on each other, I'll be damned if I'll just stand here and let you tell me you love somebody else! *(Now she is the one striding around, weeping, like a caged lioness.)* Because this isn't just some convention weekend with your secretary, is it? Or some broad you picked up after three belts of booze. This is your great winter romance, isn't it? Your last roar of passion before you sink into your emeritus years. Is that what's left for me? Is that my share? She gets the great winter passion, and

I get the dotage? Am I supposed to sit at home knitting and purling till you slink back like a penitent drunk? I'm your wife, damn it! If you can't work up a winter passion for me, then the least I require is respect and allegiance! I'm hurt. Don't you understand that? I'm hurt badly.

She stares, her cheeks streaked. Max stands at the terrace glass door, his own eyes welling. He turns to regard his anguished wife.

LOUISE Say something, for God's sake.

MAX I've got nothing to say.

He enfolds her. She sobs on his chest.

LOUISE I won't give you up easily, Max.

He struggles to restrain his tears, as she releases herself from his embrace.

LOUISE I think perhaps it would be better if you did move out. Does she love you, Max?

MAX I'm not sure she's capable of any real feelings. She's the television generation. She learned life from Bugs Bunny. The only reality she knows is what comes over her teevee set. She has devised a variety of scenarios for us all to play, as if it were a Movie of the Week. And, my God! Look at us, Louise. Here we are going through the obligatory middle-of-Act-Two scorned-wife-throws-peccant-husband-out scene. But, not to fear, I'll come back home in the end. All her plot outlines have me leaving her and returning to you, because the audience won't buy a rejection of the happy American family. She does have one script in which I kill myself, an adapted-for-television version of *Anna Karenina* in which she's Count Vronsky and I'm Anna.

LOUISE You're in for some dreadful grief, Max.

MAX I know.

NARRATOR *(off-screen)* "The Mao Tse Tung Hour" went on the air March fourteenth.

ENCINO FARMHOUSE. NIGHT.

A black LIMOUSINE winds its way up the dirt road to the front porch, where an armed guard halts it and checks it out.

NARRATOR *(off-screen)* It received a 47 share.

Slivers of light slither out from behind the drawn shades of the farmhouse, and we can hear the sounds of ANGRY VOICES.

TWO AGENTS from ICM disgorge from the limousine—a young man in his early thirties, FREDDIE, carrying a large manila envelope, and a heavy young woman, mid-thirties, HELEN MIGGS, carrying an attaché case.

NARRATOR *(off-screen)* The network promptly committed to fifteen shows.

Miggs and Freddie go up the porch and into...

THE FARMHOUSE, ENTRANCE.

Cartons, newspapers, scraps of food, cases of weapons, broken furniture and sleeping bags litter the room. A conference seems to be going on in the living room, off-screen.

NARRATOR *(off-screen)* ...with an option for ten more.

The two ICM agents head for the living room, followed by Laureen Hobbs and the three William Morris agents, Wallie, Lennie and Ed. We can see the Great Ahmed Khan, still wearing his shako, Mary Ann Gifford, wearing her bandoliers of bullets and OTHER MEMBERS of the Khan's group in fatigues and bearing arms. There is also a middle-aged lawyer from ICM named WILLIE STEIN. Everybody—with the exception of the Great Khan's retinue—is seated on broken chairs, cartons and crates.

NARRATOR *(off-screen)* There were, of course, the usual contractual difficulties...

THE FARMHOUSE LIVING ROOM.

Everybody in the living room conference studies the eighty-page contracts from which Wallie is reading.

WALLIE *(mumbling along)* "...herein called either 'the Production Fee' or 'overhead' equal to twenty percent two-o (except such percentage shall be thirty percent three-o for ninety-minute or longer television programs..."

MIGGS *(whisking through her copy of the contract)* Have we settled that sub-licensing thing? We want a clear definition here. Gross proceeds should consist of all funds the sublicensee receives, not merely the net amount remitted after payment to sublicensee or distributor.

STEIN We're not sitting still for overhead charges as a cost prior to distribution.

LAUREEN *(whose nerves have worn thin, explodes)* Don't fuck with my distribution costs! I'm getting a lousy two-fifteen per segment, and I'm already deficiting twenty-five grand a week with Metro. I'm paying William Morris ten percent off the top! *(indicates the Great Khan)* And I'm giving this turkey ten thou a segment and another five for this fruitcake *(meaning Mary Ann Gifford)*. And, Helen, don't start no shit with me about a piece again! I'm paying Metro twenty percent of all foreign and Canadian distribution, and that's after recoupment! The Communist Party's not going to see a nickel out of this goddam show until we go into syndication!

MIGGS Come on, Laureen, you've got the Party in there for seventy-five hundred a week production expenses.

LAUREEN I'm not giving this pseudo-insurrectionary sectarian a piece of my show! I'm not giving him script approval! And I sure as shit ain't cutting him in on my distribution charges!

MARY ANN GIFFORD *(screaming from the back)* Fugginfascist! Have you seen the movies we took at the San Marino jail break-out demonstrating the rising up of a seminal prisoner-class infrastructure?!

LAUREEN You can blow the seminal prisoner-class infrastructure out your ass! I'm not knocking down my goddam distribution charges!

The Great Khan decides to offer an opinion by SHOOTING his PISTOL off into the air. This gives everybody something to consider, especially Willie Stein, who becomes almost apoplectic.

THE GREAT KHAN Man, give her the fucking overhead clause.

STEIN How did I get here? Who's going to believe this?

THE GREAT KHAN *(flipping through his copy)* Let's get to page twenty-two, five, small a, subsidiary rights.

Everybody starts flipping through their contracts.

LENNIE Where are we now?

WALLIE Page twenty-two, middle of the page, subsidiary rights—*(begins to read)*—"As used herein, 'subsidiary rights' means, without limitation, any and all rights with respect to theatrical motion picture rights, radio broadcasting, legitimate stage performances, printed publications (including, but not limited to, hard-cover books, but excluding paperback books and comic books) and/or any other uses of a similar or dissimilar nature..."

CENTURY PLAZA HOTEL, BALLROOM, COCKTAIL AREA.

A huge BANNER reading "UBS AFFILIATES 1976" hangs high over the ballroom. Some thousand tuxedoed and evening-gowned PEOPLE, mostly middle-aged in the vast shuffle of cocktail time HUBBUB, intermingle and surge slowly through the doors leading into the ballroom. Here, the lights are dim as everybody, now settled at their tables, listens to an address by Nelson Chaney, in a spotlight at the podium.

CHANEY   ...Over the past two days, you've all had an opportunity to meet Diana Christenson, our Vice President in Charge of Programming. This afternoon, you all saw some of the stuff she's set up for the new season. You all know she's the woman behind the Howard Beale show. We know she's beautiful. We know she's brainy. I just think, before we start digging into our Chateaubriands, we ought to let her know how we feel about her...

An OVATION from the audience. In response to Chaney's beckoning, Diana rises from the glistening shadows of the dais and comes down to the podium. She stands there—showered with APPLAUSE, beaming, exultant.

DIANA   We've got the number one show in television! *(applause)* And at next year's affiliates' meeting, I'll be standing here telling you we've got the top five! *(tumult)*

ACROSS Hackett at the dais with Diana in background. An ASSISTANT MANAGER leans across Hackett to deliver a discreet message.

DIANA   Last year, we were the number four network. Next year, we're number one! *(tumult)*

AUDIENCE   We're Number One! We're Number One!

Hackett rises and, with apologies to his neighbors, follows the assistant manager through the shadows of the dais and heads out.

DIANA   It is exactly seven o'clock here in Los Angeles. And right now over a million homes using television in this city are turning their dials to Channel 3—and that's our channel!

MUSIC: A Rataplan of Kettledrums and a Tarantara!

COCKTAIL AREA OF THE GRAND BALLROOM.

A portable TV set is perched on a bar.

ANNOUNCER *(on TV)* Ladies and gentlemen! Let's hear it! How do you feel?

STUDIO AUDIENCE *(on TV, happily roaring)* We're mad as hell, and we're not going to take this anymore!

PULL BACK to show the vast cocktail area of the Grand Ballroom, being cleared by WAITERS and BUSBOYS: hor d'oeuvres, spreads and booze are carried away, tables and chairs packed off, linens whisked and folded. A couple of WAITERS watch "The Howard Beale Show."

STUDIO ANNOUNCER *(on TV)* Ladies and gentlemen, the mad prophet of the airways—Howard Beale!

On the TV set, the houselights dim, the curtain rises. As before, on a bare stage with the stained glass window, in an ethereal shaft of light, Howard Beale in his austere black suit trudges out and explodes.

HOWARD *(on TV)* All right, listen to me! Listen carefully! This is your goddam life I'm talking about today! In this country, when one company takes over another company, they simply buy up a controlling share of the stock. But first they have to file notice with the government. That's how CCA—the Communications Corporation of America—bought up the company that owns this network. And now somebody's buying up CCA! Some company named Western World Funding Corporation is buying up CCA! They filed their notice this morning! Well, just who the hell is Western World Funding Corporation? It's a consortium of banks and insurance companies who are not buying CCA for themselves but as agents for somebody else!

LONG WIDE-ANGLE SHOT with TV set in foreground shows the cocktail area clean-up, when across the spacious room the doors open and Hackett follows the assistant manager into the Ballroom. Hackett lingers at the doors, while the assistant manager gets a WAITER to bring a phone to one of the tables still standing.

HOWARD *(on TV)* Well, who's this somebody else? They won't tell you!

They won't tell you, they won't tell the Senate, they won't tell the SEC, the FCC, the Justice Department, they won't tell anybody! They say it's none of our business! The hell it ain't!

Hackett continues to watch as a jack phone is brought to him. People cluster around the TV set in the background, while Hackett accepts his call.

HACKETT *(on phone)* This is Mr. Hackett, do you have a New York call for me? *(calls to the group around the TV)* Do you want to turn that down, please...?

The volume goes down a very little bit in a REVERSE ANGLE ACROSS TV SET with Hackett in the background.

HOWARD *(on TV, volume lower)* Well, I'll tell you who they're buying CCA for. They're buying it for the Saudi-Arabian Investment Corporation! They're buying it for the Arabs!

HACKETT *(plays the hearty executive on the phone)* Clarence? Frank Hackett here! How's everything back in New York? How's the good lady?...All right, take it easy, Clarence, I don't know what you're talking about...When? Clarence, take it easy. "The Howard Beale Show"'s just going on out here. You guys get it three hours earlier in New York...Clarence, take it easy. How the hell could I see it? It's just on now—well, when did Mr. Jensen call you?

REVERSE ACROSS TV SET. In background, Hackett has hung up and is slowly walking toward the group watching the TV set.

HOWARD *(on TV)* We know the Arabs control more than sixteen billion dollars in this country! They own a chunk of Fifth Avenue, twenty downtown pieces of Boston, a part of the port of New Orleans, an industrial park in Salt Lake City. They own big hunks of the Atlanta Hilton, the Arizona Land and Cattle Company, part of a bank in California, the Bank of the Commonwealth in Detroit! They control ARAMCO, so that puts them into Exxon, Texaco and Mobil Oil! They're all over—New Jersey, Louisville, St. Louis, Missouri! And that's only what we know about! There's a hell of a lot more we don't know about, because all those Arab petro-dollars are washed through Switzerland and Canada and the biggest banks in this country!

Hackett peers over a WAITER'S SHOULDER to watch the show.

HOWARD *(on TV)* For example, what we don't know about is this CCA deal and all the other CCA deals! *(Hackett winces.)* Right now, the Arabs have screwed us out of enough American dollars to come back and, with our own money, buy General Motors, IBM, ITT, AT and T, Dupont, U.S. Steel, and twenty other top American companies. Hell, they already own half of England.

LOS ANGELES, UBS BUILDING. A VIDEOTAPE ROOM.

It's been a few hours, but not that long since the banquet. Now in an unglamorous room cluttered with electronic equipment, Hackett, Nelson Chaney and Walter Amundsen, all tuxedoed, and Diana, evening-gowned, sit or stand while they painfully watch a replay of "The Howard Beale Show" on the big screen.

TWO TECHNICIANS fiddle with their equipment as Howard's speech picks up where we left off.

HOWARD *(on screen)* Now, listen to me, goddammit! The Arabs are simply buying us! A handful of agas, shahs and emirs who despise this country and everything it stands for—democracy, freedom, the right for me to get up on television and tell you about it—a couple of dozen medieval fanatics are going to own where you work, where you live, what you read, what you see, your cars, your bowling alleys, your mortgages, your schools, your churches, your libraries, your kids, your whole life...!

AMUNDSEN The son of a bitch is effective, all right.

Hackett, who's seen all this already, isn't even watching. He is sprawled in his chair, eyes closed, numbed, serene with despair.

HOWARD *(on screen)* ...And there's not a single law on the books to stop them! There's only one thing that can stop them—you! So I want you to get up now. I want you to get out of your chairs and go to the phone. Right now. I want you to go to your phone or get in your car and drive into the Western Union office in town. I want everybody listening to me to get up right now and send a telegram to the White House...

HACKETT *(sighs in soft anguish)* Oh, God...

HOWARD *(on-screen)* By midnight, I want a million telegrams in the White House. I want them wading knee-deep in telegrams at the White House! Get up!...Right now! And send President Ford a telegram saying, "I'm mad as hell, and I'm not going to take this anymore! I don't want the banks selling my country to the Arabs! I want this CCA deal stopped now!"

HACKETT Oh, God...

HOWARD *(on screen)* I want this CCA deal stopped now! I want this CCA deal stopped now!

At which point, Howard keels over in his now familiar prophetic SWOON. On screen, ATTENDANTS come to carry Howard off.

CHANEY *(to a technician)* Is that it? Does he come back later in the show?

TECHNICIAN That's it. This is one of those shows he just zonks out.

CHANEY *(to the technicians)* Look could we have the room?

TECHNICIAN Sure.

The two technicians exit. SILENCE fills the cluttered room. Amundsen and Hackett sit in their chairs, Chaney leans against a side wall, Diana lounges against a rear wall. After a moment, Amundsen stretches and stands.

AMUNDSEN Well, I'd like to see a typescript and run it a couple of more times. But, as for this whole CCA deal with the Saudis, you'd know a lot more about that than I would, Frank. Is it true?

Hackett sighs.

HACKETT *(muffled)* Yes. CCA has two billion in loans with the Saudis, and they hold every pledge we've got. We need that Saudi money bad. *(He stands, so wretched he is tranquil.)* A disaster. This show is a disaster, an unmitigated disaster, the death knell. I'm ruined, I'm dead, I'm finished.

CHANEY Maybe we're overstating Beale's clout with the public.

HACKETT An hour ago, Clarence McElheny called me from New York. It was ten o'clock in the East, and our people in the White House report they were already knee-deep in telegrams. By tomorrow morning, they'll be suffocating in telegrams.

CHANEY Well, can the government stop the deal?

HACKETT They can hold it up. The SEC could hold this deal up for twenty years, if they wanted to. I'm finished. Any second that phone's going to ring, and Clarence McElheny's going to tell me Mr. Jensen wants me in his office tomorrow morning so he can personally chop my head off. *(Tears stream shamelessly down his cheeks, as he ponders his fate, a broken man.)* Four hours ago, I was the Sun God at CCA, Mr. Jensen's hand-picked golden boy, the heir apparent. Now I'm a man without a corporation!

DIANA *(comes off the back wall)* Let's get back to Howard Beale. You're not seriously going to pull Beale off the air.

HACKETT Mr. Jensen is unhappy with Howard Beale and wants him discontinued.

DIANA He may be unhappy, but he isn't stupid enough to withdraw the number one show on television out of pique.

HACKETT *(explodes)* Two billion dollars isn't pique! That's the wrath of God! And the wrath of God wants Howard Beale fired!

DIANA What for? Every other network will grab him the minute he walks out the door. He'll be back on the air for ABC tomorrow. And we'll lose twenty points in audience share in the first week, roughly a forty million loss in revenues for the year.

HACKETT I'm going to kill Howard Beale! I'm going to impale the son of a bitch with a sharp stick through the heart!

DIANA And let's not discount federal action by the Justice Department. If CCA pulls Beale off the air as an act of retribution, that's a flagrant violation of network autonomy and an egregious breach of the consent decree.

HACKETT *(liking his new train of thought)* I'll take out a contract on him. I'll hire professional killers. I'll do it myself. I'll strangle him with a sash-cord.

DIANA No. I don't think Jensen is going to fire anybody.

The phone RINGS. A moment of anxious silence. Hackett picks it up.

HACKETT *(on phone)* Hackett...yes, Clarence. I've already booked my flight...Well, can you give me a little more time than that? I've got the red-eye flight, I won't be back in New York till six tomorrow morning...That'll be just fine. I'll see you then...

He returns the phone to its cradle, regards Diana.

HACKETT Mr. Jensen wants to meet Howard Beale personally. He wants Mr. Beale in his office at ten o'clock tomorrow morning.

STREET IN FRONT OF THE CCA BUILDING.

Both dressed in banker's gray, Hackett herds Howard toward the building's entrance, and it becomes clear Howard is in a beatified state. His eyes glisten transcendentally, his smile beams from an elevated spirit. Abruptly, he raises his arms and makes a resonating pronouncement.

HOWARD   *(imbued)*   The final revelation is at hand! I have seen the shattering fulgurations of ultimate clarity! The light is impending! I bear witness to the light!

This outburst doesn't seem to bother most of the PASSERSBY, although SOME ask, "Hey, that's Howard Beale, isn't it?" The outburst does appall Frank Hackett, who stares in distress and entreats some god in the heavens. He clutches at Howard's arm to get him moving again.

ARTHUR JENSEN'S OFFICE.

An enormous space with two walls of windows towering over the Manhattan landscape. SUNLIGHT streams in. Arthur Jensen rises from behind his massive desk to greet the man he has summoned.

JENSEN   Good morning, Mr. Beale. They tell me you're a madman.

HOWARD   *(closing the door behind himself)*   Only desultorily.

JENSEN   How are you now?

HOWARD   *(as mad as a hatter)*   I'm as mad as a hatter.

JENSEN   Who isn't? I'm taking you to our conference room, which seems more seemly a setting for what I have to say to you. I started as a salesman, Mr. Beale. I sold sewing machines and automobile parts, hair brushes and electronic equipment. They say I can sell anything. I'd like to try and sell something to you...

He takes Howard's arm and leads him through oaken doors out of this office and into...

CCA BUILDING, CONFERENCE ROOM.

The darkened conference room where Frank Hackett delivered his annual report is now an overwhelming cathedral bleached by the sunlight seeping into every fold and corner. The enormous curtains are up, and an almost celestial light pours in. Being on the 43rd and 44th floors, the splendid view of the sky outside is sporadically interrupted by the towers of other skyscrapers. The double semi-circular bank of seats are all empty, and the general effect is one of hushed vastness.

JENSEN   Valhalla, Mr. Beale, please sit down.

He leads Howard down the steps to the floor level. Jensen himself ascends to the small stage and podium. Howard sits in one of the 200-odd seats. Jensen pushes a button, and the voluminous drapes slowly fall, slicing away layers of light until the vast room is utterly dark. The pinspots at each of the desks, including the one where Howard sits, pop on, lit by an unseen hand and creating a miniature Milky Way effect. A shaft of white LIGHT shoots out from the rear of the room, spotting Jensen at the podium, a sun in its own little galaxy.

Jensen suddenly wheels to his audience of one and roars.

JENSEN   You have meddled with the primal forces of nature, Mr. Beale, and I won't have it, is that clear?! You think you have merely stopped a business deal—that is not the case! The Arabs have taken billions of dollars out of this country, and now they must put it back. It is ebb and flow, tidal gravity, it is ecological balance! You are an old man who thinks in terms of nations and peoples. There are no nations! There are no peoples! There are no Russians! There are no Arabs! There are no Third Worlds! There is no West! There is only one holistic system of systems, one vast and immane, interwoven, interacting, multi-variate, multi-national dominion of dollars! Petro-dollars, electro-dollars, multi-dollars, Reichmarks, rubles, rin, pounds and shekels! It is the international system of currency that determines the totality of life on this planet! That is the natural order of things today! That is the atomic, sub-atomic and galactic structure of things today! And you have meddled with the primal forces of nature, and you will atone! Am I getting through to you, Mr. Beale? You get up on your little twenty-one inch screen, Mr. Beale, and howl about America and democracy. There is no America. There is no democracy. There is only IBM and ITT and AT and T and Dupont, Dow, Union Carbide and Exxon. Those are the nations of the world today. What do you think the Russians talk about in their councils of state? Karl Marx? They pull out their linear programming charts, statistical decision theories and minimax solutions and compute the price-cost probabilities of their transactions and investments just like we do. We no longer live in a world of nations and ideologies, Mr. Beale. The world is a college of corporations, inexorably determined by the immutable by-laws of business. The world is a business, Mr. Beale! It has been that way since man crawled out of the slime, and our children, Mr. Beale, will live to see that perfect world without war and famine, oppression and brutality—one vast and ecumenical holding company, for whom all men will work to serve a common profit, in which all men will hold a share of stock, all necessities provided, all anxieties tranquilized, all boredom amused. And I have chosen you to preach this evangel, Mr. Beale.

HOWARD   *(humble whisper)* Why me?

JENSEN   Because you're on television, dummy. Sixty million people watch you every night of the week, Monday through Friday.

Howard slowly rises, so that he is lit only by the ethereal diffusion of the light from the rear of the room. He stares transfixed at Jensen.

HOWARD   I have seen the face of God!

In the background at the podium, Jensen considers this curious statement.

JENSEN   You just might be right, Mr. Beale.

NARRATOR   *(off-screen)* That evening, Howard Beale went on the air to preach the corporate cosmology of Arthur Jensen.

NETWORK NEWS CONTROL ROOM.

The CREW are posted at their various control panels and seem, if anything, a little more bored.

On the SHOW MONITOR, Howard Beale stands in his stained-glass-filtered spotlight. Rather than his old enraged self, he seems sad, resigned, weary.

HOWARD *(on monitor)* Last night, I got up here and asked you people to stand up and fight for your heritage, and you did. And it was beautiful. Six million telegrams were received at the White House. The Arab takeover of CCA has been stopped. The people spoke, the people won. It was a radiant eruption of democracy. But I think that was it, fellers. That sort of thing isn't likely to happen again. Because, in the bottom of all our terrified souls, we all know that democracy is a dying giant, a sick, sick dying, decaying political concept, writhing in its final pain. I don't mean the United States is finished as a world power. The United States is the most powerful, the richest, the most advanced country in the world, light-years ahead of any other country. And I don't mean the Communists are going to take over the world. The Communists are deader than we are. What's finished is the idea that this great country is dedicated to the freedom and flourishing of every individual in it. It's the individual that's finished. It's the single, solitary human being who's finished. It's every single one of you out there who's finished. Because this is no longer a nation of independent individuals. This is a nation of two hundred-odd million transistorized, deodorized, whiter-than-white, steel-belted bodies, totally unnecessary as human beings and as replaceable as piston rods...*(Howard sits on a corner of the stage.)* Well, the time has come to say, is dehumanization such a bad word? Because good or bad, that's what's so. The whole world is becoming humanoid, creatures that look human but aren't. The whole world, not just us. We're just the most advanced country, so we're getting there first. The whole world's people are becoming mass-produced, programmed, numbered, insensate things useful only to produce and consume other mass-produced things, all of them as unnecessary and useless as we are...

NARRATOR It was a perfectly admissible argument that Howard Beale advanced in the days that follows; it was, however, also a very tedious and depressing one. By the end of the first week in June...

DIANA'S FOYER. THURSDAY, JUNE 19, 7:15 P.M.

Max seems depressed as he lets himself into the apartment.

NARRATOR "The Howard Beale Show" had dropped one point in the ratings, and its trend of shares dipped under forty-eight for the first time since last November.

Max enters the living room, as Diana's VOICE pours out of the bedroom.

DIANA *(off-screen)* You're his goddam agent, Lew! I'm counting on you to talk some sense into the lunatic! Nobody wants to hear about dying democracy and dehumanization.

DIANA'S BEDROOM.

Diana is on the edge of her bed, talking shrilly into the phone.

DIANA We're starting to get rumbles from the agencies. Another couple of weeks of this, and the sponsors will be bailing out!...This is breach of contract, Lew! This isn't the Howard Beale we signed. You better get him off this corporate universe kick or, so help me, I'll pull him off the air!...I told him, Lew! I've been telling him every day for a week! I'm sick of telling him! Now you tell him!

In silent rage, she slams the receiver down. She turns up the volume of her remote control unit. HOWARD's VOICE emanates from the television set across the room from her.

HOWARD *(on TV, off-screen)* ...that's the simple truth you have to grasp, that human existence is an utterly futile and purposeless thing, because once you've grasped that, then the whole universe becomes orderly and comprehensible...

DIANA Jesus Christ.

HOWARD *(on TV)* ...We are right now living in what has to be called a corporate society, a corporate world, a corporate universe. This world quite simply is a vast cosmology of small corporations orbiting around larger corporations who, in turn, revolve around giant corporations and this whole, endless, ultimate cosmology is expressly designed for the production and consumption of useless things.

Diana clicks the remote control device, and the TV set goes black. She reaches for the phone again, dials briskly. She looks up to note Max regarding her from the doorway. She regards him sullenly. They are both clearly in foul tempers.

MAX I'm sorry I'm late.

They exchange dull, sullen looks. Max turns back into...

THE LIVING ROOM.

Max sprawls morosely on one of the soft chairs. We notice that in the back of the living room, a bridge table has been set up as a makeshift desk. It has a typewriter and welter of papers, books and filing folders. Diana appears in the doorway and regards Max coldly.

DIANA You know, you could help me out with Howard if you wanted to. He listens to you. You're his best friend.

MAX *(exploding off his chair)* I'm tired of this hysteria about Howard Beale!

DIANA *(also erupting)* Every time you see somebody in your family, you come back in one of these morbid middle-aged moods!

MAX *(raging around the room)* And I'm tired of finding you on the goddamned phone every time I turn around. I'm tired of being an accessory in your life!

He finds himself by the typewriter, which he sweeps off the bridge table, sending it crashing and the papers flying off.

MAX   ...and I'm tired of pretending to write this dumb book about my maverick days in those great early years of television! Every executive fired from a network in the last twenty years has written this dumb book about the great early days of television! Nobody wants another dumb book about the great goddam early days of television!

DIANA   Terrific, Max, terrific. Maybe you can start a whole new career as an actor.

For a moment, it looks as if Max will slug her. Then he deflates.

MAX   It's the truth. After six months of living with you, I'm turning into one of your scripts. But this isn't a script, Diana. There's some real actual life going on here. I went to visit my wife today, because she's in a state of depression—so depressed my daughter flew in from Seattle to be with her. And I feel lousy about that. I feel lousy about the pain I've caused my wife and kids. I feel guilty and conscience-stricken and all those things you think sentimental but which my generation called simple human decency. And I miss my home, because I'm beginning to get scared shitless. It's all suddenly closer to the end than to the beginning, and death is suddenly a perceptible thing to me, with definable features. You've got a man going through primal doubts, Diana, and you've got to cope with it. Because I'm not some guy discussing male menopause on the Barbara Walters show. I'm the man you presumably love. I live right here. I'm part of your life. I'm real. You can't switch to another station.

DIANA   Well, what exactly is it you want me to do?

MAX   I just want you to love me, Diana. I just want you to love me, primal doubts and all. You understand that, don't you?

For one brief moment, you could almost believe she does understand. They lock eyes, and hers threaten to well with tears. There are tears in Max's eyes.

DIANA *(small voice)* I don't know how to do that.

Then the phone shatters them, and Diana promptly turns to answer it.

DIANA *(matter-of-factly)* I'll be with you in a minute, Max.

He sighs, the inchoate moment of love evanesced.

NARRATOR *(off-screen)* By the first week in July, "The Howard Beale Show" was down eleven points. Hysteria swept through the network.

DIANA'S OFFICE. MONDAY, JULY 7, 2:30 P.M.

In a wide-eyed panic, Laureen Hobbs rages all over Diana's office, as the phone RINGS and Diana answers it.

DIANA Walter, can we lay him off? Put him on vacation?

LAUREEN *(in a raging panic)* He's a plague! He's smallpox! He's typhoid! I don't want to follow his goddam show! I want out of that eight o'clock spot! I got enough troubles without Howard Beale for a lead-in. You guys have scheduled me up against Tony Orlando and Dawn! NBC's got "Little House on the Prairie!" ABC's got that Bionic woman! You got to help me out! You got to do something about Howard Beale! Get rid of the plague! Get him off the air! Do something! Do anything!

DIANA *(hanging up and yelling back)* We're trying to find a replacement for him! *(She's already out of her office as she speaks.)* I'm going down to look at audition tapes right now!

NINTH FLOOR SCREENING ROOM.

CLOSE-UP of an imposing MOSAIC FIGURE, fully bearded. He turns out to be wearing ankle-length black robes and thonged sandals, standing on a lonely mountain spur inveighing against the idolatries of the world.

PULL BACK to show the screening room half-filled with network and pro-

gramming executives. Diana is there with her top assistants—Barbara Schlesinger and Tommy Pellegrino. Frank Hackett, Nelson Chaney, Herb Thackeray, Joe Donnelly and Harry Hunter are also there.

The MOSAIC FIGURE on the console rants until otherwise indicated.

MOSAIC FIGURE And I opened the Sixth Seal, and man! I tell you, I saw it! It was heavy, baby! I saw the earthquake! And I saw the moon became like blood! And every mountain and island was moved from its place! And what in hell am I talking about! Am I talking about some Sixth Seal that was opened two thousand years ago? No! That Sixth Seal is open now! And the bottomless pit is here. And the beast that ascends is ascending! I'm talking about nuclear warheads! That's what I'm talking about! I'm talking about polluting the streams and the rivers! I'm talking aerosol cans and the mess we're making out of the ionosphere! This is now! This ain't two thousand years ago! And I ain't Saint John the Divine! But I have seen the Revelation! And I opened the Seven Seals! And I'm tell you, you boys better get cool!

DIANA *(suddenly standing into the shaft of light from the projector)* No, damn it. If we wanted hellfire, we'd get Billy Graham. We don't want faith-healers, tent-show evangelists or Oberammergau passion-players. What about that terrific new messiah ABC was supposed to have signed up as our competition?

PELLEGRINO *(indicating the monitor)* That's him.

DIANA That's him?

PELLEGRINO Yeah.

DIANA Jesus, turn him off.

The monitor screen goes black.

PELLEGRINO I've got three more, but you've already seen the best ones. I've got a guru from Spokane and two more hellfires who see visions of the Virgin Mary.

Diana sinks down in a chair and turns to Hackett in the row behind her.

DIANA We're not going to find a replacement for Howard Beale, so let's stop kidding ourselves. Fully fledged messiahs don't come in bunches. We either go with Howard or we go without him. My reports say we'll do better without him. It would be disaster to let this situation go on even another week. By then, he'll be down sixteen points and the trend irreversible, if it isn't already. I think we should fire Howard.

HACKETT Arthur Jensen has taken a strong personal interest in "The Howard Beale Show." *(sighs gloomily, to the room at large)* I'm having dinner with him tonight. Let me take another crack at Jensen and then let's meet in my office at ten o'clock tonight. Diana, give me copies of all your audience research reports. I may need them for Jensen. Is ten o'clock convenient for everyone?

Apparently it is.

LANDING OUTSIDE DIANA'S APARTMENT. 8:00 P.M.

Diana lets herself into her apartment.

DIANA'S APARTMENT FOYER.

She moves through the shadows to...

THE LIVING ROOM.

Max has fallen asleep in a chair, his newspaper in his lap. His mouth is a bit agape and he wheezes slightly, appearing, in the stark light of the lamp, to be an old man. Diana regards him with distaste. She slips off her jacket and goes to...

THE BEDROOM.

All the lights are on. Diana, scrubbed and robed, packs Max's things. A large valise lies open on the bed, and Diana is fetching Max's suits from the closet, folding and packing them. Max appears in his rumpled shirtsleeves in the doorway. She senses him there, glances, but continues with her packing.

DIANA I think the time has come, Max, to re-evaluate our relationship.

MAX So I see.

DIANA I don't like the way this script of ours is turning out. It's turning into a seedy little drama. Middle-aged man leaves wife and family for young heartless woman, goes to pot. *The Blue Angel* with Marlene Dietrich and Emil Jannings. I don't like it.

MAX So you're going to cancel the show.

DIANA Right.

MAX Listen, I'll do that.

He takes over the packing. She sits in a bedroom chair.

DIANA The simple fact is you're a family man, Max. You like a home and kids, and that's beautiful. But I'm incapable of any such commitment. All you'll get from me is another couple of months of intermittent sex and recriminations and ugly little scenes like the one we had last night. I'm sorry for all those vicious things I said to you last night. You're not the worst fuck I've ever had. Believe me, I've had worse. And you don't puff and snorkle and make death-like rattles. As a matter of fact, you're rather serene in the sack.

Max, who had gone into the bathroom for his toiletries, comes out with them, and stands, regarding Diana.

MAX Why do women always think the most savage thing they can say to a man is to impugn his cocksmanship?

DIANA I'm sorry I impugned your cocksmanship.

MAX I stopped comparing genitals back in the schoolyard.

DOWNSTAIRS FOYER.

Max is calmly pulling things from the front coat closet. Diana descends the staircase in her robe.

DIANA   You're being docile as hell about this.

MAX   Hell, Diana, I knew it was over between us weeks ago.

DIANA   Will you go back to your wife?

MAX   I'll try, but I don't think she'll jump at it. I'll manage. I always have, always will. I'm more concerned about you. Once I go, you'll be back in the eye of your own desolate terrors. You're not the boozer type, so I figure a year, maybe two before you crack up or jump out your fourteenth floor office window.

DIANA   Stop selling, Max. I don't need you.

She exits out into...

THE LIVING ROOM.

...and across that to...

THE KITCHEN.

...where a kettle is steaming. She fetches a cup and saucer from the cupboard and would make some instant coffee, but she is overtaken by a curious little spasm. Her hand holding the cup and saucer is shaking so much she has to put them down. With visible effort, she pulls herself together. She moves out of the kitchen into..

THE LIVING ROOM.

...where she stands in the middle of the room and shouts at Max through the open bedroom doorway.

DIANA *(cries out)* I don't want your pain! I don't want your menopausal decay and death! I don't need you, Max.

MAX You need me badly. I'm your last contact with human reality. I love you and that painful, decaying love is the only thing between you and the shrieking nothingness you live the rest of the day!

He slams the valise shut.

DIANA Then don't leave me!

MAX It's too late, Diana. There's nothing left in you that I can live with. You're one of Howard's humanoids, and if I stay with you, I'll be destroyed! Like Howard Beale was destroyed. Like Laureen Hobbs was destroyed. Like everything you and the whole institution of television touch gets destroyed. You are television incarnate, Diana, indifferent to suffering, insensitive to joy. All of life is reduced to the common rubble of banality. War, murder, death are all the same to you as bottles of beer. The daily business of life is a corrupt comedy. You even shatter the sensations of time and space into split seconds and instant replays. You are madness, Diana, virulent madness, and everything you touch dies with you. Well, not me! Not while I can still feel pleasure and pain and love! Oh, hell, Diana, it's over with us. I'm not sure it ever really happened, but I know it's over.

He turns back to his valise and buckles it. Diana sits on a chair. A moment later, Max comes out of the bedroom, lugging a raincoat and his valise. He lugs his way across the living room, then pauses for a moment.

MAX It's a happy ending, Diana. Wayward husband comes to his senses, returns to his wife with whom he has built a long and sustaining love. Heartless young woman left alone in her arctic desolation. Music up with a swell. Final commercial. And here are a few scenes from next week's show.

He disappears down the foyer. The CLICK of the front door opening is followed by the CLACK of the door closing. Diana pulls her shower robe around her, alone in her arctic desolation.

UBS 20TH FLOOR, LOBBY/LOUNGE/CORRIDOR. 10:15 P.M.

A solemn Frank Hackett in blue suit walks down the long, hushed corridor to the large double doors of his office. Nelson Chaney is waiting for him.

CHANEY How'd it go?

Hackett sighs, enters...

SECRETARY'S OFFICE.

...where Herb Thackeray and Joe Donnelly are lounging. Everybody follows Hackett into...

HACKETT'S OFFICE (ONCE EDWARD RUDDY'S OFFICE).

The crepuscular grandeur of Manhattan glitters in the nighttime below. Waiting on the sofas inside are Walter Amundsen and Diana. Hackett sits behind his desk. The others find places around the room.

HACKETT Mr. Jensen was unhappy at the idea of taking Howard Beale off the air. Mr. Jensen thinks Howard Beale is bringing a very important message to the American people, so he wants Howard Beale on the air. And he wants him kept on.

Nobody has anything to say to this.

HACKETT Mr. Jensen feels we are being too catastrophic in our thinking. I argued that television was a volatile industry in which success and failure were determined week by week. Mr. Jensen said he did not like volatile industries and suggested with a certain sinister silkiness that volatility in business usually reflected bad management. He didn't really care if Howard Beale was the number one show in television or the fiftieth. He didn't really care if the Beale show lost money. The network should be stabilized so that it can carry a losing show and still maintain an overall profit. Mr. Jensen has an important message he wants conveyed to the American people, and Howard Beale is conveying it. He wants Howard Beale on the air, and he wants him kept on. I would describe his position on this as inflexible. Where does that put us, Diana?

DIANA *(taking papers out of her attaché case)* That puts us in the shithouse, that's where that puts us. *(holds up a sheaf of papers)* Do you want me to go through this?

HACKETT Yes.

DIANA The Beale show Q score is down to thirty-three. Most of this loss occurred in the child and teen and eighteen-thirty-four categories, which were our core markets. It is the A.R. department's carefully considered judgment—and mine—that if we get rid of Beale, we should be able to maintain a very respectable Nielsen in the high twenties. The other segments on the Beale show—Sybil the Soothsayer, Jim Webbing, the Vox Populi—have all developed their own audiences. Our A.R. reports show without exception that it is Howard Beale that's the destructive force here. Minimally, we are talking about a ten point differential in shares. I think Joe ought to spell it out for us. Joe?

DONNELLY A twenty-eight share is eighty-thousand dollar minutes, and I think we could sell complete positions on the whole. As a matter of fact, we're just getting into the pre-Christmas gift-sellers, and I'll tell you the agencies are coming back to me with four dollar CPMs. If that's any indication, we're talking a forty, forty-five million dollar loss in annual revenues.

THACKERAY You guys want to hear all the flak I'm getting from the affiliates?

HACKETT We know all about it, Herb.

AMUNDSEN And you would describe Mr. Jensen's position on Beale as inflexible?

HACKETT Intractable and adamantine.

CHANEY So what're we going to do about this Beale son of a bitch?

A sadness settles over the top management of UBS-TV—a reluctant silence.

HACKETT *(sighs)* I suppose we'll have to kill him.

Another long, contemplative silence.

HACKETT I don't suppose you have any ideas on that, Diana?

DIANA Well, what would you fellows say to an assassination?

UBS BUILDING LOBBY. A FEW DAYS LATER, 6:00 P.M.

Lines of PEOPLE, bustling and crowding, roped four abreast as they wait to get into "The Howard Beale Show," chat occasionally with uniformed USHERS. VOICES of the network executives just interrupted CONTINUE.

DIANA *(off-screen)* ...I think I can get the Mao Tse Tung people to kill Beale for us. As one of their programs. In fact, it'll make a hell of a kick-off show for the season. We're facing heavy opposition from the other networks on Wednesday nights, and "The Mao Tse Tung Hour" could use a sensational show for an opener. The whole thing would be done right on camera in the studio. We ought to get a fantastic look-in audience with the assassination of Howard Beale as our opening show.

UBS LOBBY, ELEVATOR AREA.

The waiting, hopeful AUDIENCE is herded into elevators. The VOICES of the executive meeting continue.

AMUNDSEN *(off-screen)* Well, if Beale dies, what would be our continuing obligation to the Beale corporation? I know our contract with Beale contains a buy-out clause triggered by his death or incapacity.

UBS BUILDING, FOURTH FLOOR.

As the elevator unloads the AUDIENCE into the carpeted corridors, they pass a large wall of photographs of TV stars, glassed-in control rooms, and showpieces of electronic glory. The VOICES continue.

HACKETT *(off-screen)* There must be a formula for the computation of a purchase price.

AMUNDSEN *(off-screen)* Offhand, I think it was based on a multiple of 1975 earnings with the base period in 1975. I think it was fifty percent of salary plus twenty-five percent of the first year's profits...

HACKETT'S OFFICE.

The meeting is still going on.

AMUNDSEN ...multiplied by the unexpired portion of the contract. I don't think the show has any substantial syndication value, would you say, Diana?

DIANA Syndication profits are minimal.

THE BEALE SHOW STUDIO AND AUDIENCE AREA.

SPECTATORS fill up the auditorium. On the studio floor, the CREW is setting cameras, checking booms. The stage curtain is down. The VOICES from the meeting continue.

CHANEY *(off-screen)* We're talking about a capital crime here, so the network can't be implicated.

AMUNDSEN *(off-screen, chuckling)* I hope you don't have any hidden tape machines in this office, Frank.

THE BEALE SHOW STUDIO.

It's SHOWTIME. The stage footlights are on, the AUDIENCE is warmed up and expectant. The big wall CLOCK shows 6:29, clicks to 6:30. The ANNOUNCER strides out from the wings and bellows.

ANNOUNCER Ladies and gentlemen, let's hear it! How do you feel?

REVERSE ANGLE of the AUDIENCE. SPOT the GREAT AHMED KHAN and some of his band happily joining in the communal response.

AUDIENCE AND THE KHAN We're mad as hell, and we're not going to take this anymore!

ANNOUNCER Ladies and gentlemen! The Network News Hour! With Sybil the Soothsayer, Jim Webbing and his It's-the-Emmes-Truth Department, Miss Mata Hari, tonight another segment of Vox Populi, and starring...

MUSIC: A FLOURISH OF DRUMS.

ANNOUNCER ...the mad prophet of the airways, Howard Beale!

MUSIC: A full symphony orchestra soars into an imperial CRESCENDO.

The HOUSELIGHTS go to black. The curtain slowly rises. The bare stage, stained glass window, celestial shaft of light behind Howard Beale, in his black suit and tie, striding on to bask in the SPOTLIGHT. APPLAUSE UP.

HACKETT'S OFFICE.

The meeting continues on.

HACKETT Well, the issue is: shall we kill Howard Beale or not? I'd like to hear some more opinions on that.

DIANA I don't see we have any option, Frank. Let's kill the son of a bitch.

"THE HOWARD BEALE SHOW" STUDIO SET.

The applause for Howard Beale subsides. HUSH—suddenly, the HUSH is shattered by a HORRENDOUS ENFILADE of GUNFIRE. An embroidery of red bullet holes perforate Howard's shirt and jacket, and we might even see the impact of a head wound as he pitches backwards dead.

A BANK OF FOUR COLOR TELEVISION MONITORS.

It is 7:14 P.M., Wednesday, July 9, 1976, and we are watching the network news programs on CBS, NBC, ABC and UBS-TV. The AUDIO is ON: headshots of Walter Cronkite, John Chancellor, Howard K. Smith, Harry Reasoner, and Jack Snowden substituting for Howard Beale interspersed with tapes of the horrible happening at UBS the day before, flit and flicker across the four television screens. Television continues relentlessly on.

NARRATOR   *(off-screen)*   This was the story of Howard Beale who was the network news anchorman on UBS-TV, the first known instance of a man being killed because he had lousy ratings.

THE END

ALTERED STATES

1980

Written for the Screen by
PADDY CHAYEFSKY
as Sidney Aaron
from the novel Altered States *by*
PADDY CHAYEFSKY

Executive Producer, **DANIEL MELNICK**

Produced by **HOWARD GOTTFRIED**

Directed by **KEN RUSSELL**

CAST CREDITS

EDDIE JESSUP	William Hurt
EMILY JESSUP	Blair Brown
ARTHUR ROSENBERG	Bob Balaban
MASON PARRISH	Charles Haid
ECCHEVERRIA	Thaao Penghlis
PRIMAL MAN	Miguel Godreau
SYLVIA ROSENBERG	Dori Brenner
HOBART	Peter Brandon
THE BRUJO	Charles White Eagle
MARGARET JESSUP	Drew Barrymore
GRACE JESSUP	Megan Jeffers
HECTOR ORTEGO	Jack Murdock
OBISPO	Frank McCarthy
SCHIZOPHRENIC PATIENT	Deborah Baltzell
YOUNG ROSENBERG	Evan Richards
ENDOCRINOLOGY FELLOW	Hap Lawrence
MEDICAL TECHNICIAN	John Walter Davis
PARRISH'S GIRL	Cynthia Burr
ECCHEVERRIA'S GIRL	Susan Bredhoff
X-RAY TECHNICIAN	John Larroquette
DR. WISSENSCHAFT	George Gaynes
YOUNG MEDICAL STUDENT	Ora Rubinstein
CHARLIE THOMAS	Paul Larson
MINGUS	Eric Forst
DR. ANTONINI	Adriana Shaw
GRADUATE STUDENT	Martin Fiscoe
VERONICA	Olivia Michelle
STUNTMAN	M. James Arnett

FADE IN...

WIDE ANGLE SHOT of a sound-attenuated room with blue-steel walls. Because the lighting is subdued, most of the room is in shadows. Dominating it—in the very center—is a large, covered tank with a sacrificial, sinister appearance. The CAMERA stares at it.

NARRATOR The tank itself was unusual in that it was vertical and looked like an old boiler. Inside the tank, the subject wore a glass bubble, and you would have thought the whole contraption uncomfortable to say the least. It was however effective.

From ANOTHER ANGLE, our eyes grow accustomed to the dim lighting. We notice a few valves sticking out of the tank, cables and hoses trailing across the floor.

NARRATOR Of the twenty-three students tested, only two found it unpleasant. Some even called it exhilarating. A number of students hallucinated.

INSIDE THE TANK ITSELF.

The whitish form of a naked MAN can be distinguished, floating in the darkness, just below the surface of the inky water, like a huge dead fish with its belly up.

CLOSE-UP on the Man shows a white mask of a face, eyes closed, an austere Calvinist face, although a young man, twenty-eight years old. We may notice eight EEG leads issuing out of his scalp.

NARRATOR The others reported experiences ranging from pleasant to exhilarating.

The SCREEN suddenly goes utterly BLACK.

IMAGES flicker across the BLACK SCREEN, a sudden narrow band of color, mud-brown, much too brief to identify beyond its happening.

NARRATOR   Dr. Jessup found the encephalographic evidence especially interesting, and one Saturday afternoon in 1967, he decided to try the experience for himself.

CREDITS AND TITLE MOVE HORIZONTALLY ACROSS SCREEN:

ALTERED STATES

For purposes of identification: CLOSE-UP of JESSUP's monastic face again.

NARRATOR   Within minutes after the activating experience, well-organized alpha waves of forty to fifty micro-volts, eleven to twelve seconds, appeared in all regions.

Again, a fleeting band of IMAGERY, a broader BAND, lasts just long enough for us to see that the grains in the wooden interior walls behind the black aluminum interior lining of the tank are SINUATING, as if alive.

NARRATOR   After fifteen minutes, there was an increase in the alpha amplitude, as much as thirty to seventy micro-volts, predominantly in the frontal and central regions.

The SCREEN suddenly takes on a GRAY sheen, and just as abruptly goes BLACK.

NARRATOR   At the half hour mark, rhythmical waves of seven to eight seconds appeared, and then, suddenly...

ANOTHER FLEETING IMAGE: too quick to be really distinguishable, a vivid, baked-orange FLASH with something RED and WHITE, on-screen just long enough to recognize some kind of animal in the white.

NARRATOR   ...rhythmical theta trains, six to seven seconds, seventy to one hundred micro-volts. This EEG pattern was startling similar to those of Zen priests in zazen.

The IMAGES come with increasing frequency:

IMAGE —*A stunted, dwarfed FIG TREE, shedding its fruit—*

IMAGE —*A rocky TERRAIN, the barren Judean hills—*

IMAGE —*The ANIMAL we briefly saw, now recognizable as a white lamb, with seven eyes and seven horns. Its throat is slashed. It is dripping blood—*

IMAGE —*The entire SCREEN is suddenly WHITE, radiant, near-to-blinding—*

IMAGE —*A sudden blare of the organ, CATHEDRAL MUSIC, a snatch of Bach. A second later silence—*

IMAGE —*A twisted biblical street, empty, crooked, narrow, cobbled, twisting between the pitted white walls of small stone buildings—*

IMAGE —*The SCREEN is utterly BLACK again—*

IMAGE —*Jessup's BREATHING—*

IMAGE —*A fluttering image of a GREEN VERONICA, one of those religious handkerchiefs painted with the face of Christ, a chalk-white face of an anguished Christ with little red kewpie doll spots on his cheeks, a crown of thorns on his brow—*

IMAGE —*A surreal landscape, an endless stretch of brilliantly white beach—*

IMAGE —*The sacrificial WHITE LAMB again, this time lying on a rude stone altar. A curved KNIFE, held in a white hand, comes slashing down and cuts the lamb's throat. A BURST OF BLOOD—*

IMAGE —*A MAN dying on a white hospital bed in a lemon-colored hospital room—*

IMAGE —*A CLOSER VIEW of the man's FACE, a wax mask. A bubble of air forms on his lips which barely move; he is trying to say something. It's inaudible—*

IMAGE —*The GREEN VERONICA with the white Christ-face on it—*

IMAGE —*Beads of red BLOOD dripping against a white SCREEN—*

IMAGE —*A hailstorm of HAIL and BLOOD—*

IMAGE —*The SCREEN is BLACK again, the blackness of space. A humming, droning SOUND, resonating, getting louder, the drone of primal energy. A PINSPOT of twinkling light, a distant star it would seem moving toward us. Then we recognize it isn't a star, but a black bird. It seems to have a human face, the face of a suffering saint, an agonized, martyr's face, complete with halo. The bird is Ba, the eternal soul of Pharaonic Egypt. The face is St. Sebastian's. It veers in its flight and comes swooping horribly at us, filling the screen with its enormous black wings—*

IMAGE —*The rude stone altar with the sacrificial white LAMB. Blood drips from its slashed throat. PAN DOWN the altar to the ground where a large pool of blood has formed. A YOUNG WOMAN kneels at the edge of the pool, her back to us. She is naked and washing a white biblical robe in the pool of blood. She becomes aware that she is being watched. She looks over her shoulder at us. She is exquisitely beautiful. She stands, faces us, a striking white young woman holding her robe, which, despite its bathing in blood, is white and pure. PAN UP the altar to the sacrificial lamb lying atop it. Its throat is still cut, its blood still dripping, but its face is now the face of Christ that was on the green Veronica, the chalk-white face with the kewpie doll spots on its cheeks and crown of thorns on its head—*

IMAGE —*Total, silent BLACKNESS. Suddenly, an EXPLOSION, a shattering flash of brilliant whiteness fills the SCREEN. A high-pitched SCREAMING DRONE of energy. Waves of different colors pulsate and throb across the SCREEN. One such wave bends, wrinkles, pinches up, and the first particle of matter is created. The SCREEN is instantly filled with innumerable FLASHES, as the most primitive bits of matter smash and whirl maniacally. Flares of collision. The blinding luminosity of an earlier Universe fades into the soft glow of a cooling cloud of primordial hydrogen—*

IMAGE —*A small room with bare walls. Jessup and the beautiful Young Woman in a momentary fever of sexuality. He has seized her from behind.*

His hands clutch her breasts. He ravishes her neck with kisses and biting. She has thrown her head back, her neck arched in voluptuous pleasure—

IMAGE —A quick series of flickering images as Jessup experiences an ontological demuration: Jessup as an embryo of eight months, then as of two weeks, then a zygote, then as a single original cell; and then back up again until, with a SCREAM, Jessup re-experiences the moment of his birth, his expulsion from his mother's uterus, gasping, suffocating, screaming—

IMAGE —The small room with bare walls. A BED. On the bed, Jessup and the Young Woman, naked in the throes of exuberant intercourse. Jessup plunging, thrusting. Jessup's sweating face, his eyes wide open, his mouth agape, from the shattering metaphysicality of this experience. Beneath him, the Young Woman's white body twists, responds, her legs lock around Jessup's waist. Her head twists this way and that. Suddenly, we notice her face as the face of Christ on the handkerchief, chalk-white with red spots on her cheeks and thorns crowning her head. CAMERA MOVES IN on the Christ-face. The SOUND of Jessup's BREATHING, the short, staccato panting of a man on the verge of orgasm—

We are back inside the tank. Jessup's white mask of a face, eyes closed, cushioned in the BLACKNESS of the interior of the tank. OVER this, Jessup's disembodied sexual PANTING continues, rising to crescendo. At which point, his body suddenly thrashes; his legs kick and splash the black water on which he floats. The white mask of a face remains serene and unchanged. Suddenly, everything is silent again, silent and black, except for Jessup's white, sleeping face. Slowly, his eyes open...

ISOLATION TANK ROOM. DAY.

WIDE ANGLE SHOT of the room, the black tank isolated in the middle, shrouded in shadows.

JESSUP Arthur...Arthur!

ROSENBERG You want me to come in and get you out?

JESSUP Yeah. I want to get a look at those EEG traces.

Rosenberg gets up from his chair in the Observation Room and goes into the room containing the tank, climbing up above the tank in order to open up the tube in which his colleague Jessup has been floating.

ROSENBERG How do you feel?

JESSUP Not bad. I hallucinated like a son of a bitch. A variety of dream states, mystical states, a lot of religious allegory, mostly out of Revelation.

ROSENBERG You were in there close to five hours.

JESSUP It felt like an hour.

ROSENBERG I'd like to try that myself sometime.

JESSUP You should, you'll like it.

Trousered but still toweling himself, Jessup heads for the door and goes into...

THE MONITORING ROOM. DAY.

The small room is compactly fitted out with an oscillator and various recording machines, most noticeably a 16 styli EEG machine. Five hours of polygraph paper have piled into the cardboard bin at its side. Jessup rummages about in the bin for the beginning of the sheet, puts on a pair of wire-rimmed glasses, and studies the tracings.

JESSUP *(reading)* Did we have any communication?

ROSENBERG *(from the doorway)* Oh, sure, I kept checking you out like you told me to.

JESSUP How'd I respond?

ROSENBERG Very orderly. At one point, you were crying.

JESSUP You mean, really crying?

ROSENBERG You were sobbing, you had tears on your face. I asked you what was going on. You said you were re-experiencing your father's death.

JESSUP Did you make notes?

ROSENBERG *(indicating a loose-leaf notebook)* It's all there.

JESSUP I'd like to do this again next week, Arthur. Could you make it again next week?

YORK AVENUE, MEDICAL BUILDING. LATE AFTERNOON.

ROSENBERG What're we looking for?

JESSUP Hell, I don't know. Yet. There's really very little literature on this, or research. There's some good people in the field—Tart, Ornstein, Deikman—but most of it is radical-hip stuff, drug-culture apologias. Obviously, the first thing to do is set up some sensible methodology, see if we can't study the experiences under controlled laboratory conditions. It won't interfere with the work we're doing with Hobart.

ROSENBERG What're we getting into? Sensory-deprivation? Isolation studies? I mean, where will we be going with this tank stuff?

JESSUP We're not writing up a grant, Arthur. Strictly bootlegging just for kicks. I figure as long as we've got the use of this tank, let's play around with it, let's find out where it takes us. This is fascinating stuff, Arthur, and I think we ought to get into it.

ROSENBERG APARTMENT. SUNDAY, DAY.

Some dozen young Sixties intellectuals in denim and jeans to subdued Janis Joplin pass joints around. All are in their late twenties or early thirties, except for a gray-haired sculptress, an aggressive fifty. There is a geneticist with his wife, a biochemist with her husband, a couple clinical psychiatrists and a great deal of movement in and out of the four small rooms that comprise the Rosenberg apartment in a battered old building on West End Avenue around 95th Street.

ROSENBERG APARTMENT HALLWAY.

Arthur Rosenberg and ALAN HOBART, a clinical psychiatrist in his early thirties, are sharing a joint with EMILY FULBRIGHT, a pretty, confident young woman in jeans who doesn't look her twenty-four years. She is a physical anthropologist and our heroine. The background is full of general party activity.

ROSENBERG ...I didn't even know they had one of those isolation tanks at New York Hospital.

HOBART   Must be some guys in the psychology department doing sensory-deprivation studies. What's Jessup doing with it?

ROSENBERG   You got me. He's been taking students out of his classes and testing them. He's been doing this for three, four months, did you know he was into this kind of stuff?

HOBART   Not till you just told me.

The doorbell RINGS, and SYLVIA ROSENBERG, seven months pregnant, comes out of the kitchen into the hallway, making for the door and calling to her husband.

SYLVIA   I'll get it, honey.

ROSENBERG   *(who had started for the door, returning to Emily and Hobart)* He's the last guy in the world I figured to be screwing around with anything as flaky as altered states of consciousness.

HOBART   Well, let's face it, Jessup is pretty flaky himself.

ACROSS THEM and DOWN the hallway to the front door, where Sylvia Rosenberg is admitting Jessup with much hugging and affection.

ROSENBERG *(to Emily)* That's him.

Emily is clearly interested. She appraises him openly from her end of the hallway, liking the bespectacled, fine-featured face. Sylvia Rosenberg herds Jessup into the living room.

HALLWAY NEAR LIVING ROOM. DAY.

Twenty minutes later, Emily comes out of the kitchen, crosses into...

THE LIVING ROOM.

Emily surveys the room. Jimi Hendrix is on the STEREO. The room has not too much furniture: an overstuffed chair on which Sylvia is heavily emplanted, and a sofa where Jessup is seated. At the other end of the couch, the sculptress is making a play for the geneticist's wife. There is an open space on the couch next to Jessup, and Emily heads for it. The journey through the people lounging on Levantine cushions on the floor or perched on the enormous round coffee table is not easy.

Jessup seems distracted by his own thoughts. A joint is being passed, and when it reaches Jessup, he declines but passes it along to the biochemist on a wooden folding chair at his elbow. Emily slides into the seat beside him.

EMILY Arthur says you're very shy, and he wants me to draw you out.

JESSUP Draw me out? Doesn't sound like Arthur.

EMILY Well, what he actually said was you were a high-handed, arrogant prick, a little nuts but brilliant, and that if I ever got you talking, I would find you fascinating.

JESSUP That sounds more like Arthur.

EMILY   He says you're doing some work with him and Alan Hobart at Payne-Whitney.

JESSUP   Yes.

EMILY   What sort of work?

JESSUP   Toxic metabolite stuff.

She waits for more; he presses on with little enthusiasm.

JESSUP   We're more or less replicating Heath's and Friedhof's strategies, trying to find maverick substances specific to schizophrenia. I think we're chasing our tails. What do you do?

EMILY   I'm a physical anthropologist. I'm sweating out my dissertation.

JESSUP   Where?

EMILY   Columbia.

JESSUP   Holloway and that bunch?

EMILY   Yes.

JESSUP   You're kind of young for a Ph.D., aren't you?

EMILY   I'm twenty-four.

JESSUP   That's still pretty good. I didn't get my Ph.D. until I was twenty-five, and I'm supposed to be a whiz kid.

EMILY   I'm a whiz kid too.

JESSUP   Where's Arthur? Where's the mustard?

Emily points out the mustard.

JESSUP Anthropology seems to attract good-looking women.

EMILY So you don't think schizophrenia can be reduced to a single etiological agent?

JESSUP I'm not even sure it's a disease.

EMILY You think man is simply in another state of consciousness?

JESSUP There's a body of evidence to support that.

EMILY You don't like to talk about your work, do you?

They smile agreeably at each other and have obviously hit it off.

COLUMBIA UNIVERSITY CAMPUS. HOURS LATER. DUSK.

Emily and Jessup cross campus, engrossed in each other.

JESSUP I've always been interested in interior experiences, especially the religious experience. The one reason I'm working with schizophrenics now is because the religious experience is so significant in schizophrenia. ...And there's just so much work you can do with animals. I worked with monkeys for two years. But monkeys can't tell you what's going on in their consciousness. You need human beings for that. And you're not allowed to ablate human beings, and you can't stick electrodes in their skulls. So I have to use some kind of trance-inducing technique, and the isolation tank seemed the least risky.

Their eyes catch. There is clearly something alive between them.

JESSUP Listen, I'd like to go home with you tonight, will that be all right with you?

EMILY I have a roommate, we'll be confined to the living room couch.

JESSUP What's wrong with the living room couch?

EMILY You tend to slip off a lot.

JESSUP I'm sure we'll manage.

EMILY I'm sure we will.

JESSUP So whenever you want to go there, you let me know.

EMILY How about right now?

EMILY'S FLAT, LIVING ROOM. NIGHT.

Two white bodies thrashing around on the dark sofa to culmination. Emily thrusts up, burying her face in Jessup's shoulder to avoid crying out. His moonlit back beaded with sweat. She subsides onto the sofa, opens her eyes.

HER P.O.V.: Jessup's transfixed face. His eyes are wide, rigidly staring into space, entranced.

EMILY What are you thinking about?

At first, he doesn't seem to hear her. Then the entranced look dissipates.

JESSUP God, Jesus, crucifixions.

He rolls off her onto the floor, his back against her legs.

EMILY Well, just so long as it wasn't another woman.

Nevertheless, a curious moment and an odd thing to say. She tries to see his face in the darkness, finally slips off the sofa and joins him on the floor leaning back.

EMILY As a rule, do you usually think about Christ and crucifixions under sexual stress?

JESSUP *(considers his answer for a moment)* When I was nine years old, I used to see visions, visions of saints and angels, even Christ himself. I saw him with the eyes of faith, hanging on the cross, his vesture dipped in blood. I had a whole cult that grew up around me. People came from all over to see this kid who had visions of Christ. I got mixed up with a little Pentacostal church in South Yonkers. In the middle of services, I would suddenly become transfixed, begin to babble in voices, and I would prophesy. Of course, I don't do that anymore, not since I was sixteen.

She studies his shadowed face.

EMILY Were your parents religious?

JESSUP Anything but. My father was an aeronautical engineer, my mother a clinical psychologist.

She watches him, fascinated.

EMILY What happened? I mean, how did a little kid who saw visions of Christ turn into a physiologist teaching at the Cornell Medical College?

For the first time he looks at her, strangely but agreeably detached.

JESSUP I stopped believing. It was very dramatic. My father died a protracted and painful death of cancer. I was sixteen years old and very fond of my father. I used to race to the hospital every day after school and sit in his room doing my homework. He was very heavily sedated. The last few weeks he was in a coma. One day, I thought I heard him say something, I looked up. His lips were moving, but no sound came out. There was his yellow-waxen face on the white pillow, and his lips were moving. A little bubble formed on his lips. I got up and leaned over him, my ear an inch away from his lips. "Did you say something, Pop?" Then, I heard the word he was desperately trying to say. A soft hiss of a word. He was saying, "Terrible—terrible!" So the end was terrible, even for good people like my father. So the purpose of all our suffering was just more suffering. By dinner time, I had dispensed with God altogether. I never saw another vision. I haven't told anybody about this in ten years. I'm telling you now, because I want you to know what sort of a nut you might be getting mixed up with.

They stare at each other in the dark room.

EMILY   Arthur was right.   You are a fascinating bastard.

68TH AND YORK AVENUE. DECEMBER, 1967. DAY.

Bright and sunny. Emily, in a winter coat and jeans, flushed a cheerful red from the cold, crosses the courtyard in front of New York Hospital. She turns up a pathway to Payne-Whitney past a sign marked: Payne-Whitney Psychiatric Clinic.

PAYNE-WHITNEY CORRIDOR. DECEMBER, 1967. DAY.

Long, institutional corridor. Dr. Hobart, whom we met at the party, is now in a white coat as he brings a WOMAN PATIENT down the hall. The woman is twenty-eight years old and in ordinary street clothes but manifestly mad. She has that razor-sharp look, as she giggles and moves along with the doctor.

A stairway door opens, and Emily enters, pausing by the door to let the patient and doctor pass. They disappear into a room down the hall. Emily heads for the door just before it.

AN OBSERVATION ROOM. DAY.

Emily enters. Jessup is already there, standing before a one-way window, observing. We look into a family-therapy room, where the patient we had seen in the hall is now seated on a leather chair that can unfold into a recliner. Alan Hobart reassures the patient. We HEAR his friendly voice via a speaker on the wall.

HOBART   *(off-screen)*   You're looking really fine today, Phyllis, much less agitated than last time.   Are you feeling better?

She giggles, stares at her feet and vaguely at the floor.

As Emily joins Jessup at the window, they exchange smiles.

In the therapy room, Rosenberg, also in a long white doctor's coat, reads from the patient's records on a clipboard. A MEDICAL TECHNICIAN (a young woman, aged twenty-five) is preparing the EEG leads. They also greet the patient affably. The patient sits giggling, her head bobbing.

HOBART *(off-screen, reassuring)* We're going to do all the tests we did last time, do you remember them? Dr. Antonini is standing right here in the room with you, so there's nothing to worry about. We'll put the EEG leads on you now, if it's OK with you.

The patient responds to nothing, stares emptily at the floor. Hobart tells the technician to go ahead with the application of the leads, which she does. Rosenberg holds blood pressure equipment, as he pulls up a chair.

ROSENBERG *(off-screen)* How's it going, Phyllis?

He wraps the blood pressure cuff around her arm to take her pressure.

In the observation room, Emily and Jessup watch silently, side by side.

EMILY Well, it's settled. Metcalfe spoke to Spencer again this morning, and it's definite. The job's mine. So I'll be in Nairobi doing my postdoc work May, June and July, and, in September, I'll be teaching at Harvard.

JESSUP Terrific.

EMILY So it looks like we'll both be teaching at Harvard in September.

JESSUP Looks that way.

Unable to keep her cool any longer, Emily faces Jessup, her face aglow.

EMILY My God, Eddie, you can't get any tidier than that! We're going to be together in Boston, and I think we should get married.

JESSUP I wish you hadn't said that.

EMILY The idea had to come up sooner or later, you must've known.

JESSUP You know, of course, I'm supposed to be at least a little bit nuts.

EMILY A little bit! You're a mad monk, an unmitigated madman. So you
don't have to tell me how weird you are. I know how weird you are.
I'm the girl in your bed the last two months and even sex is a mystical
experience for you. You carry on like a flagellant, which can be very
nice, but I sometimes wonder if it's me that's being made love to. I feel
like I'm being harpooned by some raging priest in the act of receiving
God.

She would go on but VOICES issue from the loudspeaker.

HOBART *(off-screen)* ...the same?

ROSENBERG *(off-screen, rewrapping the sphygmometer)* Yeah.

Hobart makes a note in his notebook.

EMILY You're...a Faust freak, Eddie. You'd sell your soul to find the great
truth. Well, human life doesn't have great truths. We're born in
doubt, and we spend our lives persuading ourselves we're actually
alive. One of the ways we know we're alive is we love each other. Like
I love you. I can't imagine living without you. So let's get married,
and if it turns out to be a disaster, it'll be a disaster, and we'll shake
hands and say goodby.

In the therapy room, Rosenberg gives the patient a shot.

JESSUP He's giving her dimethyltryptamine. It takes effect in about
a minute, and she'll trip out for about half an hour.

*Abruptly, he leaves Emily and exits into the therapy room. Through the one-
way window, he can be seen standing over the portable EEG machine, watching the tracings. In the foreground, we see a noticeable change in the patient.*

She stops giggling and shuffling, sits stiffly, more controlled. The vaguely terrified vacuity of her expression abruptly changes to one of intense concentration, almost trance-like. Hobart is asking her his soft questions again.

HOBART *(off-screen)* Do you feel different now?

PATIENT *(startlingly response)* Yes.

HOBART Less anxious?

PATIENT Much less.

HOBART Do you have any special feelings?

PATIENT I feel like my heart is being touched by Christ.

Jessup is back again in the monitoring room. They watch Hobart draw a triangle on a slate and ask the patient to duplicate it. She manages to draw one leg of the triangle but gets stumped after that.

JESSUP There's a lot of religious delusion among acute schizophrenics. Some guys say schizophrenics are physically different from the rest of us. It's almost as if they were trying to change their physical selves to adapt to their schizophrenic image of themselves. Look we'll get married, since it's that important to you. I don't want to lose you. I'm not comfortable with women, and I'm not likely to find anyone half as remarkable as you again. I think I can make a reasonably good husband. You understand I'd rather not get married, but I'll go along with it. I don't want to lose you, you see.

EMILY I suppose that's the closest thing to a declaration of love I'll ever get out of you.

JESSUP Am I really that weird in bed?

EMILY Sometimes.

JESSUP Shall I try to change?

EMILY   No, I kind of like it.

BOSTON, PINCKNEY STREET. APRIL, 1975, SATURDAY.

Jessup is walking down Pinckney Street. Wearing neatly pressed slacks and a sleeveless sweater, he is seven years older and beginning to bald a bit. He is trundling his two-year-old DAUGHTER in a stroller with his left hand and holding a supermarket bag of groceries with his right. Hopping along behind is his five-year-old DAUGHTER. Jessup is in animated discussion with a big, fully bearded, booming bear of a man, aged thirty-eight, MASON PAR-RISH, smoking a pipe. Two young professors on a Saturday afternoon. They pause for a KID on a bicycle to wheel past them. Jessup waves to a NEIGH-BOR.

BOSTON, MYRTLE ST. APRIL, 1975, SATURDAY AFTERNOON.

Volkswagens and stationwagons are parked in front of the red-brick, ivy-covered townhouses along a pretty, tree-lined block in the Beacon Hill district. Arthur Rosenberg, also seven years older and less bohemian in a sports jacket with leather patches and a tieless shirt, is engaged in amiable conversation with his six-year-old SON. He cuffs the kid affectionately, and the boy trots back into the house they stand in front of. Rosenberg looks up the block.

ROSENBERG'S P.O.V.: Jessup and Parrish can be seen turning the corner off Revere at the end of the block. It is all too suburban for words, and Rosenberg can't help but smile. The two men are so engrossed in their conversation that they don't notice Rosenberg, until they're virtually on top of him.

ROSENBERG   If I didn't see this, I wouldn't believe it.

Jessup stops, stares.

JESSUP   My God! You weren't supposed to be here till next week! You got bald.

ROSENBERG   So did you.

They pump each other's hands.

ROSENBERG *(referring to Jessup's glasses)* Are these new?

JESSUP My God! This is sensational! *(to Parrish)* Mason, this is the Rosenberg I'm always telling you about!

PARRISH *(an ebullient good old boy from West Virginia, shakes hands)* It sure is!

JESSUP When did you get into town?

ROSENBERG About three days ago. Are these your kids?

JESSUP They are. Where's Sylvia? Is she with you?

ROSENBERG She's inside with Emily...

THE JESSUP APARTMENT, LIVING ROOM.

Sylvia Rosenberg, pregnant again, rising from the kitchen table where she's having coffee with Emily, shrieks with delight as the messy entourage enters. Sylvia tears across the living room to embrace Jessup, tears in her eyes. Everybody talks at once.

SYLVIA Oh, my God, oh my God, you look so wonderful!

JESSUP *(embracing her, notices she's pregnant)* When did this happen? Have you found a place yet?

ROSENBERG Yeah, we got a nice little place near Huntington Field.

SYLVIA Oh, my God, it's been seven years! Since we moved to San Francisco!

EMILY *(to Parrish bearing groceries into kitchen)* Arthur's going to teach at Boston U.

PARRISH So Eddie's been telling me...

The Rosenberg boy comes out of the kids' room, silently regards all this adult effusion. At that moment, the Jessup five-year-old slips into the room. Parrish, back from the kitchen, swoops her up to her shrieking delight.

SYLVIA *(releasing Jessup)* I can't believe it's been seven years since we've actually seen you people.

Rosenberg stands and beams at this jolly scene of reunion. The apartment—the ground floor, three rooms, two baths, kitchen—is a scholarly shambles. Piles of books clot the foyer and every room. Emily has set up a corner for herself in the living room, a bridge table for a desk, a typewriter barely visible among the periodicals, papers, scholarly journals, student theses, one of which flutters now onto the floor. Everybody talks at once.

ROSENBERG *(across the room to Emily)* I hear you just made Associate Professor.

EMILY Yeah, terrific!

ROSENBERG *(to Jessup)* You guys must be loaded, two professors in the family...

EMILY Listen, we've got a place in Maine you can use for the summer. I'm going to Africa again in June. Eddie'll be in Mexico.

JESSUP *(plunking himself down in a torn chair)* Listen, do you know a guy named Eccheverria, University of Mexico, says he worked with you in California?

ROSENBERG *(removing some books to sit in other chair)* Sure. A very bright young guy.

JESSUP He's here in Boston at the Botanical Museum. We'll all have to get together. I'm going back to Mexico with him in June.

ROSENBERG What's in Mexico?

JESSUP Well, Eccheverria's got this witch doctor down there, the Hinci Indians. An isolated tribe in Central Mexico, who still practice the ancient Toltec rituals, sacred mushroom ceremonies, that sort of thing. Apparently, they use some kind of hallucinatory drug that's supposed to evoke a common experience for all users.

ROSENBERG Sounds improbable.

EMILY *(enters)* Eddie, Maggie has fallen asleep on the couch. Will you take care of her?

JESSUP *(takes a beat to register)* Sure..

Jessup scoops up his two-year-old daughter sprawled on the couch.

JESSUP Did you ever get into an isolation tank since New York?

ROSENBERG No, did you?

JESSUP No, but I just found out they've got one here at the medical school.

ROSENBERG No kidding. I thought those things went out in the Sixties.

He carries the child across the living room and is followed by Rosenberg. Emily comes out of the kitchen with a tray of coffee cups and Toll House cookies. Parrish is lying on the floor pretending to be knocked cold by the Rosenberg boy and the older Jessup girl.

JESSUP *(en route carrying his kid)* I thought we did some pretty interesting stuff in that tank in New York for the couple of months we played around with it. When I come back from Mexico, maybe we'll get into it again.

ROSENBERG Why not?

Jessup disappears into the kids' bedroom. Rosenberg pauses outside the master bedroom to watch his pregnant wife in front of the mirror. This room is no more orderly than the living room. Jessup's work area is here, an honest three-drawer filing cabinet, an escritoire, a wall of bookshelves packed with texts, journals and notes in hardbound, looseleaf notebooks, neatly labeled. The rest of the room is in chaos. The double bed is unmade, and yesterday's clothing is flung over chairs or piled on the floor.

ROSENBERG *(notes to his wife)* A terrific housekeeper she's not.

Sylvia beckons him into...

THE MASTER BEDROOM.

Rosenberg joins his wife at the bureau.

SYLVIA They're getting divorced, you know.

ROSENBERG *(startled)* Who? What're you talking about?

SYLVIA I don't know if they're actually getting divorced; they're splitting up. She and the kids are moving to a furnished place in Cambridge, and that's why the place is such a mess. They're moving her stuff into storage tomorrow. Then she's going to Africa with the kids for a year, and he's going to Mexico, and, when she comes back, she's going to live in Cambridge, and he's staying here. It's him who wants the divorce, not her. Listen, I'm surprised they stayed together this long.

ROSENBERG When did all this happen?

SYLVIA She just told me five minutes ago.

Rosenberg stares at his wife, leans out into the corridor and looks toward the kids' room where Jessup can be seen gently covering his two-year-old.

ROSENBERG What happened to all those letters she kept writing us how happy they were?

SYLVIA Don't ask me. She's still crazy about him, and he's still crazy.

ROSENBERG Jesus Christ...

THE BACK CORRIDOR.

...and down that to...

THE KIDS' BEDROOM.

From the doorway, Rosenberg watches Jessup lowering the shade, darkening the room. Even in the lesser light, the room is in a packing state. Opened cardboard cartons here and there and little girls' dresses still on their hangers on beds and toys are piled haphazardly.

ROSENBERG Listen, Sylvia just told me you're getting divorced.

JESSUP Well, we're separating anyway. We probably won't get around to the divorce till next year.

ROSENBERG Look, it's none of my business, but why? You're married to one of the great women of the world, who adores you. You're obviously a devoted father. My God, if anybody's got it made, you have. You're a respected and admired figure, a full professor on the faculty of the Harvard Medical School.

JESSUP *(good-naturedly)* Oh, for God's sake, Arthur, is that how you imagine me—a respected and admired figure? A devoted father? A loving husband? Well, I've also published nearly two papers a year for the last seven years, and not a fundamental piece of work in the lot. And I don't know why you're so startled we're getting a divorce. You're the one who thought she was crazy to marry me in the first place.

ROSENBERG Well, that's true.

JESSUP Well, don't be too upset. It's an amicable separation. Nobody's mad at anyone, and the marriage itself was sufferable, as sufferable as any of the others around. I think I've played my part well. I take the kids to the zoo. I stay up with them when they're ill, I romp with them when they're well. I sit around the living rooms of other young married faculty members talking infantile masturbation, who's sucking up to the head of the department and whose tenure is hanging by a thread. Emily's quite content to go on with this life. She insists she's in love with me—whatever that is. What she means is she prefers the senseless pain we inflict on each other to the pain we would otherwise inflict on ourselves. But I'm not afraid of that solitary pain. In fact, if I don't strip myself of all this clatter and clutter and ridiculous ritual, I shall go out of my fucking mind. Does that answer your question, Arthur?

ROSENBERG What question was that?

JESSUP You asked me why I was getting divorced?

ROSENBERG Listen, it's your life. I'm sorry I even asked.

He turns to go. Jessup stands behind him by his daughter's bed, his eyes suddenly white in the gray room. The monkish, zealot cast of his face has never been more evident.

JESSUP I want to be alone again, renounce the rubbish of it all, mortify my flesh, scourge my spirit. I want to get down to the embedded rock of life. What Saint John would call the bare and barren soul.

He suddenly smiles, emerging from the room's grayness to the spill of light by the doorway where Rosenberg stands. He is honestly fond of Rosenberg and rests a hand on his friend's shoulder.

JESSUP Why don't I call Eccheverria, and we'll all go out and have dinner?

DOM'S RESTAURANT. NIGHT.

At a noisy, cheerful table, eight voluble academics gabble away, swilling their

*wine, stowing their pasta. They're all talking over each other, and we don't
need to hear anything clearly, but this is what they're saying.*

EMILY *(to Parrish's girl, a second-year med student from Mass. General)* What
differentiates man from the chimpanzee is that man needs tools for
survival and therefore evolved a cortical structure that could make use
of tools...*(to Rosenberg, who is thrusting a petition at her)* Oh, for God's
sake, Arthur, you haven't been in Boston a week, and you're already a
member of the Committee of Concerned Scientists.

ROSENBERG Just sign the damn thing, Emily.

EMILY *(signing and rattling on to Parrish's girl as she does)* A chimpanzee
might use a stick to dig into a termite hill, but he can survive as a
species without it. A baboon, whose diet is almost exclusively vege-
tarian, will take half an hour to dig up a root. It's just never occurred
to baboons they could shorten that time to five minutes if they used a
stick. Originally, man was just another savanna-living primate like the
baboon...

PARRISH *(flirting with Eccheverria's girl, a botanist from the Botanical
Museum)* Nobody really knows how memory works. Apparently, we
remember everything we sense for about fifty milliseconds. Then it
disappears or is selectively fixed in our consciousness. Now, you being
a botanist, sure as hell know puromycin can wipe out a memory, and
sympathomimetic drugs like strychnine, dextroamphetamine, et
cetera can stimulate the retention of memory. But these are all poisonous, addictive, induce convulsions, and are alien to the body. The
fact that a small chain of amino acids, ACTH four to seven, a natural
substance of the body, is instrumental in fixing memory is, I think,
particularly interesting. This, however, raises another question.
ACTH is a peptide. Its secretory rates are influenced by stress. Does
ACTH actually code learning or does it only relate to hormonal substances that formed due to stress? You really interested in this shit,
honey? Because, if you are, I'll be glad to go into it more deeply any
night this week...

ROSENBERG *(now harrassing the elegant Eccheverria with his petition)*

We scientists have a moral obligation to the public as well as to our own research. Some of those shotgun fragments could augment a bacteria's ability to produce disease. For God's sake, they're chopping up fruitflies and inserting the segments into E coli and mass-producing bacteria. We're dealing with a fistful of unknowns. We can only identify a couple of the genes. We could wipe out the planet if we don't watch out, so just sign the damn thing, Eduardo...

If we can make anything out of all this esoteric jabber, it will be Jessup's discourse to Sylvia Rosenberg, sitting at his right. Jessup, who is having a lot more wine than he usually does, is loaded and talking loudly...

JESSUP *(to Sylvia Rosenberg)* As a matter of fact, the year I spent in India was disappointing. No matter how you slice it, yoga is still a state-specific technology operating in the service of an a priori belief system, not much different from other trance-inducing techniques. What dignifies the yogic practices is that the belief system itself is not truly religious. There is no Buddhist god per se. It is the Self, the individual Mind, that contains immortality and ultimate truth...

EMILY *(interrupting her own coloquy to shout from her end of the table)* What the hell's not religious about that? You've simply replaced God with the Original Self!

JESSUP *(shouting back)* Yes, but we've localized it! At least, we know where the Self is! It's in our own minds! *(standing not too sturdily)* It's a form of human energy! Our atoms are six billion years old! We've got six billion years of memory in our minds! Hell, our hydrogen atoms are even older! *(beginning to weave a bit)* Memory is energy! It doesn't disappear! It's still in there! *(wheeling on Rosenberg, ignoring the nervous interest he's raising at other tables)* There's a physiological pathway to our earlier consciousnesses! There has to be! And I'm telling you it's in the goddam limbic system!

PARRISH *(roaring happily)* Jessup, you are a wacko!

JESSUP What's wacko about it, Mason? I'm a man in search of his true self. How archtypically American can you get? Everybody's looking for their true selves. We're all trying to fulfill ourselves, understand ourselves, get in touch with ourselves, face the reality of ourselves, explore ourselves, expand ourselves. Every since we dispensed with God, we've got nothing but our selves to explain this meaningless horror of life. Well, I think that true self, that original self, that first self is a real, mensurate, quantifiable thing, tangible and incarnate. And I'm going to find the fucker.

MEXICO, ZAPATECUS PROVINCE. JULY, 1975. DAY.

As far as the eye can see are the terrifying sierras of Central Mexico, rugged crags and violently plunging gorges, seemingly uninhabitable.

ANOTHER ANGLE ACROSS Jessup in T-shirt and khaki shorts with Eccheverria, climbing and talking. Jessup carries a Sony tape recorder on their way up the mountain. Eccheverria holds samples of leaves and roots.

JESSUP   What are their chemical properties? Are they safe?

ECCHEVERRIA   *(climbing)*   ...the mushrooms are almost certainly amanita muscaria, a very powerful psychedelic and a little dangerous. It contains some belladonna, alkaloids, atropine, scopolamine.   The sinicuiche plant is highly regarded among a number of Indian tribes. I've seen it as far north as Chihuahua. It should be especially interesting for you. The Indians say it evokes old memories, even ancient ones. The Hinchis call it the First Flower.

JESSUP   First in the sense of primordial?

ECCHEVERRIA   Yes, in the sense of the most ancient.

Jessup and Eccheverria have reached the top and THEIR P.O.V. reveals a plateau-like valley, precipitously surrounded by brutal mountains, splashes of color...

JESSUP   I'd like to try it. Do you think they'll let me join in their ritual?

ECCHEVERRIA   They seem like agreeable people.

IN THE LAND OF THE HINCHI.

*The Hinchi Indians, a tribe of pre-Aztecs, live amid the brutal barrancas of
central Mexico. Although they are descendants of the Chichimec Toltecs,
their Brujo turns out to be a Tarahumara Indian who has married into the
tribe. That helps, because he speaks a little Spanish and can communicate
with Eccheverria. Jessup and Eccheverria join up with the tribe just as they
set off on their long trek to the sacred mushroom fields. This is an expedition
lasting three weeks that winds through the colorful valleys and gorges of a
landscape filled with blue agave and yellow chaparral and that is interrupted every other night to get drunk on corn beer.*

*The Hinchi tribe, all sixty of them, cross the plateau like cotton-pickers, in
loincloths and cotton shirts and print dresses, filling burlap bags with mushrooms, branches of slender trees, leaves, petals, seed pods and white tuberous
roots, the last of which have to be dug out of the ground with bare hands.*

*They all got back to their home valley on the twelfth of July. Most of the
tribe went on a* tesguinada, *a two-day binge of corn beer while the various
powders and crumbled mushroom were stored away for a year in sealed
gourds to become sufficiently moldy.*

OUTSIDE THE BRUJO'S SHACK. DUSK.

*A SHOT or TWO showing some of the HINCHI TRIBE stretched out to
rest around their shacks and tents, swigging corn beer. Their dogs lope in and
out of view. THREE CHOSEN WOMEN, in shapeless cotton dresses,
kneel and grind roots and buds into varying degrees of fineness. In the background, the Brujo's SHACK, a ramshackle shanty with a shaky overhang
held up by two rotting pilasters.*

*The BRUJO is a shaggy old man in his late sixties, whose contact with white
civilization is evident in his shapeless gray single-breasted jacket and white
fringed prayer shawl. The fire at which he sits is actually a primitive hearth
ground. Jessup has his notebook out and is putting a fresh cassette into the
tape recorder.*

The Brujo smooths out the small blanket lying near the the fire and empties his burlap bag, item by item, spacing them with some ceremony on the blanket. First is a hunting knife, a foot in length and glistening blue in the fading light; then a soft brown leather pouch from which he extracts the ceremonial pipe, a dark reddish stem about ten inches long with a blackened bowl.

Before placing each item on the blanket, the Brujo addresses the four directions with the object, chanting in a low whine. Some of the men are biting peyote buttons and are stoned. Jessup's tape recorder WHIRS. DUSK is now descending; the valley is in heavy shadow. The last item out of the bag is a bundle of bound, white plant roots. He draws one out, splits it with his knife into a Y, humming his chant as he does. He leans to Eccheverria.

Around the fire sit Jessup and Eccheverria and FOUR ESCOGIDOS, the chosen men. ACROSS THE MEN at the fire, the fifth escogido, the man of power, the Brujo, sits in the center ready to deal with the stranger.

THE BRUJO   *(to Eccheverria)*   Quiere su amigo participar aun?

ECCHEVERRIA   He wants to know if you will want to participate.

JESSUP Yes, of course.

The old Brujo goes back to his soft chant, binding the forked ends of the split root with tendrils of a vine. Two of the Chosen Women bring a large iron pot out of the house to set it on the hearthstones. Jessup leans forward to examine the yellow sludge inside.

JESSUP Ask him what kind of an experience I can expect.

ECCHEVERRIA Qué clase de experiencia puede esperar mi amigo?

THE BRUJO Su alma regresará a la primera alma.

ECCHEVERRIA   *(to Jessup)*   Your soul will return to the First Soul.

JESSUP Ask him what this First Soul will look like.

ECCHEVERRIA Cómo es la primera alma?

THE BRUJO Es la Materia Increada.

ECCHEVERRIA *(to Jessup)* It is Unborn Stuff.

> *Jessup looks up to study the Brujo and finds himself being studied by the old man's cat-like eyes. The Brujo speaks with Eccheverria translating quickly.*

THE BRUJO Entonces, usted se lanzará en el vacio.

ECCHEVERRIA Then you will propel into the void...

THE BRUJO Usted verá una mancha...

ECCHEVERRIA You will see a spot...

THE BRUJO La mancha se convertiera en una grieta...

ECCHEVERRIA The spot will become a crack...

THE BRUJO Esta es la Grieta entre la Nada...

ECCHEVERRIA This is the Crack between the Nothing...

THE BRUJO De esta Nada saldrá su Alma Increada...

ECCHEVERRIA Out of this Nothing will come your Unborn Soul...

> *Jessup nods. The sun has disappeared. Shadows permeate the atmosphere.*

> *CUT TO VILLAGE with Jessup and ELDERS in a procession through the stone mushrooms of the landscape INTO the BRUJO'S CAVE.*

THE BRUJO Dígale que extienda la palma de la mano...

ECCHEVERRIA He wants you to hold the root. Put out your hand with your palm up.

> *Jessup edges closer and sticks his hand out, palm up. The Brujo places the*

root across the flat of Jessup's palm. Suddenly, he separates Jessup's third and fourth fingers and deftly slashes the joint with a hunting knife. Shocked, Jessup screams. He just squats, with his bleeding hand outstretched. The Brujo seizes his wrist and pulls the bleeding hand over the pot, twisting Jessup's wrist so that the root falls into the pot. He holds Jessup's hand over the pot until a few drops of blood fall into the blackness. Jessup collapses, shocked, spent and outraged.

ECCHEVERRIA *(leaning over him)* Are you all right?

Jessup nods. The Brujo and another man carry the pot to the ritual blanket. In the night, they seem like monstrous shadows. Jessup examines his bleeding hand in the darkness.

JESSUP   Jesus Christ.

ECCHEVERRIA   Are you all right?

A form looms over him. He looks up. It's the old Brujo holding out a cup of the liquid, expressionlessly. Jessup sits up, takes the cup and drinks. He gets up on his knees and then stands and EXITS THE CAVE INTO THE DARKNESS. Behind him, he can hear the Brujo and Eccheverria mumbling.

THE BRUJO   *(voice-over)* Esta funcionando la grabadora? Esta fumando tres partes de polvo de honguitos con una parte de polvo de sinicuiche y una parte de pipoloxochital...

IMAGE —*Jessup's body suddenly becomes two bodies. One remains huddled on its knees vomiting; the other takes shape outside the first body and then WHOOSHES UP into the sky until he is hardly more than a spot, visible by a curious LUMINOSITY about him. Down around the fire, the others seem entirely innocent of this extraordinary event. A dog wanders into the ring of sprawling men, sniffs at Jessup's first body, still on its knees—*

IMAGE —*The SCREEN is now a dull, matted WHITE, as if painted with heavy impasto streaks. The yellow of the lizard slowly leaks out into the whiteness, staining it. Losing its color, the lizard disappears. Then a strange pulpy shape appears, fissured and creviced, a grayish blob, recognizable perhaps to biologists as a human brain, which folds and slithers into itself to take on other shapes, changing into soft, pulsating globules of matter, insinuatingly sexual, oleaginous in movement. What we are seeing is a de-evolution of the brain, as it passes backward across the evolutionary continuum—through the brain of an alligator, then a codfish—until it oozes into the primitive, linear ridged nervous system of a worm. It disappears—*

IMAGE   *—Another biological dematuration process. Blobs of substance, grayish, constantly folding and unfolding slowly into curled up, loaf-like cracked and creviced adult brains, or the more simplified shapes of the brain of a six-month embryo; to the bulging vermiform structure of the brain of a seven-week embryo; finally the brain of a three-week embryo, hardly more than a hose-like structure with something stuck in its gullet, the bulging tip of a prosencephalon hanging down at the end of the thick snake-like thing as if it were ashamed—*

IMAGE   *—The SCREEN grows DARKER and DARKER until everything is silently, impenetrably BLACK...infinitely down below a flickering spot, perhaps the last conscious image of the fire where Jessup had been sitting...then—SUDDENLY—an unbearable FLASH of a pure white light incandescent in the fraction-of-a-second explosion of pure energy. Then it is all BLACK again—*

IMAGE   *—Enormous FLAMES, unbelievably hot, out of which emanate sudden EXPLOSIONS. One of these white-orange FLARES zigzags across the flaming face of the SCREEN, like a crevasse opening up in arctic ice—*

IMAGE   *—Suddenly, NOTHING IS LEFT to see but this jagged crack stretching obliquely up, as if the SCREEN itself were about to crack open—*

IMAGE   *—Everything else is BLACK—*

IMAGE   *—The crack is flaming red, then purple, then blue—*

IMAGE   *—A violent series of images, none lasting longer than a second—*

IMAGE   *—A flaming cloud of gasses, hydrogen and helium, WHOOSHES* *across the black screen at 90,000,000 mph, throbbing as it cools and contracts with gravity. Another such cloud. Another—*

IMAGE *—A huge spiral shaped cloud condensing into blue, condensing into a trillion soft stars, an embryo galaxy—*

IMAGE *—A blue cloud of gasses, now hotter and hotter, then redder and redder, as its trillions and trillions of atomic bits crush in on each other in a mutual gravitational attraction. The cloud is a flaming ball—a star, a sun. At the critical level of 20,000,000 °F, it ignites and burns—nuclear EXPLOSION following nuclear EXPLOSION—*

IMAGE *—A spiral arm of the Milky Way galaxy...swirling tendrils of the primal mist...a water molecule freezing into an ice crystal...a flaming yellow mass, the sun, surrounded by an iridescent halo of ice crystals and grains of rock or iron...the coalescence of small fragments into a larger fragment as the central fragment sweeps its neighboring fragments into its gravitational pull—*

IMAGE *—An endless expanse of cold, airless, waterless rock begins to leak bubbles and beads of boiling radioactivity...a cloud of yellow sulphurous steam...a falling of yellow rain—*

IMAGE *—A silent, sable SEA of water, motionless, fills the SCREEN—*

IMAGE *—All this flickering imagery is taking place across the blue, jagged crack that seems to be splitting the SCREEN. The crack never disappears but is a constant presence—*

IMAGE *—The crack ERUPTS, spewing blinding light out like lava, the first CABALISTIC emanation of LIGHT—*

IMAGE *—Everything abruptly condenses back into BLACKNESS again. The blue crack is gone. In its place, a brownish figure, a molten mass of substance, appearing to have arms and legs and a head but so protean that the limbs and distinguishing features keep dissolving or extruding, bubbling up here and there, swelling and contracting. It moves in surf-like emanations, expanding and lapping in slow exorable waves—*

IMAGE —*A high-pitched, exultant SCREAM*—

IMAGE —*The molten mass emerges larger and larger. Its substance seems to be iridescent, flaring with tiny flames*—

IMAGE —*Behind it, the screen is now GOLD*—

IMAGE —*A CLOSER VIEW of the mass: tiny flames are exploding neural matter*—

IMAGE —*Now a large YELLOW IGUANA, its pre-historic jaws slightly agape, its tongue flicking in and out. The lizard waddles across the expanse of GOLDEN SCREEN toward the pulsating, flaring mass of brown substance. It stops about halfway, suddenly wary, frightened. It edges on slowly, cautiously*—

IMAGE —*It's engulfed by the flaming molten substance. Its limbs are wrenched, ripped with a sickening SCREAM of bone and muscle, out of their sockets. The pieces of the lizard are lifted up within the molten substance by the improvisations of arms, and the shapeless head bows to devour the lizard*—

IMAGE —*It slowly surges around him*—

IMAGE —*The golden SCREEN grows reddish. The brown, orange, yellow objects lose their definition*—

IMAGE —*Again, the high-pitched, exultant SCREAM*—

IMAGE —*The screen is again BLACK*—

IMAGE —*The feeling of a bottomless shaft, a WHOOSH of precipitous descent*—

IMAGE —*We see things in what seems to be a BLACK LIGHT. The SCREEN fills with the branches of a tree. In the distance a campfire flickering in the wind*—

IMAGE —Jessup's WHITE FACE, squinting to avoid the poking of the BRANCHES—

THE HINCHI VALLEY, THE BRUJO'S SHACK. NIGHT.

In the mountains of Central Mexico, night falls on a valley where Eccheverria, the Brujo, the other four Escogidos are sprawled around their fire. Some sleep, but on the fringe of the firelight, barely visible, Jessup stands in a bosk. He is urinating.

REVERSE ACROSS Jessup, as he zips up and returns to the fire. Eccheverria looks up briefly. Nobody else notices. Under the overhang of the Brujo's shack, two Chosen Women sit in shadowy bundles of sleep. A dog drifts through the bodies, illuminated momentarily by the firelight.

Jessup joins the group, sinks onto the ground, lies back.

THE BRUJO Obtuvo la experiencia predicha?

ECCHEVERRIA He wants to know if you had the experience that was predicted for you.

JESSUP *(nods hello to the Brujo)* Tell him I did, and I also had an experience that was not predicted for me.

ECCHEVERRIA El tuvo una experiencia que no habio sido predicha.

THE BRUJO *(smiles briefly)* El se comió una lagartija.

ECCHEVERRIA He says you ate a lizard.

JESSUP How does he know I ate a lizard?

ECCHEVERRIA Cómo sabes que el se comió una lagartija?

THE BRUJO Yo lo vió comerse la lagartija. Todos lo vimos comerse la lagartija.

ECCHEVERRIA He says he saw you, they all saw you.

JESSUP   Does that mean he was with me in my hallucination? Does he have the ability to get into another man's mind?

ECCHEVERRIA   Estaba usted con mi amigo en su sueño?

The Brujo stares blankly at him.

ECCHEVERRIA   Tiene usted la abilidad de entrar en el sueño de otro hombre?

THE BRUJO   *(to Jessup)*   Yo lo vió. Todos lo vimos.

ECCHEVERRIA   He says they all saw you.

JESSUP   But I ate a lizard in my hallucination. I didn't actually eat the lizard around the fire here. If he saw me eat the lizard, he must've somehow joined me in the hallucination.

ECCHEVERRIA   El se comió la lagartija en su sueño.

The old shaman heads for the bushes where Jessup had been, some fifteen yards away. He turns back and indicates he wants them to follow. Jessup and Eccheverria start after him.

The Brujo pushes his way into the scratchy bosk, spreading the branches, holding them aside for Jessup and Eccheverria. A few paces later, the Brujo stops and points to the ground about ten yards away. Jessup and Eccheverria turn to look.

ACROSS JESSUP and ECCHEVERRIA, we see something on the ground, shrouded by the network of branches and by four dogs swarming over it, eating with the savagery of jackals. Jessup pushes into the thick tangle of bush, followed by Eccheverria, then they are struck by what they see and involuntarily close their eyes.

Behind them, the Brujo shouts at the dogs to back away. One of them has the leg of something in his mouth.

JESSUP'S P.O.V.: Lying in a gel of dried blood and leaves is the dismembered torso of the remains of a green crested iguana, terrifyingly legless, the empty white bone of the leg sockets white and flecked with blood. Half the torso has been stripped of its greenish skin, gobbets of raw flesh and exposed viscera are open to view.

Over this, the SOUND of a man retching. The Brujo shouts at the dogs snarling to get back to the carcass. Eccheverria is bent over, holding onto a branch, vomiting. Jessup turns aside and shades his eyes. The Brujo turns and makes his way out into the clearing.

OUTSIDE THE BRUJO'S SHACK. DAY.

Jessup checks his gear, his sleeping bag, tape recorder, notebooks. Eccheverria is packing, while occasional tribal activities go on in the background.

JESSUP *(no longer in good spirits)* First of all, iguanas are not mountain lizards.

ECCHEVERRIA I know.

JESSUP They are shore and jungle lizards. Somebody must've brought that iguana up here, and this whole hideous business is just a joke the Indians have played on me just to make the gringo look like a fool...

ECCHEVERRIA You asked me what happened, and I told you. You were crawling around on your hands and knees for awhile. Then, around seven-thirty, you got up and went to those bushes to urinate, I thought. Then it sounded like some of the dogs had jumped you. There was a great deal of yelping and snarling and growling. Then you screamed. Or something screamed. And I and a couple of the women went to see if you were in any trouble. We had just about gotten to the bushes when the screaming stopped, and the old Brujo yelled at us to come back and forget it.

Jessup scowls and lashes his gear tightly into one bundle.

JESSUP Do you think they'd let me take some of that mixture I smoked back to Boston?

ECCHEVERRIA We can only ask.

JESSUP I'd like Arthur to analyze, maybe synthesize it.

ABRUPT SHOCK-EFFECT CUT TO:

A BIO-FEEDBACK ROOM.

A volcanic terrain wrenches and crevasses—SOUND of rock being wrenched out of place—suddenly a white, steaming shaft of rock roars up, followed by another shattering emergence of rock the size of a small skyscraper, crushing the first shaft, forcing it to fold and crack and bend under the new weight.

JESSUP *(off-screen)* My God! It's cracking, it's cracking, the whole thing cracking! Enormous masses of rock!

ROSENBERG *(off-screen)* Are you okay, Eddie?

JESSUP *(off-screen)* I'm fine! Get this stuff! This is new!

The black water of a vast lake is heaving and bubbling when out of this sable sea, an enormous volcanic cone of rock surges up, ERUPTING with flame and boiling rock, tons of plutonic EXPLOSION, a fantastic fountain of rock and scalding water rising two thousand feet into the air. Another plutonic EXPLOSION.

JESSUP *(off-screen)* Deafening! The noise is deafening! Can you hear me above this noise?! My God!

DEAFENING, AGONIZING SOUND accompanies the eruptions of earth crust, the breaking land with its rupturing of rock and mantle—each one piling on top of each other, steaming, white hot, folding, buckling, building. The air is filled with poisonous gases—

JESSUP *(off-screen)* ...the most unbelievable thing I've ever seen! I'm watching the birth agony of a mountain! I can't believe this!

BRIGHAM HOSPITAL, BIO-FEEDBACK ROOM. NIGHT.

ACROSS Jessup on a leather reclining chair, wearing a T-shirt and jeans, with bare feet. Eight EEG leads issue from his scalp. His face is contorting into fierce grimaces, his mouth opening into silent, strangulated rictus. The lighting is subdued and the room sound-attenuated and empty but for the chair. Through an observation window (two-way) in the background, we see Rosenberg and Parrish in the observation room.

JESSUP My God! Can't you hear it! The noise is stupefying!

THE OBSERVATION ROOM. DAY.

Compactly and densely fitted out with recording equipment. Three sheepskin-lined coats are piled on the floor. Rosenberg fiddles with controls; Parrish stands watching Jessup through the window, disturbed by what he's observing.

JESSUP *(over the amplifier)* ...a whole mountain range is being born in front of my eyes!

THE BIO-FEEDBACK ROOM. DAY.

REVERSE ACROSS Jessup, eyes wide open, bulging, madly staring...

JESSUP ...and the sun became black as sackcloth! The full moon became like blood! And a great mountain, burning with fire, was thrown into the sea! And the beast ascends from the bottomless pit! His name in Hebrew is Abaddon!

Sudden silence.

THE OBSERVATION ROOM. DAY.

Silence while through the window Jessup's face again becomes serene. The wheels of a Sony cassette recorder slowly whirr.

ROSENBERG *(clicks the intercom)* Are you okay, Eddie?

JESSUP *(off-screen, dispassionate, calm)* I'm fine. Really, I'm fine.

PARRISH *(still disturbed)* Jesus Christ...

ROSENBERG *(into intercom)* Do you want me to bring you down?

There is no response, only an uneasy silence settling over the room.

PARRISH What happens now?

ROSENBERG He's blacked out. These blackouts can get very freaky. Sometimes, they last as long as four hours. When he comes out of it, he's as chipper as a bird, but he doesn't remember a thing.

Parrish checks the EEG machine.

ROSENBERG All the vital signs are normal. He just blacks out.

PARRISH How did you explain my coming over here tonight?

ROSENBERG I told him you called and asked how everything was since we hadn't seen each other in so long, and I said, "Why don't you come over tonight and bullshit for awhile?" and you said terrific.

PARRISH *(cutting him off)* Just how dangerous is this stuff he brought back from Mexico?

ROSENBERG I didn't say dangerous. I said it was weird. It hangs around too long. It goes to all the wrong places. This stuff doesn't degrade. I must've shot up two dozen rats by now. We're retrieving sixty, seventy, sometimes eighty percent. And what's really screwy is it heads straight for the brain. I never saw a psychoactive drug that didn't wind up in the liver or in the kidney. There's nothing in that stuff I don't know. A lot of alkaloids. Principally cryogenic, some harmine... They're all known hallucinogens.

PARRISH *(fed-up, cutting Rosenberg off)* Well, I don't believe this! You guys are shooting up with an untested drug that stacks up in the brain and works in the nucleus of the cell—and you don't call that dangerous?

ROSENBERG For the record, we don't actually shoot up. Eddie drinks a ten milligram per cc solution of the stuff.

PARRISH Well, it's going to stop right now!

ROSENBERG What're you yelling at me for? I've been trying to get him to stop for months!

PARRISH You guys are supposed to be reputable scientists, for God's sake, not two kids in the dorm freaking out on Mexican mushrooms!

ROSENBERG Let's see you stop him. What do you think I called you for?

DISSOLVE to later the same day, same place: They clean up the room, getting ready to leave, gathering up the rolls of polygraph paper, putting on their coats.

PARRISH *(arguing for some time with some temper)* This ain't LSD, goddammit! This ain't no serotonin antagonist you're drinking! How many grams of that stuff do you figure you've already got in you? Two, three? You could be working up one hell of a case of cancer with a truckful of antimetabolites in you like that!

JESSUP *(heading for the door)* The Hinchi Indians have been smoking that stuff for centuries with no special incidence of cancer.

Parrish follows Jessup out into the...

THE FOURTH FLOOR CORRIDOR. DAY.

...where Jessup slips into his sheepskin coat.

PARRISH Fuck the Hinchi Indians. You don't know anything about those mushrooms. It sounds to me like they have fantastic staying power.

Rosenberg turns off the lights in the bio-feedback room and joins them, his tape recorder slung over his shoulder. Jessup locks up. They head out.

JESSUP We've shot up at least thirty rats with that stuff. Some of them have a whopping load in them, and none of them have been noticeably affected...

He leans into the Departmental Office, the only lit room on the floor. He drops off the key.

JESSUP *(to someone inside)* Thanks.

HARVARD MEDICAL SCHOOL, CENTRAL COURT. DAY.

The three dark figures of our heroes cross the quadrangle for B Buildings. Parrish is still quite exercised.

PARRISH Now what's all this shit about an isolation tank? For God's sakes! You guys get flakier every time I see you. I thought all that isolation tank stuff went out in the Sixties with Timothy Leary and all the other gurus. Where is this dumb isolation tank?

They climb the steps of B Building and into...

HARVARD MEDICAL SCHOOL, B BUILDING, FOYER. DAY.

...and head for the stairway, where they pause as Jessup expounds.

JESSUP Mason, shut up for a minute, and let somebody else say something. What happens during this blackout period is you get the feeling of phenomenal acceleration, like you're shot out over millions, billions of years. Time simply obliterates. You sense the hallucination is going on, but you get no images. Well, I want to break through that blackout barrier. I'd like to know what those images are that I know are going on but I can't see.

He opens the door to...

THE STAIRWELL.

...and they go clattering down the steps.

JESSUP We can't raise the dosage of the drug because we're close to toxic levels now. So the only way we can intensify the experience is to take the two hundred milligrams in conjunction with the tank.

BASEMENT CORRIDOR.

It has that basement look. It's after hours, only a few other people are about.

PARRISH There's a lot of things I'd like to do to that drug before you take anymore. We should do a half-life determination. I'd like to know the transport system. I'd like to find some analogues.

JESSUP ...and that could take us a year! All I know is this Mexican stuff is an extraordinary substance, and every instinct I have says I'm on to something hot here. And another two hundred milligrams isn't going to kill anybody.

He's found the room. He tries the door, but it's locked. He inserts a key he's brought. It turns. He opens the door. He enters...

THE ISOLATION TANK ROOM. DAY.

He turns on the flight. Overhead fluorescent lighting flickers on. To the left is a brightly lit observation room, small and emptied of most equipment. With the exception of an EEG machine and its panel up against a sound-proofed wall, the aluminum shelving is all bare. Directly in front, the door leading to the tank room itself is opened when Jessup finds another key. This room is pitch black. A switch on the wall is found, and it allows graduated levels of light. Subdued, hidden light comes up. There seems to be a bed with a naked striped mattress and pillow in the middle of the room.

JESSUP They were doing sleep studies here.

The room is now well lit, picking up some cartons and empty animal cages along one wall, and a coffin-shaped black box, four by four by eight feet.

JESSUP There it is.

ROSENBERG Oh, it's horizontal. It's smaller than the one we had in New York.

JESSUP I don't think anybody's used it in years. But I connected it up yesterday, and it works. It won't take a week to get this place cleaned out and functioning.

PARRISH You could get your ass in a sling if it ever gets out you're using an untested drug on human subjects.

JESSUP Don't worry so much, Mason. Nothing's going to happen to me. Let's go get a quick hamburger. I told a kid in one of my classes I might see her tonight...

He heads back to the door, turning the light switch so the room darkens.

PARRISH *(exploding as he follows)* All right! Do what you want to do! I think you're both irresponsible as hell! So don't call me any more, Arthur, to tell me you're worried about Eddie putting all this shit into him. I'm telling you now—don't put any more of that shit into him till you find out a hell of a lot more about it! I offered you the use of my lab and all the rats you can use. And that's as much as I want to be implicated in your dumb experiments. And go get your own hamburger. I got my own date I'm already an hour late for!

He storms out.

C BUILDING, PARRISH'S LAB. DAY, TWO WEEKS LATER.

A small Christmas tree is in evidence in an endocrinology lab. Parrish, a Grad Student and an ENDOCRINOLOGY FELLOW are standing by a scintillation counter, a large square aluminum contraption that looks like a dishwasher except it has a digital recording device, which rattles off red digits. In the background, a second Grad Student and two lab technicians, each at their desks, cut microtomal sections or tend to the rats, or whatever one does in endocrinology labs. They are variously dressed.

Parrish has on a long, white lab coat. He has been doing rounds today, evidenced by the stethoscope sticking out of his pocket, an ophthalmoscope, a pen light, fountain pens. In one hand, he holds a stack of computer programming cards. Parrish glances at his watch.

PARRISH *(to the Endocrinology Fellow, extending the cards)* You want to do these today?

ENDOCRINOLOGY FELLOW *(takes them)* Sure.

B BUILDING, BASEMENT, ISOLATION TANK ROOM. DAY.

The brightly lit room has been cleared of everything but the black tank. Rosenberg is on a footstool bent over the tank checking the EEG leads on Jessup's skull. The open doorway suddenly fills up with Parrish, unbuttoning his coat. Rosenberg, carefully straightening out the wire leads, notices him.

ROSENBERG Couldn't resist, right?

PARRISH Somebody's got to keep an eye on you two sorcerers.

He looks into the tank, CAMERA looking with him. Jessup lies in it, floating naked just below the surface of inky black water, an imperceptible shimmering of white. His ankles are resting on what seems to be a surgical dam, his head on a headrest. He smiles up at Parrish.

PARRISH What have you got in there? Some kind of salt solution?

ROSENBERG Ten percent magnesium sulfate, for buoyancy. *(bringing the lid for the tank)* Give me a hand with this, Mason.

REVERSE looking up from JESSUP'S P.O.V.: Parrish and Rosenberg loom over the tank, carefully fitting the lid into its hinges. They slowly lower it. The SCREEN goes shocking BLACK. Parrish stands looking down at the covered black coffin of a tank.

PARRISH Weird, man...

OBSERVATION ROOM. DAY.

Rosenberg has flicked the lights off and is back in the observation room. There is polygraph paper in the EEG machine, and the styli are scrawling. An audio speaker is on the top shelf in one corner. A one-way window looks out into the tank room where the coffin-like tank lies in penumbral shadow. Jessup's and Rosenberg's sheepskins are piled on the floor in a corner. Parrish adds his to the pile. Rosenberg clicks the intercom on.

ROSENBERG *(into the mike)* One-two-three-four...

JESSUP *(on the speaker)* One-two-three-four...

ROSENBERG *(on the mike)* Okay, you're fine. *(clicks the tape recorder on, speaks into it)* Wednesday, January seventh, four twenty-eight P.M.

Jessup's VOICE CHANTS over the speaker...

ROSENBERG *(indicates the EEG machine)* We went into theta like a shot, no spindling, nothing.

JESSUP *(off-screen, overriding)* Hey, this is terrific. A plateau or a lowland, grasslands, savannas. I feel I'm actually alive and inside this landscape...

Parrish looks through the one-way window. The black coffin-like box lies silent. He can see his own and Rosenberg's reflections superimposed on the tank.

JESSUP ...a density of woodlands about a mile away, beyond that mountains that seem to be smoking—newly born mountains, Cenozoic, latter Tertiary, I'm in an edge-area—utter tranquility, but alive, life in the trees, life in the sedge, paradise, the Garden of Eden, oh my God! The birth of man! That's it! The birth of man! That's got to be it!

REACTION SHOT of Parrish getting nervous. To his left, Rosenberg writes in a notebook.

JESSUP *(off-screen)* My God!—there it is! A proto-human! The first and original truly human form! Tiny! Perhaps four feet high! Barely visible above the sedge grass! Completely furred, chimp-like, but erect, no knuckle-walking, shorter arms, moving along rather gracefully—there's two, three of them! Bipedal, tiny, little furred humanoid creatures, a rock, some kind of basaltic rock, a chunk of lava in their hands, they're stalking or hunting, that's it! It's a hunt, they're hunting something—it's me! It's me they're hunting! It's me!

Annoyed, Parrish looks over to Rosenberg putting a new tape into the recorder.

JESSUP *(off-screen)* Beautiful! Beautiful! I'm racing through the grass! I'm trying to get to the trees! They're on my flank! I'm struck by a stone! I'm down! They're on me! No, just one of them! It's his kill. The others have to wait their portion. He's beating me with the lava. He's gouging me.

PARRISH For Chrissakes...

ROSENBERG *(clicking his mike)* Are you okay, Eddie?

JESSUP *(off-screen)* Ripping at my flesh! I'm the hunter now! I'm the killer! I'm killing! I'm eating! I'm eating the blood-hot flesh of a giant goat! I'm eating a goat I just killed! I'm eating a goat!

The hysterical fluency of Jessup's report abruptly deteriorates into a curious CROAK and then a series of quick CLICKING NOISES and then a strangulated sort of HOWL. It's too much for Parrish. He wrenches the door open, strides into...

TANK ROOM. DAY.

...where he crosses to the tank, pulls the hinged head-section up.

PARRISH'S P.O.V.: Jessup's white mask of a face, cushioned in the rectangle of blackness, serene as a saint.

PARRISH Are you okay?

JESSUP It's beautiful, beautiful...

ROSENBERG *(right behind Parrish)* Do you want to come down?

JESSUP No.

Rosenberg lowers the lid. Parrish pulls out his cigar case, extracts one, heads back to the...

OBSERVATION ROOM. DAY.

...as Rosenberg enters...

PARRISH Sounded like he was having a bad trip to me.

ROSENBERG Some of these tank trips can get pretty creepy.

The speaker emits another croaking GRUNT, a series of CLICKING SOUNDS, then some LIP-SMACKING SOUNDS. Parrish rises nervously.

PARRISH What the hell was that?

ROSENBERG *(into the mike)* You okay?

JESSUP *(off-screen)* Beautiful.

Parrish lights his cigar.

ROSENBERG Do you want to stop this?

JESSUP *(off-screen)* No.

ROSENBERG Do you want me to leave you alone?

JESSUP Yes.

B BUILDING, BASEMENT CORRIDOR. NIGHT.

Parrish comes out of the men's room adjusting his trousers. He walks down the corridor, glancing at his watch. He enters...

ISOLATION TANK ROOM, ENTRANCE.

...and left into...

OBSERVATION ROOM.

...where Rosenberg perches on a stool, reading a mystery novel.

PARRISH I thought you said these things don't last more than four hours. It's a quarter to nine...

A guttural sound erupts from the speaker.

ROSENBERG *(into mike)* Are you okay, Eddie? *(looking through window)* He's coming out...

THE TANK ROOM. NIGHT.

ACROSS the isolation tank as Jessup stands up, holding the lid, then setting it down against the side of the tank. Parrish and Rosenberg rush in, Rosenberg helping him to clamber out of the tank.

ROSENBERG *(removing the EEG leads)* I don't like being out of contact for these long periods of time, Eddie.

Parrish hands Jessup a hooded terrycloth robe. Jessup slips into the robe, towels his hair. He nods at Rosenberg, a strange monkish figure in the dark room, a cowl over his head, only his white, wet eyes visible in the coped blackness of his face. He is trying to say something. His jaws move, but nothing comes out except a rasping primitive noise. His eyes stare mutely at them. He tries again to talk, but produces only CLICKING SOUNDS. He sinks slowly to his knees, his eyes staring in blank shock out of the black oval of the robe's cowl.

ROSENBERG I think he's in shock.

He flips on the rheostat, and the light rises. Parrish pulls the hood back. As the LIGHT strengthens, we see Jessup in the middle of the room, on his knees, his robe hanging limply from his white body, his face blank, his cheeks and mouth wet with red blood, smeared where he has towelled his face—looking for all the world as if he has just ravened a carcass.

PARRISH He must've bit his lip.

He towels away some of the blood, then slips out of his lab coat, strips off his shirt, leans over to the tank, wets it in the tank, uses it to clean Jessup's face. By now the LIGHT is up, and the room well lit. Parrish fetches his examining light from his coat, pokes it into Jessup's mouth and up his nose.

PARRISH Must've had a seizure, hit his head or something.

Jessup seems to be coming out of shock. He is trying to talk. All that comes out is a WHISTLE and a CLICKING SOUND. He reaches out his hand to Rosenberg. His two friends finally get him standing. The shock is gone. His eyes respond intelligently. They glisten with excitement. He smiles and heads for the observation room, indicating that, since he can't talk, he must communicate in writing.

THE OBSERVATION ROOM. NIGHT.

By the time Parrish and Rosenberg get there, Jessup is seated on Rosenberg's chair and scrawling something in his notebook. Rosenberg leans over to read the message.

ROSENBERG What do you want blood tests for?

PARRISH Can you hear me? Can you understand me?

Parrish reaches forward to palpate his neck. Jessup angrily brushes Parrish's hand away, scrawls a long message in Rosenberg's notebook.

PARRISH What's he say?

ROSENBERG *(reading what Jessup writes)* He says, "A buccal smear and blood for a karyotype. Also blood samples for the Goodman and Sarich labs. Pictures of my neck. A whole series of films. Now. Before I reconstitute." Exclamation point.

PARRISH *(slipping back into his lab coat)* Before he what?

ROSENBERG Before he reconstitutes.

PARRISH Well, take his damn blood, and then maybe he'll let me take a look at him.

Rosenberg fetches a vacu-tainer from the airline bag he always carries, and some tubes and a rubber tourniquet. He sets about taking blood samples from Jessup's left arm.

PARRISH *(to Jessup)* Do you mind if I examine your neck for a moment?

Jessup, who is in a state of excitement, rolls his eyes in exasperation but allows Parrish to palpate his neck.

ROSENBERG *(inserting the syringe)* Any masses?

PARRISH No.

*Parrish auscultates Jessup's neck, shines his ophthalmoscope into his eyes.
Jessup submits with little grace, only because he is confined by Rosenberg
drawing blood. His inner turmoil is obvious. He balances precariously on the
chair in his bulky robe, his legs crossed, one swinging nervously, finally he
pushes Parrish aside and scrawls in the notebook again. Parrish leans over
to read.*

PARRISH *(losing his temper)* Oh, stop talking shit! Are you saying your
dumb hallucination has externalized?

ROSENBERG *(inserting a new tube)* What'd he write?

PARRISH *(reading)* Not common aphasia. Time-space fallout from the
hallucination. *(bends so that he is nose-to-nose with Jessup)* You are a
fucking flake, Jessup, so get dressed, and I'm taking you over to the
Brigham to do a complete work-up on you! *(as Jessup shakes his head,
Parrish explodes)* You are a very sick dude, you dumb son of a bitch!
And I want to look down your throat, get some skull films, do a CAT
scan, maybe even an arteriogram, and I'd like an unbiased eye to look
at those EEG tracings.

*Jessup shakes his head—an arctic, imperious no. He scribbles a brief message
and stabs it with two exclamation points.*

ROSENBERG *(inserting a new tube)* What'd he say?

PARRISH He just wants X-rays. Okay, finish up with him, Arthur, and let's
get him over to X-ray.

THE TANK ROOM. TEN MINUTES LATER.

*Parrish, in his jacket, is cleaning up in the tank room. He rolls his torn shirt
into a ball with Jessup's bloody robe, goes over to make sure the valves have
been shut tight, then goes into...*

THE OBSERVATION ROOM.

...where Rosenberg and Jessup are also tidying up, packing polygraph paper, etc.

PARRISH *(indicating Jessup's robe)* I'll be right back. I just want to get rid of this stuff.

He exits.

SUB-BASEMENT TUNNEL. NIGHT.

Empty except for the three of them, a quixotic trio, shambling, bulky Parrish, tiny Rosenberg carrying his airline bag, Jessup in Levis, his shirttails not entirely tucked in. They are moving through the bowels of the building. They walls are lined with huge, thick, hot water pipes. They pass the open incinerators, wells dug deep into the foundations of the buildings. Flames leap up from the depths.

ROSENBERG *(as they go)* Is it possible it's purely mechanical?

PARRISH Well, neurologically, he's grossly intact, and if it isn't neurological, then it's got to be mechanical...

They push through swinging doors. Parrish pulls an exit door open.

PARRISH I'd like to get a look at his cords and do a barium swallow...

A STAIRWELL. NIGHT.

They head upstairs.

PARRISH Maybe I'll run down to Emergency and pick up an ENT bag.

BRIGHAM HOSPITAL, A CORRIDOR. NIGHT.

The three of them coming down the otherwise empty yellow-tiled hospital cor-

ridor to a door which has a little wooden marker sticking out of the wall above it, reading X-RAY. They turn into...

THE X-RAY DEPARTMENT, OUTER ROOM.

A TECHNICIAN looks up at this late interruption.

PARRISH I want some plain films of this guy's neck: a PA, a lateral and an oblique.

TECHNICIAN Jesus, Doctor, I'm backed up to my ass for tonight...

PARRISH *(snapping)* Take the damn pictures! This is an emergency.

The technician leads Jessup into an X-ray room and closes the door. Parrish leans back against a wall.

ROSENBERG I guess we'd better not tell Eddie he had blood on his face when he came out of the tank. He'll claim it was goat's blood from that goat he was eating in his hallucination.

PARRISH Oh, for Chrissakes! You really are getting as weird as he is.

ROSENBERG Well, what do you think happened?

PARRISH *(fishing out a cigar)* He's not the type for an hysterical conversion, so I'm thinking seizure. He came out of the tank in a fugue state, and he had blood all over his face. He must've had a seizure in the tank, bit his tongue while convulsing and is post-icticly aphasic. I thought maybe he had a vascular insult, a stroke or flipped an embolus. But neurologically, he's intact, so I'm thinking seizure now...

INSIDE THE X-RAY ROOM.

The technician clips up the X-rays for Parrish, Rosenberg and Jessup to see. They huddle, and Jessup points with excitement to the throat area.

PARRISH Take it easy. None of us are terrific at reading X-rays.

TECHNICIAN What're you guys looking for?

PARRISH *(indicating the X-rays)* Put these things in an envelope, and who's reading tonight in radiology?

TECHNICIAN Dr. Wissenschaft.

Jessup puts his hand on Parrish's arm and shakes his head.

PARRISH *(barely controlling his temper)* I want someone to look at those X-rays who can read them, Eddie.

Jessup indicates he wants to talk outside. He and Parrish go out into the...

HOSPITAL CORRIDOR.

The two of them stand in a long, empty hospital corridor.

JESSUP I'd rather not have everybody in the Brigham in on this. It's bad enough we've got this nosy X-ray technician.

It takes Parrish a moment to realize Jessup is talking again.

PARRISH Are you all right?

JESSUP I'm fine, Mason. I tried to indicate this was just a transient thing.

PARRISH A transient ischemic attack, that's what it was...*(leans into the X-ray department to say to Rosenberg)* He's got his voice back.

Rosenberg comes out into the hallway carrying the large manila envelope containing the X-rays.

JESSUP It wasn't an ischemic attack, it wasn't a seizure. You saw the X-rays, Mason. There was a clear fusion of the digastric muscles to the hyoid bone, and the larynx was in an unusually forward position.

I'm not sure, but I think the digastric muscles which are looped in humans, are fused directly to the bones in apes. I obviously regressed to some quasi-simian creature.

Parrish takes the envelope of X-rays from Rosenberg.

PARRISH *(trying not to explode)* I'm taking these over to someone who can read them right. We're reading them wrong, that's all there is to it. Because nobody's going to tell me you de-differentiated your goddam genetic structure for four goddam hours and then reconstituted...*(The more he tries to keep his voice down, the more apoplectic he gets.)* I'm a professor of endocrinology at the Harvard Medical School. I'm an attending physician at the Peter Bent Brigham Hospital, a consulting editor to the American Journal of Endocrinology, a fellow and vice-president of the Eastern Association of Endocrinologists, the president of the journal club...*(He erupts into full-blown rage.)*...and I'm not going to listen to any more of your cabalistic, quantum, frigging, dumb, limbo mumbo jumbo! *(brandishing the envelope)* I'm going to show these to a radiologist.

He turns, strides down the hallway to another door which is marked RADI-OLOGY, thrusts the door open, enters...

DEPARTMENT OF RADIOLOGY. NIGHT.

DR. WISSENSCHAFT, an unhappy resident, is poring over a stack of X-rays. Parrish hands him an envelope, working to keep himself under control.

PARRISH Do me a favor, take a look at these.

WISSENSCHAFT *(extracting the films)* What's the story in this case?

PARRISH Thirty-five-year-old white man, acute onset of aphasia, no history of trauma.

WISSENSCHAFT *(affixing the X-rays to the light)* What're you looking for?

PARRISH It looks to me like the architecture is somewhat abnormal.

WISSENSCHAFT   *(peering at the film)*   Somewhat?   This guy's a fucking gorilla!

JESSUP'S FLAT, BEDROOM. NIGHT.

CLOSEUP of Jessup asleep, then his eyes slowly open. Despite the darkness in the room, his eyes glisten with terror. His mouth opens slowly till it is agape with terror, as if he is about to scream.

CAMERA SUDDENLY PULLS BACK, as he abruptly rises, throwing the blanket off him. He stares at his body. Under his pajama bottoms, something terrible seems to be happening to his body. It is swelling and contorting as if forces inside his body were trying to break out.

On the other side of the bed, now in view, the young female MEDICAL STUDENT he had mentioned is asleep, her back to us.

CLOSER ANGLES of Jessup's body: his arm shrivels into a bent little furred arm, much like a rat's paw, suddenly his feet are webbed then furred and a second later back to normal. His face is a mask of pain. He touches his head and feels the bones of his skull: his jaw, the bones above his eyebrows, moving under his skin, are all reassembling into new formations. He bends forward clutching the back of his neck, as if he'd been struck. The musculature of his chest surges and subsides. Cracks appear and spread throughout his body.

The medical student stirs.

MED STUDENT   *(drowsily)*   Are you okay, Dr. Jessup?

JESSUP   *(on his elbows and no longer in pain as he observes the deformations of his body)*   Yes.

He forces himself to sit up, his legs hanging over the side of the bed, and almost falls to his knees. Carefully he makes his way to the bathroom, all the while his body crumbling and buckling, as if it were dry earth, as if seismic forces were at work within him. He gets himself into...

THE BATHROOM.

...where he closes the door, turns on the light and stares in the full-length mirror.

JESSUP'S P.O.V.: In the dull yellow bathroom light, he sees a series of disjunctive evolutionary images of himself, flickering one after the other, lasting only a fraction of a second. They are mostly hominid and protohuman images, Ramapithecine figures in which he is no more than three feet tall. Several reflections reveal him as a delicately-fingered, insect-eating, lemur-like animal with enormous soft eyes, in a tree and clutching a branch.

As quickly he is his realistic self again, a slight, white-skinned young man in his late thirties, wearing pajama pants. It all lasted perhaps five seconds.

MED STUDENT *(off-screen, calling through the closed door)* Are you all right, Dr. Jessup?

JESSUP *(staring at his own reflection)* I'm fine.

He opens the door and sees a momentary vision of apocalyptic formations. He reels back, observes it closely, then comes out into...

THE BEDROOM. NIGHT.

The Med Student stands, holding the blanket around her, more asleep than awake. Jessup heads for his desk.

MED STUDENT Are you all right, Dr. Jessup?

JESSUP I just want to make a few notes.

He sits down, clicks on the desk lamp, reaches for a notebook and begins to write. Behind him, the Med Student sinks back onto the bed and is instantly asleep. Jessup writes—then pauses to look again at his naked right arm. CAMERA PANS DOWN to the arm. A protoplasmic substance bulges out and moves up his arm under the skin like a mole and disappears into his elbow. He regards this with blank astonishment, then returns to his meticulous noting of what has just happened.

LOGAN AIRPORT. APRIL, 1976. SUNNY DAY.

A KLM jumbo jet touches down.

LOGAN AIRPORT CUSTOMS, ARRIVAL GATE.

Emily and the girls, brown from a year of African sun, with a year's worth of luggage, cartons, crates, bags accompany a porter wheeling their gear toward the arrival gate. Jessup is among the crowd awaiting the passengers.

REVERSE from Emily to the greeters, where Jessup can be easily spotted. Emily points out their father to the girls, who race to him. He embraces them both, hugs them individually, and embraces Emily too as she gets to the gate.

JESSUP My God! You all look so marvelous!

Emily studies his face, detecting a feverish enthusiasm.

EMILY How've you been, Eddie?

He pauses before answering.

JESSUP I don't know. Strange things have been happening.

He seizes both squealing kids, one under each arm, and heads off.

GRACE Are you going to drive us to our new house?

JESSUP You bet your life. And I'm going to help you unpack, and, depending on how nice you are to me, I may take you all to a Chinese restaurant.

Concerned by the strange, almost mad and uncharacteristic exuberance of her husband, Emily follows with the porter and luggage.

EMILY'S NEW HOME, LIVING ROOM. DUSK.

*Several hours later, the whole flat—the bottom floor of a Cape Cod house on
Avon Hill in Cambridge—is a wild disarray of packed and unpacked luggage. Cartons and valises lay open in every room. Clothing is piled on beds
or heaped on the floor. Books and notebooks, cans of film and stacks of tape
recorder cassettes and reels are massed in mounds on beds, chairs and tables.
Through the windows, we can see dusk descending. We might even catch
glimpses of the Jessup children on the front porch.*

*Amidst this disarray Emily follows her own private pattern of efficiency, pil-
ing and sorting. She turns on a lamp with an orange shade, casting a warm
light. All the while she chats away with Jessup back in the kitchen at the rear
of the living room. He sits at the formica table, legs crossed, sipping coffee.*

EMILY Anyway, don't let anybody tell you baboons aren't occasionally
carnivorous. I personally observed two instances of predation which
involved the unmistakable behavior of hunters. A pair of baboons
killed young Thomson gazelles and ate them. There was a rudimen-
tary communication between the two baboons that was noticeably different from the usual baboon vocalizations. So I've become fascinated with the work on non-verbal communication being done with apes.
I've been corresponding with the Gardners at the University of
Nevada. I may just go out and spend a couple of weeks there this summer. I've got nothing else to do except write up my report.

JESSUP I don't suppose you recorded any of those baboon sounds.

EMILY Yes, of course, I did, why?

She comes into...

THE KITCHEN. DUSK.

...where she pours herself a cup of coffee.

JESSUP I'd like very much to hear them.

EMILY Of course.

She pulls up a chair to join him at the table.

JESSUP Mrs. Tully said she'll be here tomorrow morning at ten-thirty to help you put everything away. She wanted to know if you wanted her to come back to work steady, and I said I was sure you would.

She nods. A silence falls between them. They sip at their cups. She steals a glance at him.

EMILY I got a letter from Mason about a week ago, just before we left Nairobi. He says you've been working with a very complex drug you brought back from Mexico. It hasn't been tested yet and it's dangerous as hell.

JESSUP What else did Mason write you?

EMILY He says that over the past year you've taken about two grams of that drug yourself, and that you had a very unusual instance of genetic regression about three months ago. You may have leukemia or lymphoma. He's been trying to get you into the hospital for a complete workup, but you refuse to go. He's worried stiff that you're cracking up. He thinks you're behaving very strangely, and he begged me to talk to you about this when I got back.

JESSUP Mason is pathologically incapable of keeping his mouth shut about anything.

EMILY He's worried about you.

JESSUP He's also a stupid, starched, doctrinaire idiot.

EMILY Mason is a first-rate doctor.

JESSUP It's not leukemia. Or any other kind of cancer.

He stands, flushed with fury, his hands trembling with his effort to control a mounting rage.

JESSUP I let him do a liver-spleen scan on me and a CAT scan. I've been probed, scoped and palpated! Parrish has had a mirror down my throat or up my ass every half hour for three months! And there is no evidence, no suggestion whatsoever of cancer!

She says nothing. He strides off into the living room and is suddenly back.

JESSUP What else did he write you? Which of these has the baboon vocalizations on them? I'd like to hear them.

EMILY Why?

JESSUP Did Mason write you that during that incident of regression I went through, I had an aphasic experience for about four hours? The only sounds I could get out were clicks and grunts. I've got a hunch they're very much like the baboon vocalizations you have on your tapes.

EMILY Mason says that you took blood tests, and the lab report showed some characteristics of simian blood group systems.

JESSUP They also picked up antigens, specific to man.

EMILY I'd like to see that data.

JESSUP We also took a buccal smear. The chromosomal count was forty eight...

EMILY Are you serious?

JESSUP And the structure of the karyotype was also non-human. I mean, for God's sake, the thing to do is for me to get back in that isolation tank and try it again! Let's see if it happens again! I mean, none of us really believes it happened! After three months, I'm beginning to wonder if it ever happened myself! But oh, no! They won't go back in the tank! Mason's taken over the whole project! He's got Arthur up in his lab every day, fractionating rats' brains! What the hell am I supposed to do, while they're fractionating rats' brains?!

His daughter appears in the doorway, fearfully watches her father ranting and raving.

GRACE Mommy...

JESSUP *(quiets down for her)* Everybody thinks your daddy's going nuts.

GRACE Mommy, when are we going to eat?

EMILY *(rushing to scurry the child away from the tense discussion)* Go on upstairs and get dressed.

Emily moves to the kitchen to prepare supper.

JESSUP I was convinced the regression was triggered by an act of consciousness. While I was in the tank, I entered another consciousness. I became another self. And the drug, in some way, triggered the externalization of that other, more primitive self.

Jessup gets increasingly furious with Emily's actions away from him to prepare food and he yells.

JESSUP At least look at my data.

EMILY Of course. Maybe tomorrow afternoon. Would tomorrow afternoon be all right?

JESSUP Don't patronize me.

EMILY I'm not...

JESSUP It's just possible I'm not mad, you know! I'm asking you to make a small quantum jump with me! To accept one deviant concept: that our other states of consciousness are as real as our waking state and that that reality can be externalized!

EMILY You're screaming.

JESSUP I know. But I've been getting this patronizing shit from Arthur and Mason for three months now, and I'm sick of it. We've got millions of years stored away in that computer bank we call our minds! We've got trillions of dormant genes in us, our whole evolutionary past! Perhaps I've tapped into that! For God's sake, all I'm saying is I want to get back to that tank and repeat the experiment. The most elementary laboratory behavior! Repeat the experiment! Confirm it! I would like other responsible scientists with me when I do it. I'd like a little consensual validation on this! We may have demonstrated a whole new force in nature. My God, don't you agree it merits further investigation? I've got all the tapes, notes and everything at my place. What time would you like to come over and look at the stuff tomorrow?

EMILY Two, two-thirty? *(smiles nervously)* I just want to get the girls. I'll be right back.

Carrying Margaret, she goes out into the...

ENTRANCE FOYER.

She is very nervous and a little frightened. She opens the front door and goes out onto...

THE FRONT PORCH. DUSK.

...where she stands scouring the area for her other daughter. She spots her down the block a bit talking to a NEIGHBOR with a small BOY. She moves quickly down the porch steps and out to...

AVON HILL. DUSK.

...where she sets Margaret down and heads across the street.

EMILY Grace...

The woman turns to her, smiling.

NEIGHBOR I'm Linda Sandys. *(She points to a gray clapboard down the block.)* I belong to that house over there.

EMILY I'm Emily Jessup.

NEIGHBOR And you've just come back from Africa today. Grace has been telling me and Georgie all about it. My husband's in French Classics.

EMILY I'm in Anthropology.

NEIGHBOR Would you like to come over and have some coffee?

EMILY *(forcing a smile)* I'd love to really, but I've got a hungry husband back in the house. *(to her daughters)* We're going to a Chinese restaurant.

The children race back to the house.

EMILY We're still unpacking...

NEIGHBOR Of course.

EMILY I'll take you up on that coffee tomorrow morning, if I may.

NEIGHBOR Please. The gray house there.

EMILY Thank you. Excuse me.

She hurries back down the street. When she gets to the front path, both kids are coming out of the house onto the porch.

EMILY *(frightened)* Is your father all right?

GRACE Where is he?

EMILY Oh God...

GRACE   Are we still going to the Chinese restaurant?

EMILY   Yes of course.   I just want to make a few phone calls...let's get
inside.

ISOLATION TANK ROOM. NIGHT.

*The SCREEN is BLACK. A door in the back of the blackness opens, and
Jessup enters silhouetted in the rectangle of light made by the open doorway.
A moment later, subdued lighting comes on. We are in...*

THE ISOLATION TANK ROOM.

*ACROSS the black tank, we see Jessup entering. He wears a jacket, sweater
and shapeless chinos from the previous scenes and carries Rosenberg's airline
bag. He turns on a valve. Water RUMBLES into the tank. He checks the
thermostat, opens the bag, extracts a jar of magnesium sulfate, pours it into
the spume gathering at the bottom of the tank. Stripping off his jacket and
sweater, he keeps checking the water level. He takes a Mason jar of clear liquid out of the bag, measures four cc's of the liquid into a syringe, squirts that
into a beaker. He drains the beaker in a single gulp. He walks to a shadowy
corner where a white porcelain bowl is sitting, stripping as he goes. He adds
his shirt to the piles made by his jacket and sweater. He goes into...*

THE OBSERVATION ROOM.

*...where he sits, checks the time on his watch and makes a notation in a note-
book. He unclips his watch, stands, walks back into...*

THE TANK ROOM.

...where he drops the watch on his clothing, checks the water level in the tank.

No. 22 AVON HILL, EMILY'S HOUSE. NIGHT.

*A taxi pulls up. The door opens, and Grace and Margaret tumble out and
head for the porch. They are followed by their mother.*

EMILY'S HOUSE, PORCH.

EMILY *(unlocking the front door)* It's eight-thirty, so get washed and changed right now, and I'm in no mood for any trouble from either of you tonight, do you understand?

The phone is RINGING inside. She gets the door open, the kids scoot in. Emily hurries across...

THE FOYER. NIGHT.

...and into...

THE LIVING ROOM.

The phone is still RINGING. She picks it up, snapping on the lights as she does.

EMILY *(on phone)* Yes, hello. Oh, Mason, thank you for calling. I assume you've spoken to Arthur...No, I just got back from dinner with the kids...Well, I just don't know what to say. I think you're absolutely right. I think he's on the verge of a breakdown. He was here all afternoon and carried on like a madman and then just disappeared. Ordinarily, I wouldn't be this panicky, but I just am.

THE OBSERVATION ROOM. NIGHT.

We are looking through the one-way window into the tank room at the black coffin-like tank, shrouded in shadow. We watch it for a beat. Then the lid starts to rise. It's being raised by what seems to be a furred arm—

THE TANK ROOM.

ANGLE looking down on the tank, as the lid is raised out of its grooves and pushed thudding to the floor, revealing a four-foot high creature, covered with a fine fur, standing waist-deep in the water—its stance human, bipedal if a bit sloping in the shoulders—definable features except for a massive projecting ridge of bone above the eyebrows and a prognathic jaw, a somewhat flattened skull, a low brow, chinless. A creature just tall enough for its little red eyes to barely see over the walls of the tank. It GRUNTS, makes a CLICKING SOUND.

B BUILDING, CADAVER ROOM. AN HOUR LATER, 9:30 PM.

HECTOR ORTEGA, thirty-nine years old, one of the janitorial staff at the medical school, gathers trashbags.

This is the room where they keep the cadavers hanging on hooks like sides of beef for the morning's dissection classes. There are two such naked, death-white cadavers hanging now. Ortega carries out the trash into...

B BUILDING, BASEMENT CORRIDOR.

...where he unloads them into the can of his cleaning cart. Then he trundles the cart along the corridor, trying doors as he goes. All are locked until he gets to the door of the Isolation Tank Room, which is marked Electroencephalography. It is unaccountably open. Interested, Ortega goes into...

THE ISOLATION TANK ROOM, ENTRYWAY. NIGHT.

The lights are on here and in the observation room. The door between them is closed. Ortega goes into...

THE OBSERVATION ROOM.

He looks through the one-way window into the tank room at the sinister coffin-like, uncovered tank. Ortega shrugs, starts to go back into the corridor, opens the door, changes his mind, turns and opens the door to the tank room.

He is immediately knocked against the wall by a hurtling, ferocious little animal, which, in his confusion, Ortega takes to be a dog. At least, he mutters imprecations in Spanish about who the hell down here is keeping a fucking dog. The animal has gotten out the door just before it closes. Ortega goes back out into...

B BUILDING CORRIDOR.

What he sees now about fifteen yards down the hall is an apelike creature, covered with a fine fur, that is unmistakably human. It stands upright. Its eyes are small and red but not deep-socketed like an ape's. Human intelligence seems to be in them. The creature is no bigger than Ortega's own nine-year-old son, but it is fierce, making a savage, rumbling SNARL, curling its lip and baring its teeth, which are yellow, even and very human in appearance.

Ortega is getting a little scared. He reaches for his janitor's broom and begins to unscrew the long handle.

ORTEGA *(calling hopefully to a colleague)* Hey, Jameson! Hey, Jameson, are you still there? Come here!

His voice echoes in the empty basement corridor. No response. Holding the broom pole, he takes a step toward the strange animal watching him.

ORTEGA Hey, Jameson, in the name of God, come over here and see this! *(brandishes his pole at the creature)* Es mejor que salgas de aquí antes de cometa una locura!

The creature's face flares with rage. It raises both furred fists and screams in fury. Ortega turns and bolts up the corridor to another hallway leading to D Building.

CONNECTING CORRIDOR TO D BUILDING.

Ortega comes tearing halfway down to a door marked Security Office. Behind him, he can hear enraged SCREECHES echoing off the walls. He knocks on the door of the Security Office, looking back up the connecting corridor, clutching his broomstick. The corridor is empty but still echoing. The door opens, and the bulky figure of Sergeant GEORGE OBISPO, a tall, uniformed man, appears.

OBISPO Que pasa?

ORTEGA   *(breathing hard, figuring out what's the matter)* Hay un animal suelto en el edificio B.

OBISPO Qué clase de animal es?

ORTEGA *(takes a moment to sort things out)* Un mono, creo.

A SHRIEK from the distant bowels of Building B ricochets off the walls.

OBISPO Carajo.

He strides up the corridor, unbuckling his nightstick. Ortega follows, holding his broom pole. Halfway down, they both pull up short, because in front of them, where the corridors to the buildings cross, the strange little creature suddenly lopes into view, silhouetted in the diffused yellow light. It regards the two men, then bursts into a shrill BARK. Its GROWL clearly signifies its frustration with the situation. It moves off with startling quickness. Obispo and Ortega break into a trot to get to...

B BUILDING CORRIDOR.

They pause, look down the length of the corridor to the right. It's empty. There is an exit door at the far end.

OBISPO   *(pulls out his walkie-talkie, speaking into it as he moves slowly up B Corridor into the set)* Charlie, Charlie Thomas, where are you? In the library?...Who you with?...Okay, listen, we got an animal loose in B Building basement, so you and Mingus come over here right away. We'll be in the north corridor that goes back to the nurses' residence, so you guys come down the other way, and we'll meet you at the door. We'll keep him cornered, but he's a pretty good-sized ape, and I better call the animal rooms and see what he's doing down here. But be very careful, because he looks dangerous. And come in fast, because I don't know how long we can hold him down here.

Obispo and Ortega have reached...

THE NORTH CORRIDOR.

Empty. This area is poorly lighted. An overhead neon tube is blown. It serves as a sometime storage area. A corrugated metal door leads to the Longwood Street loading platform on the left side. Huge empty cardboard cartons stand against this door. It's also an auxiliary changing room for the students, and both walls are lined with green and gray lockers. About sixty yards down, there is a set of doors with wire-reinforced windows in the upper halves.

ORTEGA He's hiding in there somewhere.

OBISPO No sé. *(nods at exit)* You think he could've got out that way?

Ortega tugs at the heavy door. It's stuck and takes all of Ortega's strength to open it.

ORTEGA He could never open this door.

Nevertheless, he leans into the stairwell and looks up to the street level and down to the sub-basement level. Behind him, Sergeant Obispo puts his walkie-talkie back into the case and, holding his club, moves into the shadows between the lockers, poking them with his club. CAMERA DOLLIES with him.

A terrifying SHRIEK and the creature leaps down upon him from the top of the lockers. Sergeant Obispo falls to the floor with a shout of terror. His club clatters on the cement.

THE STAIRWELL.

Ortega, who has gone down a landing, is petrified by the SHRIEKS. He starts climbing back up, tugs open the heavy door and bolts into...

THE NORTH CORRIDOR.

...where he stops, stares. ACROSS Ortega to where the hideous little creature is battering away at the fallen, SCREAMING Sergeant Obispo with

the Sergeant's own nightstick. The creature spots Ortega, whirls, and charges at the poor man. He bolts for his life down the B Building corridor.

NORTH CORRIDOR, THE OTHER SIDE OF THE DOORS.

Security Officers THOMAS and MINGUS break into a run, hearing Obispo's SCREAMS. Thomas is pulling out his chain of keys, tries to unlock doors. It is difficult to tell what is going on, because the wire-reinforced windows deform the view.

THEIR P.O.V. through the windows: A confused flux of shapes on the floor. The creature's high-pitched SCREAM and Obispo's BELLOWS of pain. Suddenly, the rectangular window is filled with a savage, hairy face, deformed by the quality of the glass.

Thomas and Mingus startle back from the door. Mingus pulls at his gun holster. Thomas gets the door open. The two guards fling themselves into the other corridor. Obispo is on his knees, a hulking black silhouette, holding his head and bleeding heavily. He slowly sinks unconscious to the floor. At the juncture of the corridors, the heavy exit door is slowly wheezing shut. The creature, whatever it was, is gone.

ROXBURY, CEDAR STREET. NIGHT.

Three WILD DOGS slink along the wet, black streets of this Boston ghetto. The houses are one-family frame and brick, and lit, emitting faint sounds of television. Cars are parked at the curb. A row of shops lines one side of the street, and on the corner is a bar with a neon sign. The rain has almost stopped, but men still wait, lounging in the doorway of the bar. One of them throws an empty beer can at the dogs. The can misses, clanks tinnily on the street.

The dogs barely notice. They pad softly past the row of store fronts, almost disappearing after about thirty yards. Into the darkness behind them, a form slips out from a recessed store front and trots along after the dogs. It is the creature last seen clubbing Sergeant Obispo.

ROXBURY, ANOTHER STREET. NIGHT.

This area is burned-out. The occasional six-story tenement with smashed, gaping black windows stands opposite demolished rubble. The three dogs pick and slink their way across this expanse. Keeping a distance behind them, JESSUP lopes along. He pauses to pick up a piece of jagged brick. A surreal scene in the derelict heart of the city. A hunt for prey.

BLUE HILL AVENUE, FRANKLIN PARK ZOO.

Mist. On the west side of the street, the high iron fence of Franklin Park Zoo opposite a row of small apartment houses. Jessup, his fine fur soaked through, holds his club and a piece of brick, hearing the TRILLS and CROAKS of birds. The dogs on the other side of the street are marauding garbage cans and plastic trash bags, sniffing up alleys and down basement steps in search of rats.

A small, snarling flurry among the dogs indicates a fight over something. It's over in seconds. A car whisks by, its windshield wipers stroking back and forth. The dogs slink over to the zoo side of the street.

Jessup watches them—filthy, skulking animals. Alert, Jessup doesn't move a muscle. They are twenty yards south of him, poking about for a hole in the zoo's fence. One suddenly wheels toward Jessup, baring its teeth, its yellow eyes wide. The other dogs snarl softly, turn their heads toward the curious little ape-like creature.

With a SHRILL SHRIEK, Jessup dashes at the dogs, brandishing stick and stone. They scatter, slink back, keeping their distance. His cry rouses the birds in the zoo, as a FLUTTERING of distant wings and BIRD CALLS signal danger to the caged animals.

The lead dog, a MONGREL MASTIFF with white markings on its brow, growls softly, pads into the street, moving up on Jessup's flank. Jessup watches him warily, responding with a SNARL of his own. The mongrel leaps at Jessup's throat. Jessup batters at the red-tongued maw. Two other dogs lunge in. Jessup wheels on them, SHRIEKING with fury, smashing at them with his club and brick.

A SCREECHING of tires on the wet pavement. A car, headlights blazing, veers around the corner, dispersing the dogs and disappearing up the street.

Silence, then the dogs slink back to continue the feral battle. But the ape-like creature is gone. They soon spot him again—squatting on the stonework that forms the top of the fence.

Ape-like, he taunts the dogs. He soon tires of it and with agility climbs down on the zoo side.

THE ZOO. NIGHT.

Jessup finds himself on grass and ground. The street lights of Blue Hill Avenue spill over enough to let Jessup see bushes and trees. He GRUNTS with pleasure at this familiar terrain. He can see a low wattled fence and grass receding into darkness and silence. The zoo is asleep.

On the crest of the slope is a RED GLOW. Jessup stands stock-still, listening for the distant BURR of a crane. He moves forward, finding himself on a walkway. Puzzled by the hard feel beneath his feet, he follows the path for a ways, until he sees water—the wild fowl pond—glistening blackly.

The air hangs heavy and fetid with animal smells, the silence weighted by the massive sensation of sleep.

He moves further, cutting between trees and bushes, until he reaches an open area and is startled by the abrupt stone building, rearing up and made visible by the light-colored stone. Further along, he sees the RED GLOW again off to the right and slips softly in that direction. What he sees are a building's night lights given a red hue by the tinted windows, the small mammals building. He approaches the low stone building, stretching around him in a soft, red haze. He peers inside.

JESSUP'S P.O.V.: An empty hallway bathed in a soft red light cast over cages of mice, porcupines, sloths and shrews, curled up in balls of furry sleep. An occasional slithering movement heads toward a watering trough. All of it is incomprehensible to Jessup; he is quickly bored.

THE ZOO, ANOTHER SECTION.

Jessup makes his way around empty round cages with thick iron bars—the great apes building—and down macadam paths lined with protective railings. He hears the croaking BURR of a crane, much closer. He freezes, waits, listens. To his left, a stone outcropping is barely discernible in a fenced area for the giraffes.

Suddenly behind him to the right, he senses movement and a CROWNED CRANE prances into his vision. It is sufficiently lit to be recognized by the glistening red and white spots on its face and straw-colored topknot of feathers. It stares blankly out of its button eyes, turns and disappears. Jessup stands staring back at it with his club and bit of brick. Reaching the low wooden fence, he squints into the darkness trying to see the crane again. It's gone, he moves on.

THE ZOO, THE AFRICAN PLAINS.

Jessup stands in front of a four-foot HEDGEROW used to disguise a wooden fence enclosing this section of the park. The dark is impenetrable, but he hears SOUNDS—of East African grasslands, movements of animals, the startled flurry of veering herds.

Forcing his way through the bramble of hedgerow, he crawls beneath the horizontal poles of the fence. He soon finds himself on the edge of a shallow moat, some four feet deep and ten feet wide.

The spill of STREETLIGHT from Seaver Street allows Jessup to make out that he is on high ground with a tract of savanna stretching out before him. At the bottom of the slope, he can see a waterhole. On his right is a sparse woodland and a group of sleeping blesboks. He grunts with pleasure.

Letting himself down into the moat, as high as he is tall, he moves along until he finds an overhanging limb to pull himself up onto the other side. Landing on a small stone outcrop, he startles a herd of some forty mouflon huddled for the night near the wooden palisade of their paddock. The herd of sheep skews madly into the open grass.

Jessup stands stock still, holding his club and brick, waiting for his presence to become part of this world. Silence. At a waterhole on his left, a single hartebeest humps forward, lapping quietly at the water.

Through the wet grass, Jessup heads for the end of the waterhole furthest from the hartebeest. Pausing at the edge, he tries to sense the presence of other predators. The hartebeest raises its head, watches him, prepared to bolt. Jessup get down on his knees and begins to lap the water. The hartebeest returns to its own drinking. We watch the two animals, sharing the waterhole, each drinking warily.

From a dark slope, Jessup watches the herd of mouflon huddled in a sparse little grove about twenty yards away. They're edgy, trembling even as they sleep. A skittish few on the periphery of the flock flit here and there like butterflies. The zoo sleeps.

Nothing moves anywhere. The air is heavy and wet. He waits. A flicker of movement in the herd. A lamb bounds away, rejoins the herd. Three sheep run, whirl, fluttering shadows of movement followed by silence. Jessup waits. In one hand he holds his club and bit of brick, in the other are two round stones that he suddenly pitches into the trees where the herd lies. With the first rustle of leaves, the herd explodes dementedly, scattering.

Half a dozen leap and skitter past Jessup. He takes after them with a SHRIEK, driving their agitated wild shadows before him past the waterhole straight for the moat. At the lip of the moat, all but one veer and shoot off into the safety of darkness. The one tries to leap the chasm. It falls in a heap to the bottom of the moat, crippled. Jessup jumps after it and, with a single stroke of his club, smashes the animal's skull.

THE ZOO, THE MOAT.

Jessup scrapes away the sheep's hide with his jagged chip of brick, stripping a good-sized piece off its haunch. He pauses, looking up, sensing danger. A low GROWL can be heard, not far away. He stands, picks up his kill by a leg and moves softly, quickly up the wide, dark moat until he finds an overhanging branch.

He places the sheep carcass on the lip of the moat and hauls himself up to it. He picks up his club and brick, checks the terrain, then squats down, raising the carcass to his face, clamps his teeth into the hot, bloody flesh. He twists his head back and forth, wrenching the gobbet of flesh free. He chews at it, then looks up, again sensing danger.

Led by the mastiff with the white markings, the three dogs are moving up the slope from the waterhole. These lumps of black movement in the black grass halt a few yards from him, GROWLING. Jessup makes a NOISE of his own and brandishes his club. They keep away.

CAMERA PULLS BACK for the image of Jessup, squatting in the grass, eating the sheep in the night with a sullen satisfaction, keeping the snarling dogs at bay—a primal animal at one with his elemental world.

THE ZOO. NIGHT, 2:00 A.M.

In the CLEAR MOONLIGHT, a jeep crawls along the pathways, parking lights on. A zoo SECURITY GUARD on night duty spots some movement on the African Plains. He stops, lets the jeep idle, gets out and peers over the wire fence enclosing the area.

ACROSS the guard looking up the slope, something is going on. The rain is long over, the moon bright. From here it looks like the three dogs are ravening at something.

The guard climbs over the fence and starts up the slope, drawing his revolver. The dogs see him and scatter. He moves in to see what they were eating: the remains of the mouflon. The guard looks to see if the dogs are still skulking around.

They are gone, but the guard's eye is caught by a WHITE BLUR in the dark grass some twenty yards away under a tree. He cocks his gun and moves cautiously. It is a naked man. It is Jessup—sleeping, his chest rising and falling evenly. There is a beatific smile on his face.

FRANKLIN PARK PRECINCT, SQUAD ROOM. 3:30 A.M.

In the typical, old, battered police station house, a COP brings Jessup out of the bowels of the building, dressed and carrying an empty overnight bag that he hands to Emily, who, along with Parrish, has been anxiously waiting for him.

JESSUP See what you can do about getting me out of here.

EMILY It's all done. Mason has his car outside...

OUTSIDE THE PRECINCT STATION. NIGHT.

Jessup is getting into the front passenger seat.

JESSUP *(vague, stunned)* I'd like to stop by the medical school. I left all my clothes in the tank room.

EMILY *(sliding into the car beside him)* Let's just get you home. It's three thirty in the morning.

JESSUP I have my watch and my wallet there. My keys are there. I'll need them to get in the apartment.

EMILY I've got my keys. I had to stop off to get you some clothes.

PARRISH *(sliding behind the wheel)* I'll go back and get your stuff later.

Parrish starts the motor, and they move off.

PARRISH'S CAR, EN ROUTE. NIGHT.

Emily glances surreptitiously at her husband sitting between her and Parrish. He seems to be in a state of shock, distracted, oddly placid, lobotomized as he stares through the windshield, almost unaware of her or Parrish.

EMILY What were you doing in the tank room? *(He doesn't seem to hear her.)* Do you remember anything at all about last night?

JESSUP *(staring at her blankly for a moment)* I remember large fragments of what happened, but not all of it. You'll have to be patient with me.

He turns back to stare out the windshield again.

EMILY I've had Mason looking all over Boston for you all night.

She lets her head sink onto his chest and cries.

JESSUP *(murmurs into her hair)* It's okay, I'm alright...

JESSUP'S APARTMENT, KITCHEN. NIGHT.

Emily sits at the kitchen table, sipping coffee and nibbling at cookies from a box. She looks up as Jessup enters, swathed in a towel-robe, patting himself dry. He makes himself a cup of instant coffee. He seems in a very good mood, excited, exhilarated.

JESSUP *(affably)* I suppose getting a call from the police at three o'clock in the morning to the effect your husband has been found sleeping naked in the city zoo might have caused you some concern.

EMILY Yes, I think you could say that.

JESSUP And Mason's been writing you all this time telling you I'm having a nervous breakdown, and you figured I finally flipped out altogether.

He sits across from her and begins to say something, he laughs—a full, open, exuberant laugh. After a bit, he wipes his eyes.

JESSUP I'm sorry, Emily, forgive me. I know what a harrowing day I've caused you. I'm sure you've been sitting here all this time while trying to figure out how to get me to a psychiatrist.

EMILY As a matter of fact, I have.

JESSUP I don't know how you've put up with me all these years.

EMILY I loved you.

He stands, cries out in exultation.

JESSUP Oh, my God, Emily! I don't know how to tell you this! I really don't! Bear with me, Emily! The implications are staggering.

He strides off into the living room. She follows to the doorway.

THE LIVING ROOM. NIGHT.

He is moving erratically around the room, so exhilarated that his arms and legs seem out of control.

JESSUP *(trying to keep his voice calm)* I don't remember all of it. Apparently, I entered a very primitive consciousness, and all I can remember of last night is what was comprehensible to that consciousness. I don't remember, at least not clearly, how I got out of the tank room. The first thing I remember are the dogs. I followed a pack of wild dogs to the zoo. That's how I got there. In the zoo, I hunted down and ate a small sheep. I was utterly primal. I consisted of nothing more than the will to survive, to live through the night, to eat, to drink, to sleep. It was the most supremely satisfying time of my life. *(He is up again, moving around the room in a gathering frenzy of creativity.)* On a strictly physiological level, I suspect we achieved an observable momentum at enough nuclear locations to alter the actual form. The drug probably affects the bonding. But even if we could establish a biochemical setting for this, so what? Suppose we get some cells, crack them open, get some assays. Okay, so we get all kinds of whacked out polyribosomal profiles. Fantastic enzymatic activity. I'm making protein at an unbelievable pace. I mean, let's face it! This whole thing is biologically impossible! We're not just talking about one cell or even a colony of cells going wild. We're talking about a massive mutation of my entire biological system, a process that took millions of years to evolve reversing itself in a matter of hours if not moments. Some extraordinary transfer of energy has occurred. We may be into some kind of exotic relativistic physics here in which consciousness snapped me into some new sharp attribute. Don't we have a physicist in our circle of friends? I'd like to bounce this off a quantum guy. Because, you see, Emily, what I think happened is I somehow got into a quantum state where there is no matter, only the potential of matter. It makes sense, doesn't it? Some original and universal state of energy potential. I somehow tapped into that original consciousness of pure potential. My God, what an implacably beautiful thought!

He stands glowing, radiant, frozen by his vision, his eyes closed, staring into eternity, his face as masklike as an icon's.

JESSUP   It must be true. Anything that beautiful must be true. *(He doesn't even know she's in the room anymore.)*

He sighs as if in sexual consummation and sinks into the embrace of the soft chair.

EMILY   You still haven't told me what happened tonight.

He sprawls in the chair, seeming to be almost asleep.

JESSUP   After I left you this afternoon, I went to the isolation tank room, took two hundred milligrams of the stuff, got into the tank, and at some point during the evening, I transformed my matter into some form of early human life.

The doorbell RINGS.

EMILY   That must be Mason.

She sits frightened by the madness she has just heard. The doorbell RINGS again. Emily stands, starts for the door.

JESSUP   I may have killed a man tonight, or damn near killed him. I remember beating somebody bloody.

Emily pauses at the door, sighs, then opens it. Parrish booms into the room, carrying Jessup's clothing over his arm.

PARRISH   Man! You don't know the trouble I had getting these clothes! I had to go to the security office for them! They want you to call them right now. There was some kind of ape in your isolation tank room tonight, do you know anything about that? This ape almost killed a security guard. You didn't bring an ape down to the tank room tonight, did you? Your watch and stuff are in the jacket pocket. *(dumps the clothing on a chair, senses something is wrong)* Is everything all right? Is he okay?

EMILY   If he's okay, the rest of us are in a lot of trouble. *(pauses as she moves toward the kitchen)* Tell Mason what you've been telling me. I'd like to hear Mason's views on all this.

JESSUP   I think Mason's views will be predictable.

EMILY'S HOUSE, FRONT PORCH. SUNDAY. DAY.

It is two days later, a pleasant Sunday afternoon in April. Emily, Parrish, the Rosenbergs all lounge on the porch. Sylvia is nursing an infant. The Jessup kids and the Rosenberg boy can be seen in the background. Parrish's predictable views are being expounded by him at the moment.

PARRISH   *(to Rosenberg)* He wigged out, had a toxic delirium, ran around the streets of Boston naked and wound up sleeping in the zoo. This is hardly the first instance of drug-induced delirium any of us have heard of.

EMILY   What worries me is he actually believes his hallucination. I mean, he actually thinks he turned into an apeman. He can't tell hallucination from reality anymore.

PARRISH   As for that strange ape they found in the tank room that night, I'm sure it'll turn out to be some local kid who broke in to steal some drugs, or something like that.

EMILY   I called him yesterday morning and last night, and I spoke to him this morning again. He sounds absolutely fine. He's going over to M.I.T. to brainstorm with some physicists on Wednesday. I told him he ought to spend some time with the kids. He hasn't seen them in a year, they've been asking for him. This has got to be the most hideous weekend I ever lived. I'm still not unpacked. My husband has had a breakdown, and do you know the only thing I can think about right now is I've got to place the kids in a school tomorrow morning?

PARRISH   And now he wants to do it again, and he wants us to watch him.

EMILY   For God's sake, you're not going to let him do it again.

ROSENBERG   How do you plan to stop him?   Listen, if you're worried about his flipping out again, we can always bring him down with a little benzodiazepine. But the point is there is no way we're going to talk him out of going into that tank again. He's going to do it with us or without us, and I think it'd be a hell of a lot better if it was with us.

The point is arguable.

PARRISH   *(to Emily)*   When're you going over to look at his data?

EMILY   Thursday, while he's with the kids.

JESSUP'S APARTMENT, LIVING ROOM. DAY.

Emily reads a sheaf of papers—the blood analysis reports from the Goodman labs. Jessup's notebooks, X-rays and stacks of audio cassettes are stacked on the coffee table in front of her as she sits on the sofa. There is a tape playing of Jessup's aphasic experience.

JESSUP'S VOICE   *(on cassette)*   He's beating me with his chunk of lava! He's gouging gobbets of me with his chunk of lava!

ROSENBERG'S VOICE   *(on cassette)*   Are you okay, Eddie?

JESSUP'S VOICE   *(on cassette)*   No pain! No pain! I tell you, no pain...

We can see that Emily is not actually reading, but has been caught by the theatricality of the tape.

JESSUP'S VOICE *(on cassette)* He's devouring me! Ripping my flesh! Of course! It's me! It's my primordial me devouring me! I'm returning to my original me! Unbelievable sensation! Ineffable! Beatitude! Absolutely transcendental! I'm it, and it's me! I'm the hunter now! I'm the killer! I'm killing! I'm eating! I'm eating the blood-hot flesh of a giant goat! I'm eating a goat I just killed! I'm eating a goat!

Jessup's voice breaks into a CROAK and some CLICKING noises, then a HOWL. Emily lets the tape run, just long enough to know there's nothing more. She quickly rewinds and plays the GRUNTS and CLICKING SOUNDS and HOWL again. She rewinds yet again, plays it, listens with the most intense interest.

McDONALD'S RESTAURANT. NIGHT, 9:30 P.M.

The Jessups seem to be a typical American family among a large dining room of typical American families. It's late.

Emily and Jessup are down to their coffee, and Margaret is cranky and whining, and Jessup has to hold her. He is talking, and Emily is fascinated.

JESSUP   Physicists see the whole thing in terms of particles and energy states. You get situations in particle physics, where you have something in one state and then suddenly you'll find it appearing in another state. It has apparently zipped through a forbidden region between the states. What I may have done is reduce my uncertainty in energy to zero or near enough to zero, so that the time available to me to tunnel through had been infinite.

In background, Grace, who has been roaming around the restaurant, falls and cries. Jessup rises and gets her, without letting it stop the flow of ideas he's trying to communicate.

JESSUP   Where I differ from the physicists is they conceive of consciousness as a particular force exerted by a particular person. I see it as a cosmic, perhaps *the* cosmic force. Our universe exploded into being some twenty billion years ago, a fantastic explosion of hydrogen, so it all began with an actual act of creation. What did the creating? That original creative force is what I call consciousness. You can call it God if you like, but there's a difference. Consciousness is not a noumenal process; it's phenomenological. It can be reached, tapped, manipulated. Lord knows, I believe I tapped into it.

EMILY   I think I better get the kids home.

She gets the sleepy kids jacketed and on their way. Jessup watches her movements: her saucy ass, the long legs, her natural physical sensuality.

JESSUP   I'd like to go home with you tonight, would that be all right with you?

She pauses, turns, smiles at him.

EMILY   Do you know, I think that's exactly what you said to me the first night we met, do you remember? In Arthur and Sylvia's apartment back in New York?

JESSUP   Yes, and you said we'd have to make do with the couch. The couch is still okay with me.

EMILY   I've finally made my peace with this divorce, Eddie. It's been a very painful year for me, and I think it would be dumb to reintroduce sex between us. So thank you for what really has been a fascinating day. I'll drop you off.

EMILY'S APARTMENT, HER BEDROOM. NIGHT.

Emily is asleep. Suddenly she sits bolt upright, propelled out of her sleep by an insufferable nightmare, for the terror lingers in her eyes. After a moment, she lies back again, but her eyes are open. There is no more sleep for her now.

She sits, swings her legs over and slumps there in her pajamas, trying to subdue her fear. She looks at her watch on the bedtable, goes out into...

THE HALLWAY.

...and down to the door of her kids' room. She watches them sleep, then heads back down the hallway to...

THE LIVING ROOM.

...where she slumps into a chair. But she is immediately up again wandering around the dark room, distraught. Finally she goes to the phone and dials.

EMILY *(on phone)* Did I wake you? It's Emily...Eddie, I'm in kind of a wild panic. I need to talk to you...

OUTSIDE EMILY'S HOUSE. NIGHT.

Jessup's Toyota pulls into the driveway. He gets out, cuts across the lawn to the porch, up the stoop to where Emily is waiting for him. They go into...

THE FOYER.

The lamplight from the living room spills into the darkness.

EMILY I don't even know how to put this into words, but I'm beginning to think that what happened to you last Friday night was not just a hallucinatory experience. I've got this gut feeling something phenomenological did actually happen, that there was some kind of genetic transformation. I don't know why I think that in defiance of all rationality. But I do. And now that I do, I'm terrified. I mean, really terrified, petrified.

JESSUP So am I.

EMILY *(as soon as she closes the door)* I don't want you doing this experiment again next week.

JESSUP We've got to find out if it actually happened, Emily.

They move to the threshold of the shadowy living room.

EMILY I'm suggesting that you put the experiment off until we understand a little more in order to minimize the risk.

JESSUP There is no way we can understand this before the event. We can only work back from the event itself.

EMILY You may be causing yourself irreversible genetic damage.

JESSUP I don't think we're dealing with genetics. We're beyond mass and matter here, beyond even energy. What we're back to is the first thought.

EMILY Something monstrous is going to happen.

JESSUP All our evidence indicates nothing irreversible is going to happen. None of my experiences have lasted longer than four hours, and I have always reconstituted completely.

EMILY I'm trying to tell you that I love you.

JESSUP I know that. And I'm trying to tell you this is an all-bets-are-off sort of thing! We may be opening a black box that could scrap our whole picture of space-time! We might even have a link to another universe. For God's sake, Emily, you're a scientist! You know how I feel!

And, of course, she does.

EMILY *(sighs)* Yes, I know how you feel. It's very late Eddie. Would you like to stay here tonight? I could do with a little love and a little reassurance right now. You'll stay, won't you?

EMILY'S HOUSE. FRIDAY, APRIL 30, 7:30 P.M. STORMY.

The rain and thunder create a befittingly Gothic night. Thunder RUMBLES. Rain lashes through the streets. LIGHTNING bleaches the scene. Emily comes out of her house in a raincoat with an umbrella and braves her way to the car.

MEDICAL SCHOOL, B BUILDING, BASEMENT. NIGHT.

Emily comes in through the exit door at the end of the corridor, shaking her umbrella out.

CORRIDOR TO THE TANK ROOM.

She heads up the corridor to the tank room. There is considerable traffic of hospital personnel on such a rainy night, all going about their individual duties. Emily turns into...

THE OBSERVATION ROOM.

Rosenberg stands beside an examining table with an attached I.V. stand, loading it. On the examining table, there are a narrow tray, a biopsy tray, a prep kit, a 35mm Nikon and videotape setup, camera and console, along with two gooseneck standing lamps. Through the window, we see Parrish by the isolation tank talking to Jessup. He smiles at her. She responds with a nervous smile of her own.

ROSENBERG *(indicates the I.V.)* If it happens, we'll give him a big bolus of amytal for starters...

EMILY *(raw nerves exploding)* What do you mean, if it happens? If it happens? Everybody keeps saying if it happens. Do you think something's going to happen, Arthur? Because if you do, then I think—I'm sorry, Arthur. I'm nervous as hell.

ROSENBERG Listen, so am I.

She goes into...

THE TANK ROOM. NIGHT.

In the subdued lighting Parrish is by the uncovered tank, staring down into the water, as Jessup is taking off his clothes.

JESSUP *(to Parrish)* If I come out of that tank anthropoid, I'll be in a very primitive consciousness and impossible to relate to, so sedate me while I'm still in the tank. Otherwise, you'll have to chase me around and subdue me.

PARRISH Okay.

Jessup goes into the observation room to continue undressing. Emily comes down to examine the tank, seeing it for the first time.

PARRISH I'll tell you this, if he comes out of that tank looking like an ape, I'm going straight over to Mass Mental and commit myself.

ISOLATION TANK ROOM/OBSERVATION ROOM. NIGHT.

Emily sits with Parrish, lighting up a cigarette. Rosenberg enters with a brown paper bag.

ROSENBERG Anything happen?

PARRISH *(shakes his head)* I just checked him ten minutes ago.

Rosenberg has apparently come from the local deli and unloads coffee and sandwiches and Danish. Emily abruptly goes into...

THE TANK ROOM.

...where she goes down to the tank, lifts the hinged headpiece, looks in.

EMILY'S P.O.V.: From deep within the square blackness exposed by the open lid, Jessup's white face stares blankly out, framed, cadaverous, like a plaster cast sunk into a cushion of blackness.

MEDICAL SCHOOL, B BUILDING, CORRIDOR.

Several hours later, Emily is manifestly agitated and walks aimlessly about the corridor smoking. She looks at her watch, crushes out the cigarette, returns to...

ISOLATION TANK ROOM/OBSERVATION ROOM.

...where Parrish is cleaning up the mess from the deli, gathering half-eaten sandwiches, empty containers, etc., into a brown paper bag. Rosenberg is reading a mystery novel.

EMILY *(no longer able to contain herself)* Look, I've got nearly ten. That's more than two hours now. Is there any way we can stop this? I tell you, frankly, I'm really frightened. We could be screwing around with his whole genetic structure. How do we stop this?

HALLUCINATORY BLIP —A WHITE-ORANGE JAGGED FLAME shears diagonally across the entire length of the screen, seeming to rip it in half—the same JAGGED CRACK that occurred in Jessup's Mexican hallucination.

Neither Emily, Rosenberg nor Parrish seems aware of this extraordinary invasion of their reality.

PARRISH Can you bring him down, Arthur?

ROSENBERG He's going to be sore as hell.

EMILY *(in full-fledged panic)* We never should've let him do it! How did we let him talk us into this?! We were humoring him. But we know he's not crazy! And we all know deep in our hearts he may be on to something that is beyond our own comprehension. Because I believe him! I want this stopped!

SUDDEN HALLUCINATORY BLIP —*Out of a sable sea an enormous VOLCANIC cone of ROCK surges up, ERUPTING with FLAME and BOILING rock, hundreds of tons of plutonic EXPLOSION, a fantastic FOUNTAIN of ROCK and SCALDING WATER rising two thousand feet into the air. Again, the others seem unaware they are being invaded.*

ROSENBERG *(clicking on the mike)* How're we doing, Eddie?

He waits for a response. There is none.

EMILY Oh, Jesus...

HALLUCINATORY IMAGE —*An EXPLOSION, a shattering FLASH of brilliant WHITENESS fills the SCREEN. Emily, Rosenberg and Parrish are made almost invisible, bleached out. We see just enough of Emily to realize she is slowly becoming aware of the reality of her husband's hallucination.*

A high-pitched SCREAMING DRONE of energy. We are back to the reality of the observation room again, except that WAVES of different COLORS pulsate and throb across the SCREEN. Neither Rosenberg nor Parrish are aware of this; but Emily is staring blindly ahead—seeing and hearing it all. The SCREAM abruptly stops.

Suddenly, over the speaker on the top shelf, we hear a rasping kind of GRUNT and a series of CLICKING SOUNDS. Emily turns to the two men, her face in panic, and pleads.

EMILY *(almost screaming)* Please!!

Parrish unwinds himself from his sprawled position, gets up and goes to...

THE TANK ROOM.

...where he moves to the tank and lifts the headpiece.

Parrish looks down into the tank, this time into the sleeping mask of a somewhat gorilla-like face, its skin a black and shining hide. The close-cropped scalp extends down almost to the heavy simian ridge bulging slightly across the brow. The facial fur is finer than that found on apes and does not entirely cover the ears. The lower jaw is prognathic, the lips extended and open, revealing strong yellow but very human teeth. The eyes, even closed, are more human than apelike, larger and not sunk into deep sockets. The neck, shoulders and part of the chest visible are all covered with a fine, short fur.

REACTION SHOT shows Parrish...sighing for lack of any other reaction.

PARRISH *(to himself)* There is no way no how that this can be explained on any physical level. *(raises his voice but maintains a calm)* Have you got your needle ready, Arthur? He said to nail him while he was still in the tank.

A moment later, the door opens and Rosenberg is framed in the bright light.

ROSENBERG *(nervous)* What do you mean?

The eyelids of the creature open slowly, revealing malevolent little red eyes.

PARRISH *(seeing this in the tank)* Goddammit, Arthur, bring your goddam syringe over here.

OBSERVATION ROOM. NIGHT.

Emily stands at the one-way window, peering into the tank room and reaches over to hand Rosenberg his airline bag. HOLD on Emily long enough to see tears streaming down her face.

TANK ROOM.

Unzipping his bag, Rosenberg joins Parrish at the tank, stops and stares in astonishment at the proto-human face looking back at him.

ROSENBERG *(babbling)* How...do we define this? I mean, there is no coherent schemata for this. We need a whole new language, Holy God Almighty, we need a whole new space-time picture. We...

Abruptly he stops as a penetrating DRONING SOUND emanates from somewhere about them. He and Parrish look around with a growing terror, as they face a line of BLUE LIGHT moving across the increasingly darkening room toward them.

Swiftly the BLUE LIGHT sweeps through the tank in SHOCK WAVES, and the four walls of the tank fly apart, as if a nuclear blast had been detonated inside of it. Both Parrish and Rosenberg are flung against the walls of the room. The water GEYSERS to the ceiling in a SCREAMING MUSH-ROOM CLOUD, crashing with a CLAP as loud as thunder, and then floods the room ankle-deep.

INFRA-RED WAVES of light sweep back and forth across the room, accumulating in intensity to ORANGES and YELLOWS that seem hotter than the sun, and the whole of the tank room FLARES molten with heat.

THE OBSERVATION ROOM.

Emily is stupefied.

HER P.O.V.: Where the tank had been is a pulsating WHITE MASS rising out of the thin layer of BOILING WATER. This grotesque, unformed white thing has been gouged, revealing a skeletal structure underneath. Emily SCREAMS in terror. She lunges at the door to the tank room and wrenches it open and plunges, SCREAMING, into...

THE TANK ROOM.

...splashing ankle-deep into the room, she—like Rosenberg and Parrish over at the far wall—gapes stupefied at what is happening.

The MASS of SUBSTANCE seems to be assuming form: stumps of arms and legs, misshapen and misplaced, BULGE and RECEDE. The substance itself changes color, BUBBLING and BOILING, as if cooked by an interior fire. Then it begins a PIERCING, AGONIZED SCREAM.

Emily's hysterical immobility is overcome, as she hears this SCREAM, and she splashes toward her husband. The room is COSMIC BLACK, PUL-

SATING with *WAVES* of force, *SHUDDERING BANDS* of *RADIA-TION*, and *DRONING* with *ENERGY*.

Jessup's form is recognizably human still, but seems caught in a PINCH of ENERGY WAVES, temperature differences, changing his coloration from LUMINOUS WHITE to FOGGY INFRA-RED, then BURNING RED of ultra-violet radiation to blurred CHIAROSCURO BLACKS and GRAYS, the quality of X-rays.

Jessup's form appears to DISSOLVE in SHIMMERING VIBRATIONS, then suddenly SWELLS until it DISTENDS into a sphere of gas, shocking YELLOW GAS turning RED, collapsing back under the weight of its own gravity. His bowels erupt into flames, rekindling the maniacal CARNAGE of COLORS, becoming WHITE HOT. He begins to SCREAM again in terror, sinking to his knees as if he were melting, imploding as if he were being sucked into his own black hole.

Emily flings herself upon this SHUDDERING, SHAPELESS anti-matter and embraces her husband. Not fifteen seconds have elapsed since the first explosion.

In Emily's arms, Jessup's form THROBS and CRACKS and RES-ONATES, as he SCREAMS his primal SHRIEK. His eyes stare blindly at some unspeakable horror. Then the fluctuating extensions that are almost the shape of arms flow out and unform themselves around his wife. They kneel together on the flooded floor, two terrified figures alone in the dense, black, spaceless DRONE of energy—clinging to each other against the horror of human origins.

Abruptly, the demented HUM of entropic forces stops. The COSMIC BLACK RECEDES, snatched away as Emily presses to her the entirely reconstituted naked form of her husband. They remain locked in their desperate embrace amid the wreckage of the tank room. Fragments of wood are everywhere, floating listlessly.

Jessup is no longer screaming. There is NO SOUND at all. The silence is palpable, as Emily looks down at the ashen face resting on her breast, apparently in a coma. She turns her own harrowed face to Rosenberg and Parrish, lumbering to their feet, mutely asking them for help.

Parrish sloshes over to her to disengage Jessup's limp form from Emily's embrace and carry it to the door.

MYRTLE STREET, JESSUP'S HOUSE. 45 MINUTES LATER.

Parrish's car pulls up to the curb. Between him and Emily, they get Jessup, now clothed, out of the car. Parrish carries him in in total shock.

PARRISH Bring my bag.

Emily reaches into the car for the doctor's bag, then leads the way up the walk and opens the door. They go into...

JESSUP'S HOUSE, FOYER AND HALLWAY. NIGHT.

Carrying Jessup, Parrish follows Emily into...

JESSUP'S LIVING ROOM/BEDROOM.

Emily turns on the lights for Parrish to bring Jessup to his bed. Parrish gets out his stethoscope, begins to take Jessup's pulse and examine him. Emily goes out into the...

LIVING ROOM.

...and crosses it to the...

KITCHEN.

...where she rummages for the instant coffee. Dazed, she stands there in the middle of the kitchen, tears streaming down her face.

LIVING ROOM. FIFTEEN MINUTES LATER.

Parrish sprawls on the couch, sipping from a mug that he rests on his stomach. Emily moves aimlessly around the room, verging on hysteria.

PARRISH His signs are all good. He'll probably sleep a day or two, come out of it a little stuporous. He's got a whopping load of drugs in him. It's not uncommon for a psychedelic experience to whack you out for a couple of days.

EMILY You'd hardly call this just a psychedelic experience.

She goes into...

THE BEDROOM.

In the darkness she looks down at her husband with his eyes closed. He is motionless and yet somehow not asleep. She turns back to...

THE LIVING ROOM.

PARRISH His heart's good, his pulse is good, his pressure's good. I'm more worried about you than I am about him.

EMILY *(sinks into the soft chair)* I'm all right, Mason.

Obviously she's not. A spasm of shudders racks her, and she doubles forward in the grips of a cramp, her head on her knees. And she cries. Parrish slowly moves to her, placing a comforting hand on her back, and she starts to her feet like a frightened doe.

EMILY *(crying out)* Of all the goddamned men in this world, why do I have to love this one?! I can't get him out of me. Do you know how many men I tried to fall in love with this past year? But it won't work! No matter whom I'm in bed with, I have to imagine it's him, or nothing happens. No matter whom I'm eating with or walking with, there's always that pain, because it isn't him. I'm possessed by him! It's crazy!

PARRISH I think that's the way it's supposed to be.

EMILY He doesn't give a damn about me.

PARRISH Oh Emily, you're the only thing he really cares about outside his work.

She manages to remain contained, but the sensation of hysteria remains imminent.

EMILY No, Mason, he's a truth-lover, a God-fucker. I was never real to him. Nothing in the human condition was ever real to him. Reality to Eddie is only that which is changeless, immutably constant. What happened to him tonight—that was Eddie's idea of love. That was consummation. He finally got it off with God. He finally embraced the Absolute, was finally ravished by Truth. And it fucking near destroyed him! *(On her feet again, she's yielding to the hysteria.)* He never loved me! You knew him as well as I did. We were all bits of transitory matter to him!

She sits abruptly on the couch, frozen. Parrish observes her.

PARRISH You're going into shock, I'm going to give you something.

FOYER. SEVERAL HOURS LATER.

Rosenberg comes down the hall to the apartment, starts to ring the bell, thinks better and knocks. Just as he's about to knock again, Parrish opens the door.

ROSENBERG How is he?

PARRISH Same. She's a wreck though.

ROSENBERG Who isn't?

He goes into...

THE LIVING ROOM.

Emily is stretched out on the couch, resting but not asleep.

PARRISH   Did you get the place cleaned up?

ROSENBERG   Yeah. What a mess.

EMILY   There's sandwich stuff and coffee in the kitchen, if you want anything, Arthur.

ROSENBERG   No, I'm okay. How're you doing?

EMILY   I'll be all right. I called Sylvia to tell her not to worry about you.

ROSENBERG   Thanks.

He sits. Parrish sits. All are silent, subdued, still overwhelmed. All the lights are on, but it does little to relieve the tenebrous sensation that makes the air around them so dense.

ROSENBERG   Look, it's got to be said. What the three of us witnessed tonight was one of the most fantastic instances in the history of science. Analogous perhaps to the first time somebody looked through a microscope lens and discovered solid matter wasn't solid. We reached a point tonight where physical science just breaks down. We're in blue skies. Tonight was history, and what're we going to do about it?

PARRISH   I'm doing nothing about it. Tonight scared the hell out of me, and all I want to do is go home and go to sleep and wake up and forget about the whole goddam thing.

ROSENBERG   Maybe you're right. Maybe we ought to drop it till tomorow.

He stands, goes into...

THE KITCHEN.

...where he slaps together a cheese sandwich from what's on the table, but the suppressed excitement within him takes over, and he drops the sandwich and comes back into...

THE LIVING ROOM.

ROSENBERG *(getting excited)* That tank just blew up. Whatever happened inside that tank released a hell of a lot of energy.

PARRISH *(flaring)* For God's sake! Let's drop the goddam thing! I don't want to talk about it!

ROSENBERG *(flaring back at him)* I can't help it. You may want to go to sleep, but the way I feel right now, I don't expect to go to sleep for a year! I'm on fucking fire! I'm in there mopping up that goddam tank room, and I've got to know why! Do you believe in supernatural agencies, Mason?

PARRISH No!

ROSENBERG Then what we saw tonight was a physical phenomenon, an inexplicable physical phenomenon, and, if it's phenomenological, it's got to be explicable, and I've got to know why! Let me talk, for Chrissakes! I've been in there mopping up that tank room for three hours, and I want to tell you what I'd like to do.

PARRISH Arthur, I've had all I can take tonight. Just leave me alone.

ROSENBERG We've got to repeat this! We've got to repeat this with other human subjects. We need a selective sample! We'll put up a notice for volunteers in the Student Union, something like that, get five or six subjects, and just go back to square one with them, step up the doses of the drug in a graduated fashion, check them against Eddie's values! I'll bet you we could even get a grant! We'll give them some kind of bullshit about checking this drug for renal clearance, some shit like that!

PARRISH *(bellowing)* God Almighty! This is Arthur Rosenberg talking, right! The conscience of the scientific community! The guy with all the petitions against genetic engineering and protests against nuclear power! The big, moral, science-for-the-people man! And here he is, ready to test an untested drug on innocent human beings!

EMILY *(stands, cries out)* Please stop shouting!

Grumpy, the others subside. She moves across the room into...

THE BEDROOM.

...to see if all the yelling has had any effect on Jessup. He still lies motionless. She closes the door, darkening the room even more, and moves silently around the bed to raise the shade on the window and look into the sleeping backyards of the houses on the next street. She turns to look at her husband.

Jessup has turned his head on the shadowy pillow, his eyes open. He is look-ing at her. She is momentarily immobilized by the fact that he is awake. They just look at each other, then she kneels on both knees by the bed and examines his long, ashen face.

EMILY *(softly)* How are you?

JESSUP *(whispering)* Wiped out.

EMILY Would you like to go back to sleep?

JESSUP Yes.

EMILY Would you mind if Mason had a quick look at you?

JESSUP *(can barely whisper)* Good idea.

His eyes close. She gets to her feet, gently touches his face and goes to get Parrish. She opens the door to...

THE LIVING ROOM.

EMILY   He's awake. Maybe you ought to have a look at him, Mason.

THE BEDROOM. HOURS LATER. 6:00 A.M. DAY.

The shade on the window is up, and the gray passionless light of dawn filters into the room. On the bed, Jessup awakens. Eyes open, he lies there letting the sanity of daylight enter him. The living room door is open, but the apartment is utterly still.

He sits up, moves his legs over the side of the bed and stands. He seems okay. Barefoot and wearing the T-shirt and jeans he had slept in, he goes to the living room.

From the doorway, he looks into the living room. Rosenberg and Parrish are obviously gone. His wife lies sleeping on the couch under a twist of blanket, her leg protruding. The blinds are drawn and she seems very white in the stillness. Her face is drawn in pain, and her sleep seems not a pleasant one.

REACTION SHOT on Jessup, filled with solicitude. He brushes away a tear from his face. Moving to the stuffed chair opposite her, he sinks into it and watches her.

She turns in her sleep, and the blanket slips onto the floor. She curls up into herself in an automatic reaction to the chill of her nakedness. He gets up, crosses the room and picks up the blanket to cover her again. Then, lifting her head, he squeezes onto the couch under her, taking her into his arms, warming her with himself. She shudders and, still desperately asleep, begins to whimper and cry.

Emily suddenly clutches at him out of the terror of her own nightmare, fevered by some frightened sensuality, making strangulated cries and arching panic-stricken up within his embrace. Her cheeks are streaked with tears, her eyes clenched closed, and she is sucking at his mouth with the rapacity of a vampire.

He locks her in his arms. Quickly, the moment is over. Her head sinks back onto his chest then into his lap and again into sleep.

THE KITCHEN. TWO HOURS LATER. DAY.

Jessup sits at the kitchen table, eating a sandwich and sipping coffee. His legs are crossed, and he is in the depths of thought. The sun is higher and brighter now, breaking through the slats of the window blind.

The phone RINGS. It takes a moment for the sound in the living room to penetrate Jessup's mind. It RINGS again, and he starts from his seat, moving to...

THE LIVING ROOM. DAY.

Emily is already sitting up. She smiles briefly at him and sighs.

EMILY   Oh, God, I hope it isn't the kids...

She stands and crosses the room, gracile, shamelessly naked except for her almost indiscernible panties, picks up the phone, ending its THIRD RING, and perches on the arm of the chair.

EMILY   *(on phone, listens)* ...Everything's fine, Arthur. He's fine. *(to Jessup)* It's Arthur. Are you fine?

Jessup nods, goes back into the kitchen.

EMILY   *(on phone)* I was sleeping...No, I don't know if he's eaten anything...

She looks up as Jessup returns from the kitchen, bringing her a mug of coffee. She nods her thank-you.

EMILY   *(to Jessup)* Arthur, the indestructible Jewish mother, wants to know, have you eaten anything.

JESSUP   Yes.

EMILY   *(on phone)*   Arthur, I'll call you back when I'm more awake. Everything's fine.

She hangs up, notes the sun fragmenting itself through the blinds.

EMILY   God, what time is it? I should call the kids. Eddie, could you throw that blanket over here? I'm freezing.

JESSUP   I love you, Emily.

EMILY   You said that last night too, you know.

JESSUP   I know.

EMILY   I think those have been the first unsolicited words of love you've ever said to me.

JESSUP   I love you. I love the kids. I can't tell you how much the three of you mean to me, how much I need you. I just wanted you to know that.

EMILY   Why don't you just come back to us?

JESSUP   It's too late.

He picks up the fallen blanket, brings it to her, tucks it around her. She tries to read his face.

JESSUP   The point is what happened last night was more of a religious experience than a scientific one.

EMILY   Yes, I know.

Jessup returns to his corner of the couch, where it's darker. The widening shaft of sunlight divides them.

JESSUP   You saved me. You redeemed me from the pit. I was in it, Emily. I was in that ultimate moment of terror that is the beginning of life. I found the final truth. I found it, touched it, ate of its flesh, drank its blood. I've seen it face to face, and it's hideous. It's insufferable! The pain cannot be described. It is nothing, simple, hideous nothing. The final truth of all things is that there is no final truth. Truth is what's transitory. It's human life that is real. This is real. You and me sitting in this room. That is real! That is substance! That is the only truth there is.

He emerges out of the cucullate shadows to stand in the band of dust-moted white light streaking across the floor from the slatted window.

JESSUP   I'm trying to tell you why I love you, that without you, I would have disappeared into unspeakable terror.

She stands, pulling the blanket around her.

EMILY   I suppose that's why anybody loves anyone.

JESSUP   For God's sake, Emily, don't be so facile.

EMILY   I'm not being facile! My God, do you think you're the only one who has experienced despair? The only one who has experienced the nothingness of life? We are all creatures of despair, Eddie. Life for all of us is a flight from the unspeakable terror. Life is an act of faith for all of us! That's why we love each other. It's the only act of faith most of us are capable of. At least, it's the only act of faith I'm capable of.

JESSUP   I can't live with it, Emily. The pain is unbearable.

EMILY   We all live with it. That unspeakable terror is what makes us such singular creatures. We hide from it, we succumb to it, mostly we defy it. We build fragile little structures to keep it out. We love, we raise families, we work, we make friends. We write poems, we paint pictures, we build beautiful things. We make our own universe, our own truth, our own reality. And every now and then, someone like you comes along who goes out and challenges it face to face. Passionate

men. Poets, philosophers, saints and scientists. What the hell do you
think makes me love you so much?

JESSUP I don't want to frighten you, Emily, but what I'm trying to tell you
is what happened to me last night can happen at any time, even now,
right now, while I'm talking to you. The drug I've been using must
have a latency factor. I don't know how much of it has accumulated in
my limbic nuclei. It could be self-perpetuating. The chemical potential is there. I've attained a critical mass. Any act of consciousness
could kick it off. Because whatever act of consciousness occurred last
night is embedded in me just as much as the drug is. So it could happen at any time.

They stare at each other. He is crying openly, his face glistening with tears.

JESSUP It's too late, you see.

*He slowly raises his right arm and extends it for her to see. The vivid sun-
light bleaches into a sepulchrally white limb where a bulge of protoplasmic
substance moves under the skin like a mole. She stares, stunned.*

*We hear a HUM resonating, the throbbing SOUND of the pulsing primal
energy we had heard the night before.*

EMILY *(screams)* Defy it, Eddie! You made it real! You can make it
unreal! If you love me, Eddie, defy it!

*He stands immobilized, crying helplessly. His body RUMBLES, CRACKS
and BUCKLES, as if forces inside it were about to break through the surface. He begins to change forms, some recognizable, some merely monstrous.*

*His substance seems not more real than a photograph, a projected illusion, a
demented kaleidoscope of instant, transitory, transparent images, flickering
madly in the wide shaft of sunlight.*

*The DRONE has become unbearable. She clutches her ears. She sees a quick
fleeting image of her husband reaching out his arms to her for help, but she*

is petrified. His arms turn to stumps. She finally forces out a HISSING sibillant SOUND.

EMILY *(barely a whisper)* If you love me, Eddie!

Suddenly, she is convulsed herself, clutching at her stomach, as some pain explodes within her. Her arms bulge and swell and discolor. A jagged crack appears on her forearm and shoots up the length of her arm, as if it were splitting open. She forces her arm up, as if to show it to her husband. It is now a stump and losing its definition as the lines become wave-like and melt into the shrieking air.

She feels a massive shock just inside her skull above her eyes. A RED-HOT FLAME erupts from her bowels. She seems to be burning alive. Her EYES DISAPPEAR. She would scream, but her mouth has disappeared as well.

The SCREEN has become total, impenetrable BLACKNESS.

We HEAR a distant echo of a scream, lightyears away in the ultimate blackness. It grows louder, but is no longer a scream. It is now rather a roar of rage, the fury of a raging animal.

Light begins to penetrate the total blackness. Forms begin to take shape. Jessup's human form, flickering in and out of the madness of all his other shapes, reasserts itself.

The blackness is now gone, and we are back in the living room. Jessup stands, a completely human form again, naked, as immobile, enmarbled as a statue, stark white.

He looks at his wife and sees her disintegrating into the shapeless anti-matter that had been his condition the night before. With a shocking wrench of effort, he takes a step toward her, forcing himself into the human who will take one step, two—reaching out to embrace the shapelessness of his wife.

Instantly, abruptly, it is over. The drone, the lunacy of illusion, the whole shattering moment is done.

What we see, standing in the sunlight in the middle of their living room, is a young married couple—he, a slight, light-haired man of thirty-seven, beginning to bald just a bit but looking boyish at the moment in his jeans and T-shirt with a slim, gracefully naked young woman, her face pressed against her husband. Her arms are wrapped around his waist, a pair of young living humans, standing embraced in the white sunlight of their living room.

JESSUP *(after a moment)* I love you, Emily.

THE END

The Collected Works of Paddy Chayefsky

The Television Plays

HOLIDAY SONG

PRINTER'S MEASURE

THE BIG DEAL

MARTY

THE MOTHER

THE BACHELOR PARTY

"Paddy Chayefsky makes it a habit of writing for television as if he had invented the medium....**A SINGULARLY ENDOWED CRAFTSMAN!**"

— VARIETY

"TELEVISION'S FINEST DRAMATIC WRITER."

— THE NEW YORK TIMES

ISBN: 1-55783-191-2 $12.95 Trade Paper

The Collected Works of Paddy Chayefsky

The Screenplays

Volume 1

MARTY **(Winner of the Academy Award)**
"One of the most true and touching stories ever told on film. **WONDROUS!**

— William K. Zinsser, NY HERALD TRIBUNE

THE GODDESS
"It is unlikely that a stronger and more penetrating study of a human soul will come along soon...AN UNCOMPROMISING FILM...So powerful that it should **BE SEEN BY ANYONE WITH A SERIOUS INTEREST IN FILM AS ART**."

— NEW YORK HERALD TRIBUNE

THE AMERICANIZATION OF EMILY
"Some of the wildest, brashest and funniest situations and cracks at the lunacy of warfare...**FASCINATING AND REMARKABLE**."

— THE NEW YORK TIMES

ISBN: 1-55783-193-9 $16.95 Trade Paper